Rasa in Aesthetics

Rasa in Aesthetics

An Application of Rasa Theory to Modern Western Literature

Priyadarshi Patnaik

with a foreword by
K. Krishnamoorthy

DK PRINTWORLD
Publishers of Indian Traditions

Cataloging in Publication Data — DK
[Courtesy: D.K. Agencies (P) Ltd. <docinfo@dkagencies.com>]

Patnaik, Priyadarshi, 1969-
Rasa in aesthetics.
Includes bibliographical references (p.)
Includes index.
ISBN 13: 9788124600818

1. *Rasa*s. 2. Literature – Aesthetics.
3. English literature – History and criticism.
I. Title.

ISBN 13: 978-81-246-0081-8 ISBN 10: 81-246-0081-3
First published in India in 1997
2nd impression, 2004
3rd impression, 2013

Printed and published by:
D.K. Printworld (P) Ltd.
Regd. Office : *'Vedaśrī'*, F-395, Sudarshan Park
(Metro Station: Ramesh Nagar)
New Delhi - 110 015
Phones : (011) 2545 3975; 2546 6019; *Fax* : (011) 2546 5926
e-mail : indology@dkprintworld.com
Web : www.dkprintworld.com

आनन्दरूपता सर्वरसानाम्।

(*अभिनवभारती*, १.२९२)

ānandarūpatā sarvarasānām ।

***Abhinavabhāratī*, I.292**

All *rasa*s lead to (are of the nature of) Bliss.

Foreword

I AM glad to write this Foreword to Dr. Priyadarshi Patnaik's brilliant study entitled *Rasa in Aesthetics* : *An Application of Rasa Theory to Modern Western Literature.* Apparently, it is addressed to literary critics of modern literature, a group to whose membership I cannot lay any claims. My studies have been in the area of Sanskrit poetics and since Dr. Patnaik bases his whole work on the *rasa* theory as perfected by the ancient masters, I might view it only as a modest scholar.

The actual examples of applied *rasa* theory, even in Sanskrit and other Indian languages, are very few. To the extent the *rasa* theory is universal in its application — with the concept of *sādhāraṇīkaraṇa*— it must be adequate to analyse any worthwhile literature of any century. But when applying that theory we are faced with problems, not subjected to detailed studies so far, of intermixtures (*saṅkara*) and of appearances (*ābhāsas*), and of part-whole relationship (*aṅgāṅgībhāva*). For example, while we have *raudra* and *vīra* in the *Gadāyuddha* episode of the *Mahābhārata*, we have a shade of *karuṇa-bhayānaka* in Draupadī's *Vastrāpaharaṇa* episode and *karuṇa* in Abhimanyu's death episode. All these are overlaid by *adbhuta* as the episodes have epic stature. But, none of them is taken as the *pradhāna-rasa* or the Master Passion of the entire epic by Indian theorists like Ānandavardhana amd Kuntaka. They make out a case for the acceptance of *śānta* as a *rasa* on the basis of this epic itself. But what exactly is the positive *sthāyībhāva* of *śānta* is an open question.

Similarly, in the *Rāmāyaṇa* we have *śṛṅgāra*'s *ābhāsa* in the

Sūrpaṇakhā episode and Rāvaṇa's overtures to Sītā. They are only psuedo-*rasas* and not real *rasas* though enjoyable as instances of the comic. Regarding *saṅkara* (blending) of *rasas*, the theorists are very rigid in disallowing any delineation of inimical *rasas* consecutively. *Śṛṅgāra* and *bībhatsa*, *hāsya* and *karuṇa* are tell-tale examples.

These are some of the basic problems that arise while attempting application of old rules to new instances. The complexity of the problems is enhanced by the subjectivity of the critic also. I must admire the perseverance and probity of Dr. Patnaik in subjecting modern classics to a *rasa* analysis — an exercise, first of its kind, as my knowledge goes. Franz Kafka, Mayakovsky, Ernest Hemingway, Conrad, Lorca, T.S. Eliot, Neruda, Albert Camus are only some of the writers whose work is subjected to an in-depth analysis, besides a number of works broadly coming under the 'Absurd'. But the question remains if *rasas* identified in parts can explain the over-all *rasa* pervading the entire work satisfactorily, not to mention the nebulous yardstick of *rasaucitya*, *bhāva-sandhi*, *bhāva-śānti* etc.

While the recapitulation of the *rasa* theory in the first two chapters is quite scholarly and dependable, the bulk of the work devoted to a vivid account of *navarasas* with their paraphernalia, is a major breakthrough. It is bold in conception, strewn with insights and brilliant in execution. The dimension of *śānta* is explored in depth to accommodate the modern literature of alienation with its inability to locate Man in the metaphysical sense. Several questions are raised and possibilities are discussed with profound insight. In particular the areas of *karuṇa*, *bībhatsa* and *bhayānaka* have been enlarged and shown in a wider perspective as providing the key to a literature concerning Man's identity crisis. The metaphysical is also covered in the analysis of the worldly *rasas*.

This study would be of great help not only to academicians and literary critics, but to the general readers also, as it gives extensive excerpts which can be critically assessed as well as enjoyed from the *rasa* perspective. In a sky where criticism is becoming a meaningless jargon of specialists, this work opens up a new horizon for understanding modern literary pieces of great writers.

I wish the work will reach the hands of enlightened readers and that it will stimulate further attempts at a deeper understanding of literature.

K. Krishnamoorthy

Preface

WHEN I first began reading Indian Poetics, the various types of literary figures (*alaṁkāras*), the do's and don'ts of good literature, the various styles followed in different parts of the country confused me. For a person with linguistic inclinations, these were immense wealth. But for a man like me who read a book because he enjoyed it, what was immediately understandable and comprehensible was the theory of *rasa* which essentially dealt with the various kinds of emotions, how they are depicted, inferred and transmitted though a work of art. It made more sense because emotion was common to all the literatures I had ever read. I was further convinced because it did not leave anyone out. It took into account the writer and his genius (*pratibhā*), the reader and his response (*āsvāda*) and obviously the work itself, which was there to be savoured.

More probing showed that the *rasa* theory had tremendous linguistic potentials as well, which I could make out even with my limited knowledge of linguistics. For an emotion cannot ever be shown or communicated directly. It can only be suggested (*dhvani*) through words or their equivalents.

Further, in an academic world where theories were getting more and more technical, where dry intricate dialectic was hounding modern critics as it had once hounded some of our ancient grammarians and logicians, the *rasa* theory was refreshingly understandable. Not only that, it looked to me that it had, for these very reasons, a very strong need to be revived in a modern context.

The present work is an affirmation of such a stand. What I have tried to do here is elucidate the *rasa* theory as lucidly as I could and then apply it to various modern Western works.

I do not deny that some work has been done in this light before me. But I think this work is the first book-length application of the ancient canons of *rasa* to a wide range of modern European texts. The idea of the work was suggested to me by my *guru* Dr. P.G. Rama Rao. It was also he who was always there at times of difficulty with valuable suggestions as the work progressed. Without his presence this book would never have been written. Professor K. Krishnamoorthy, whose works on Sanskrit aesthetics I had always read and admired, was kind enough to go through my manuscript and agreed to write a 'Foreword' without having ever known or met me. I have no words to express my heartfelt gratitude to him. Professor C.D. Narasimhaiah and Dr. D.P. Pattanayak both motivated my interest in Indian aesthetics. I am grateful to both these esteemed scholars for the active interest they have shown in my work. Finally, I would like to thank my publisher M/s D.K. Printworld without whom this book would not be before you.

Priyadarshi Patnaik

Contents

Foreword v

Preface ix

INTRODUCTION 1

Is the *rasa* theory relevant?
Rasa theory among other Indian theories
What is *rasa* theory about?
Causes for its decline

1. RASA 13

The word *'rasa'* : a short introduction
Rasa : a chequered career
Rasa in the *Upaniṣads*
Rasa in *Nāṭya Śāstra*
What is *rasa* made of?
Sthāyībhāvas — *Vyabhicārībhāvas* — *Anubhāvas*
Rasa and *bhāva* : which one came first?
The world of stimulus and response
Then what is the nature of *rasa*?
The sympathetic perceiver

2. THE RASAS AND THEIR RELATIONSHIP 53

The eight *rasas*
Śānta rasa

3. ŚṚṄGĀRA RASA 69

Love-in-union
The permanent emotion in *śṛṅgāra* — The causes of *śṛṅgāra* — The effects and consequences of *śṛṅgāra* — Violence, terror

and love — Inanimate objects and love — Union in love

Deviant relations, incomplete relations and other problems

Love-in-separation

Effects and consequences of separation — Separation and longing — Hope and despair — The problem of interpretation — Love between friends — One-sided love — The problems of view-point — More than one *rasa*

4. HĀSYA RASA 99

One of the oldest emotions

Disorder, cruelty and laughter

The nature of the disorder

Cruelty beyond the laugh

Satire and *hāsya rasa*

Causes of laughter

The need for distancing

High and low comedy

The comedy of the grotesque

Hāsya vs. *śṛṅgāra*

5. KARUṆA RASA 121

The causes of *karuṇa*

Who is the aggressor?

Tragedy and *karuṇa rasa*

Karuṇa vs. *vipralambha śṛṅgāra*

Subjectivity

Pity

Bībhatsa vs. *karuṇa*

Alienation

Karuṇa and the other *rasas*

Hope and *karuṇa rasa*

The states that accompany *karuṇa*

How can *karuṇa* be relished?

6. RAUDRA RASA 143

The stable and accompanying states in *raudra*

Anger through words

Injustice and *raudra*
The accompanying states
Raudra and other *rasas*
Raudra and *vīra*
Raudra and *karuṇa*
Impotent rage and suffering
Raudra, the frenzy and the grotesque
Fury and waste
Fury and disgust as responses

7. VĪRA RASA 159
The manifestations of *vīra rasa*
Firmness and patience — Strength — Correct perception — Dynamic energy
The causes of *vīra*
The responses of *vīra*
Determination in the face of odds — Humility
Wonder
Weakness — Absence of confusion
Associated emotions of *vīra*
Love, anger and *vīra rasa*
Vīra and the other *rasas*

8. BHAYĀNAKA RASA AND BĪBHATSA RASA 175
Neglected *rasas*
Bhayānaka rasa
Causes — What causes fear?
Bībhatsa rasa
Metamorphosis to the unknown — Ugly-distortion — Incomprehension
Metaphysical disgust
Towards *śānta* — The absurd
Bībhatsa and *hāsya*
Bībhatsa and black comedy
Fear and disgust
The states that accompany fear and disgust
Relation with other *rasas*
Wonder and disgust — *Vīra*, *bībhatsa* and

bhayānaka — *Karuṇa* — *Śṛṅgāra*

Problems

9. ADBHUTA RASA 205

Surprise and delight

Causes of *abdhuta*

Skill and wonder

Adbhuta rasa and love

Wit and wonder

Surprise and delight

Which way does wonder move?

Vīra, adbhuta and *śānta*

Adbhuta and terror

Wonder beyond terror

Effects of *adbhuta rasa*

Adbhuta and the other *rasas*

10. ŚĀNTA RASA 225

The uniqueness of *śānta*

Is *śānta* really a *rasa* — The stable state in *śānta* — Causes of *śānta*

What is really the *sthāyībhāva* of *śānta*

Harṣa or laughter — *Śoka* or sorrow — *Krodha* or anger — *Utsāha* or dynamic energy — *Bhaya* or fear — *Jugupsā* or disgust — *Vismaya* or wonder — *Rati* or love — Cause and effect of *śānta* — Accompanying emotions

Śānta in meditative literature

The seeker of peace

Śānta and *mokṣa*

11. CONCLUSION 251

Bibliography 257

Glossary 269

Index 273

Introduction

Is the Rasa Theory Relevant?

A valid literary theory is always one that has practical applications. The reason is clear. A literary theory is about literature. Unless it can be applied, it has very little practical relevance. Then it usually stagnates or dies. If it survives at all, it does as a mere fossil. In most cases, a good literary theory has a double potential. It can lead to further theories, to newer philosophical speculations. At the same time it can also be applied to literary texts.

But this is not enough. The theory must cover a wide enough area. In other words, it must have a general applicability. Not merely that. It should also be made of something that is not a matter of vogue. When interests have shifted, such a theory would be left nowhere. And finally, it must be flexible enough to take the wear of time, to be malleable to interpretations and newer needs.

The *rasa* theory, one of the oldest theories in Indian tradition, fulfils most of these conditions. First expounded in Bharata's *Nāṭya Śāstra*, it influences the entire discussion of dramaturgy there as the very essence of good writing. It is, in fact, considered the soul of literature. The theory of *rasa* essentially deals with the various kinds of emotions, and how they are depicted, inferred and transmitted through a work of art. It holds that finally literature is essentially about life (simulated or imagined) and its emotions. And the problem that confronts a critic is to find out how, in a work, emotion is depicted, suggested and how it is finally communicated to the reader or audience. The strength of this theory lies in that it deals with what is common to all mankind at all times — emotion.

Secondly, it is a theory which is considerate of the entire literary process from its very conception in the mind of the artist to its final perception in the heart of the perceiver or reader. No one is left out. The artist is of prime importance. It is his genius (*pratibhā*) only that leads to an excellent text which has the capacity to transport the essence of aesthetic enjoyment — *rasa*. The text is of great importance, for here it is that we see how emotions are suggested through words or actions. Finally, without the reader who perceives, savours (*āsvāda*) and enjoys, the text is useless. In the *rasa* theory, each of these factors is acknowledged for its indispensability. It is this total world-view that makes up this lucid theory.

Thirdly, the *rasa* theory has a tremendous linguistic potential, for an emotion cannot ever be shown or communicated directly. It can only be suggested (*dhvani*) through words or their equivalents.

Fourthly, it is one of our oldest and most influential theories that has grown over the centuries. Subjected to a rich tradition of dialectics and interpretation over a period of more than a thousand years, it has become richer and more complete. And not a couple of centuries back it influenced our regional writers and critics powerfully.

Finally, it seems, now it is time our own rich canons are revived. It was probably with the advent of English education that our writers and critics came under the very strong influence of European writings and canons. Unfortunately, until recently, there was hardly anything to show that we had such a powerful critical tradition. Since the last few decades things are changing. We have a fairly large number of theoretical works on the *rasa* theory. And these days some good work in the field of practical criticism is also being done. It is essential in the present context to restore our rich tradition. And the best way of doing so is to apply it to an alien culture and prove that it works.

The need to reinstate the *rasa* theory has a different kind of implication as well. In European criticism, New Criticism, a movement which got its momentum from the works of I.A. Richards and later grew in America in the hands of William Empson, Cleanth Brooks and others, was perhaps the last of the critical schools which could be easily understood by any perceptive reader. In a traditional sense, it aided the reading of literature by focusing on the various meanings and implications a work could generate. But in the sixties started a movement called Structuralism which focused on the linguistic implications of the text. Post-Structuralism, that followed, could be accused of nihilism since it denied a writer his authorship (Michael Faucault and Ronald Barthes), and, where a work was concerned, questioned its ability to *mean* (Jacquies Derrida). Such works had strong philosophical implications, no doubt. But as a well-known contemporary novelist and critic, David Lodge, points out in his book, *After Bakhtin*, what followed was a kind of technical and jargon-oriented criticism which was understood by only those who had had some training in that area of scholarship. In other words, practical criticism and critical writings on literature became so dense and difficult that only the academics read them. This is the present scene. Unfortunately, most modern critical writings read like writings in Physics or Mathematics. There are innumerable words, technical terms, and what make things worse is that very few of them can be found in a dictionary. This trend has certain alarming implications as far as readership is concerned. Bluntly put, no one reads the modern critics except themselves and those who are working on them.

At present, Post-Modernism and Post-Structuralism are slowly expending themselves. What follows could be a vacuum. Movements like Formalism or New Criticism are too close in history for them to be reinstated. In such a situation, an updated application of some of our ancient critical traditions could come as a fresh breath. And it applies both to our as well as European critical tradition. This is another of the chief underlying reasons why the *rasa* theory has been taken up here.

Before we discuss the *rasa* theory elaborately, a brief history of its development and a discussion of its place among other ancient Indian theories might be useful.

Rasa Theory Among other Indian Theories

Nāṭya Śāstra of Bharata (written somewhere between the first century BC and AD the 4th century) can be considered the first extant work that deals with poetics in Indian tradition. Prior to it we find no treatise that discusses poetics in any comprehensive manner. And though *Nāṭya Śāstra* deals primarily with drama and its various elements, in the context of a specific kind of drama (*vācikābhinaya*), it deals with poetry. Bharata specifically mentions that good literature must fulfil ten conditions of good writing (*guṇas*), abstain from ten faults (*doṣas*) and maintain certain literary characters (*lakṣaṇas*). He lists thirty-six of these characters. He also discusses the use of literary figures (*alaṁkāras*), all of which separate literature from other kinds of writings. But over and above all, he again and again emphasizes that they must have the essential *rasa* which is the soul of any literature. Thus, according to him, *rasa* is the aesthetic objective of dramatic representation.

After this significant treatise, we do not have any extant work until we come to Bhāmaha. Bharata, in *Nāṭya Śāstra*, sets apart a separate chapter for dealing with the ornaments (*alaṁkāras*) of poetry. Thus, it seems, dramaturgy, as a school, had a separate existence from poetics. But unfortunately, no such work on poetics survives. We can hardly even be certain of the names of such works if they existed at all. In fact, the first extant treatise that deals with poetics proper belongs to the seventh-century and is written by Bhāmaha. In his *Kāvyālaṁkāra*, he highlights *alaṁkāras* as a separate school. Bharata, no doubt, deals with certain important elements of poetry like *alaṁkāra*, *doṣa*, *guṇa* etc. But they are clearly subservient to the principal aim of generating *rasa* in a work. But for Bhāmaha, the poetic embellishments form the principal objects of study. He considers them the soul of poetry. For him poetry must have a definite sense which is made charming by various turns of expression. In his hands *rasa* is reduced to *rasavat*, another of the many literary figures. In the following centuries, Udbhaṭa and Rudraṭa highlight this school of thought. Udbhaṭa has virtually nothing to say about *rasa*. And though Rudraṭa is considerably influenced by the *rasa* doctrine, it is for him more or less extraneous.

In the eighth-century Dāṇḍin wrote *Kāvyādarśa*. This can be considered the first work on what later developed into the *guṇa-rīti* theory. Though Dāṇḍin was strongly influenced by Bhāmaha and the *alaṁkāra* school, his emphasis was on *mārga* (syonymous to *rīti* used by Vāmana) which broadly means diction or style. He also explored the associated *guṇas* or canons of good writing. According to him poetic writing can be divided into two categories — *svabhāvokti* (plain and direct description) and *vakrokti* (indirect or figurative language). For him, style or diction is the essence of poetry. This school — the *guṇa-rīti* school — later developed in the hands of Vāmana, a contemporary of Udbhaṭa. He defines *rīti* as that which separates poetic speech from ordinary speech. In fact, his treatise gives us the first confident, well thought-out and carefully laid scheme of poetics. Elaborating on *guṇas*, he distinguished between *śabdaguṇas* or skilful use of words and *arthaguṇas*, or qualities of good writing or style. Unfortunately, he has very little to say about *rasa*. For him it is a mere figure. Rather, Dāṇḍin gave some prominence to *rasa* by including it as one of the marks of excellence of diction or style (*guṇa*).

Rasa seems to have been explicitly alluded to and discussed for the first time by Rudraṭa. But as we said earlier, he has very little to say about its theoretical implications and its importance though he devotes four chapters to it. It was sometime between the seventh and the tenth century that *rasa* finally shook off its strong psychological attachment to drama and came broadly within the discussion of poetics proper. Bharata's *sūtra* on *rasa* being vague and ambiguous, many controversies regarding its exact implications raged over the centuries. Four distinct interpretations seem to have existed including that by Abhinavagupta. Abinavagupta informs us about three of these — the discussions by Bhaṭṭa Lollaṭa (eighth-century), Śrī Śaṅkuka (ninth-century) and Bhaṭṭa Nāyaka (tenth-century). Unfortunately, their works are lost to us. But these interpretations indicate that *rasa* gradually grew in strength and became all powerful when it was fused with the theory of *dhvani* (suggestion) by Dhvanikāra and Ānandavardhana.

In the ninth-century came *Dhvanyāloka* by Ānandavardhana where he claims that *dhvani* (suggestion) is the soul of poetry. The several expressed parts of the poem, he holds, reveal the unexpressed deeper sense. Interestingly, he combines *rasa* with suggestion to call it *rasadhvani*. This, the right combination of suggestions to emote an aesthetic mood, is to be the aim of all good poetry. This combination of *rasa* and *dhvani* is especially a happy one since an emotion or aesthetic state (*rasa*) cannot be expressed directly through words, but can only be suggested. The theory was a very well-accepted one and it later influenced Abhinavagupta.

Abhinavagupta wrote two significant commentaries, one on *Nāṭya Śāstra* and the other on *Dhvanyāloka* (*Abhinavabhāratī* and *Locana*). In his hands, the emotional and aesthetic states that a poem represented were recognized for their importance. It was thus, with him, that *rasa* theory not only regained its former glory but, along with *dhvani*, became the most influential theory to affect all theorists to come.

By the end of the eleventh-century we have two other significant schools. Kuntaka expounded *vakrokti* (indirection), which was already there in Vāmana, as the essential feature of poetry. Kṣemendra, a student of Abhinavagupta, propounded the theory of *aucitya* (propriety) as the soul of poetry.

The significant writers who followed took up these older schools and discussed them. But no other distinct schools of thought appeared after this point. Thus, we have *Sāhityadarpaṇa* of Viśvanātha on *rasa* and *dhvani*. We have *Kavyaprakaśa* by Mammaṭa. And the last significant work that discusses all the earlier theories, chiefly *rasa*, is *Rasagaṅgādhara* by Paṇḍitarāja Jagannātha in the seventeenth-century. This, in brief, is the history of poetics in ancient India.

What is Rasa Theory About?

Before we discuss the *rasa* theory elaborately, a broad sketch could be helpful. *Rasa* can be roughly translated as aesthetic relish, pleasure or rapture on the part of the reader which is derived from (in response to) a work of art. But what is it that gives rise to this aesthetic rapture? According to Bharata, it is from a combination of *bhāvas* (in the work) that *rasa* arises. *Bhāvas* can be roughly translated as psycho-physiological states in a man and they are broadly of three kinds — *sthāyībhāvas*, *vyabhicārībhāvas* (or *sañcārībhāva*) and *sāttvikabhāvas*. *Sthāyībhāvas*, which can be translated broadly as stable or permanent states, are those which dominate or persist throughout a work. In other words, they can be said to set the mood of the work — angry, sad, terrifying etc. The various fleeting or transitory states accompanying them or generated along with them — *sañcārībhāvas* — are short-lived mental states. These can be panic, fear, anger, trembling, paralysis, stuttering etc. The *sāttvikabhāvas* are very similar to the *vyabhicārībhāvas* or *sañcārībhāvas*. But in dramatic enactment, they are harder to imitate.

But for these emotions to be generated, there must be some cause or stimulus which will give rise to an effect in the character or the subject. The causes, antecedents or stimuli are known as *vibhāvas*. For instance, a tiger in a forest can be the cause of fear in a lonely traveller. In this case, the tiger and the man's aloneness can be considered the *vibhāvas* which generate fear. And the consequences, manifestations or effects of fear will be many like trembling, panic, horripilation, paralysis etc. These are known as the *anubhāvas*.

Bhāvas or states may or may not be perceivable to our senses directly. For instance, anger in one can never be communicated directly to another. It can only be suggested through various manifestations. Thus, whereas *vibhāvas* and *anubhāvas* can be seen or observed directly, the states or *bhāvas* need not necessarily be directly perceivable. It is, in fact, to suggest the *bhāvas* that *anubhāvas* and *vibhāvas* are used.

This is broadly what *rasa* implies in Indian aesthetics. I use the word aesthetics since *rasa* can also be said to exist in music, dance, sculpture and painting — for all these four forms are capable of suggesting emotions or psycho-physiological states.

Though Bharata has used *rasa* almost exclusively in the context of drama, later on it came to be applied to all kinds of literature and especially to poetry. Rudraṭa was the first to use it in his *Kāvyālaṁkāra*. Later, however, it was through the efforts of Ānandavardhana and Abhinavagupta that *rasa* was applied to poetry in a very important manner.

This is not unusual since drama was chiefly written in verse form. As P.V. Kane points out, both *kāvya* (poetry) and *nāṭya* (drama) were considered synonymous by Bharata (*Nāṭya Śāstra*, XVI.169; XVII.17). Both used metre, and dramatic verse also used figures and other literary devices (Kane, 355). Besides, many emotions and states can be suggested by words or by the way they are used. For instance, a sentence like "I . . . I . . . can't stand . . . I can't . . . move" in the presence of a tiger can suggest the state of fear. A description of a man frozen to the ground in the presence of a tiger can also indicate fear. This is in fact what is impled when Abhinavagupta says in his commentary on *Nāṭya Śāstra* :

> To the extent that poetry resembles drama, *rasa* is also to be found in poetry. Our teacher said that *rasa* arises in a poem if we see things as if they were happening before our very eyes.
>
> — *Aesthetic Rapture*, Vol. II, p. 71

It is thus that *rasa* can be applied not only to poetry, but also to any literature that fulfils the above conditions — "as if they were happening before our very eyes".

Causes for Its Decline

As mentioned earlier, around the 17th century, a dialectical tradition came to an end — a tradition that contained many original aestheticians and poets like Bharata, Dāṇḍin, Śaṅkuka, Mammaṭa, Bhaṭṭa Lollaṭa, Bhaṭṭa Tauta, Ānandavardhana, Abhinavagupta, Rudraṭa, Kuntaka, Viśvanātha Kavirāja, Jagannātha Paṇḍitarāja, etc. In fact, Jagannātha's *Rasagaṅgādhara* can be considered the last important work in this tradition. At this time, discussions on not only *rasa*, but also various other theories like *alaṁkāra, guṇa-rīti, vakrokti, dhvani* etc., came to an end. Of course, this does not mean that discussions about poetics came to an end. Almost all regional literatures incorporated and elaborated upon what had been written before them in Sanskrit, but the outcome cannot be considered very significant.

Why was it so? Was it because these different theories (including *rasa*) lost their relevance? Or could there be other reasons?

Briefly, a few observations can be made. Sanskrit, which was the language in which this tradition had sustained itself, gradually became — like Latin — obsolete. Around the seventeenth-century and eighteenth-century, the regional languages of India also became more powerful. They started growing and the court language was no longer Sanskrit (for this the Muslim invasion of India in the twelfth century was also responsible to a certain extent). Sanskrit became the language of the elites, of a select few. On the other hand, it had hardly ever seen any interaction with the other major important Asian languages — Chinese, Japanese etc. True, Chinese and later Japanese cultures were influenced by Buddhist religion and literature. But in India, we never ever see any influence of Chinese literature or philosophy.

Thus, on a wider scale, hardly any exchange of ideas and philosophies took place. Even in the twentieth-century, with so many translations that are accessible, there has been very little dialectical interaction among these cultures.

But these could not be the only reasons. Perhaps there were no powerful minds to harmonize such disparate cultures as Muslim, French, Portuguese and British. But here we can only speculate.

What is of much greater importance is that in the present century, Sanskrit literature (leaving apart theory) hardly lives as a dynamic force. Regional languages and literatures have developed — though most of them are profoundly influenced by Sanskrit. In fact they carried on the spirit of Sanskrit critical tradition along with them. But in the present century, almost all our regional literatures are soaked in European influence. Earlier, they had borne a striking resemblance to Sanskrit works of literature. But they were now also strongly influenced by European canons. This is never bad, but what was in the process very noticeable was a lack of harmonization of the traditional canons and the modern Western canons in our critical tradition. These are some of the reasons that could have led to the relegation of the ancient Indian theories of literature and art to the background.

It is my effort in this work to first elucidate the theory of *rasa*. Next, I will attempt to critically examine its validity as an aesthetic (more specifically a literary) theory and to make an application of its canons to modern Western literature. That is the best way of validating a theory — showing that it works.

In the process of this validation certain modern problems relating to text, meaning and the reader's response will also come up. Sometimes, the theory will be inadequate to resolve some of these issues. On occasions, certain changes will seem necessary and reinterpretations will have to be made. But this is nothing strange to our tradition. Bhartṛhari (4th century AD), an ancient philosopher of language, in his work *Vākyapadīya* (II.314) has said that "meaning of words are determined from . . . propriety, place and time, and not from the mere form". (*Vākyapadīya*, p. 84)

This brief introduction will suffice for those who are not very keenly interested in the intricacies of the *rasa* theory. They can skip the first two chapters devoted to *rasa* and the relation among the various *rasas*, and move directly to the practical application of the *rasa* theory to modern Western works which takes up the rest of the book.

Finally, in this work the translation of Bharata's *Nāṭya Śāstra* by J.L. Masson and M.V. Patwardhan has been followed. In the process, their translations of *bhāvas* and *rasas* as **emotions** have been retained though in my own writing *bhāvas* have been translated as **psycho-physiological** states and the use of the original Sanskrit word *rasa* has been retained.

1

Rasa

The Word 'Rasa' : A Short Introduction

WHAT does the word *rasa* mean? Any word, in itself, does not really mean anything. Its associations with time, context and other words only give it a cloud of meanings. And the older a word becomes, the richer its associations, its resonance, its cadence. So it is that a word can mean various things at various times since its emergence. It can at the same time have in its umbra the vibrations of its earlier meanings or the seed of what it is destined to mean in, perhaps, the next century. This might seem a little confusing. But this is the way it is. And perhaps this is what makes a word very rich and exciting.

Rasa at one time meant 'water', 'juice' or 'wine'. At another time it implied 'essence'. In another context it meant 'relish' or 'savouring'. There was a time when it indicated the primary constituents of medicine. It also meant 'aesthetic pleasure' or 'enjoyment' — a meaning or association of meanings with which we are essentially concerned. But to really understand this last said implication, it is important to know its other associations, the other possibilities through which it has travelled — for, as I said earlier, a word is made up of its journey in time, its associations and its context.

Rasa! Where did it come from? In other words, we are asking a question about its origin. To answer this overwhelming question is futility itself. Where did I come from? Where did you come from? Where did the world come from? Any question about an origin only gives way to innumerable questions. In a way, it questions the very essence of question itself. We should never try to undertake such a task. What we could do instead is try to analyze the word with what we have.

Rasa as a meaningful word has floated in the air of ancient India for a very long time. It figures in *Ṛgveda*, it figures in the *Upaniṣads*. It is also to be found in our ancient treatises on chemistry and medicine. It must be at least five thousand years since it was codified to be chanted in hymns by man. Perhaps it floated much earlier than that in the air of ordinary conversation.

But the particular *rasa* with which we are concerned came much later and is to be found in *Nāṭya Śāstra* of Bharata — a work on art in general and dramaturgy in particular. Prior to this, *rasa* might have been used in other works of aesthetics — in fact, evidences point that way. But if it has been so, unfortunately, all such works are lost. The first extant work in which *rasa* has been used in an aesthetic context and with an aesthetic purpose is *Nāṭya Śāstra*. If we date this work roughly between AD first and fourth-century, then we may say that after this very important discussion of *rasa* as an aesthetic concept in *Nāṭya Śāstra*, it again degenerated into a mere figure of poetry for more than six centuries. But between the tenth- and the seventeenth-century it found itself in currency once more and grew in stature in the hands of Ānandavardhana, Abhinavagupta, Rājā Bhoja, Viśvanātha, Jagannātha Paṇḍitarāja and others.

A little earlier, we said that *rasa* meant a lot of things at some time or the other. Now, if we narrow down our area to aesthetics, we find that even here it meant many things at many times. For Bharata, it meant a distinct school of thought. It implied a very distinctive way of looking at and perceiving aesthetic objects. Later, in the hands of Bhāmaha it was a mere figure of speech. Again, in the tenth-century it combined with *dhvani* or suggestion to mean something more in the hands of Ānandavardhana.

What did *rasa* really mean in an aesthetic context? For that, what does anything mean in any given context? Perhaps in a temporal flow there is really no end to meanings — meaning is a continuous and living process. But we have to start and stop (not begin and end) somewhere. We have to start with *Nāṭya Śāstra* because that is where we first find *rasa* as an aesthetic concept. Next, we can take up the important later writers who have looked at and commented on Bharata's work. And then we can try to reinterpret *rasa* in a modern idiom.

Rasa : A Chequered Career

We have talked so much about *rasa* and *Nāṭya Śāstra* that one might, by now, have formed the opinion that *Nāṭya Śāstra* contains nothing but discussions about *rasa*. On the contrary, it devotes only one small chapter of its thirty-six chapters to the discussion of *rasa*. It assumes that we already know a lot about *rasa*. In fact it quotes certain ancient verses, called *ārya* and *anuvaṁśya* verses, to the effect. It talks about the origin of drama from the gods, about the various forms of acting, of the different dance forms, of rhythms in musical instruments, of meter. It talks about the various kinds of plays, the different kinds of heroes and heroines in a play, the numerous forms of speeches and gestures to be shown on stage. It is, in fact, an encyclopaedic work which talks about a number of art forms like music, dance and percussion in relation to drama. *Rasa*, considered from this point of view, does not really form a part of its main subject. It is only in the context of plays, primarily, that Bharata talks of *rasa*. But what he says about *rasa* implies that it is indispensable not only to drama but to all forms of art.

In an off-hand way Bharata says that without *rasa* there can be no drama, that it is the soul of any play (*Nāṭya Śāstra*, VI.31). *Nāṭya Śāstra*, thus, assumes that we know about this theory called *rasa* from earlier works which are devoted to it, and hence know how important it is in any form of art. It is here that we come to feel exasperated. For we know of no other work on *rasa*. Time betrays us and we are left with missing and lost manuscripts. And so, we have to fall back again and again on what Bharata has said about *rasa* and face difficulties. This is so since Bharata, assuming that his readers are knowledgeable about *rasa*, is not very careful or rigorous with his words. Some expressions are ambiguous, some enigmatic and *rasa* is transmitted down to us among a cloud of amorphous interpretations. Interestingly, we are not the only ones to face such difficulties. Ten centuries back, Abhinavagupta also faced the same problems — for Bharata's work was the most ancient extant work on *rasa* that Abhinavagupta had. In his works, *Abhinavabhāratī* and *Locana*, he talks of critics who came between him and Bharata — Bhaṭṭa Lollaṭa, Śaṅkuka and Bhaṭṭa Nāyaka — who also, like him, tried to interpret *Nāṭya Śāstra*. But from that quarter we have little help — their works are also lost to us. All that we know of their interpretations we know only through Abhinavagupta.

Abhinavagupta's interpretation became so influential that the later writers and critics, instead of focusing their attention upon Bharata, preferred to work upon Abhinavagupta's interpretation instead. Thus, an important tradition of interpretation on *Nāṭya Śāstra* which included Śaṅkuka, Lollaṭa etc., came to an end with Abhinavagupta.

So where do we stand? At one end we have *Nāṭya Śāstra*. At the other end are Abhinavagupta's works. In between are lost works of which we know a little from Abhinavagupta's *Abhinavabhāratī*. On the other hand, we know of the use of the word *rasa* in Vedic, Upaniṣadic and culinary contexts prior to *Nāṭya Śāstra*. These are all the evidences and tools we have in our hands to try and re-analyse the concept of *rasa* which Bharata handed down to us.

Rasa in the Upaniṣads

The earliest use of the word *rasa* is found codified in the *Ṛgveda*. In it, *rasa* was used to mean 'water' (III.48.1), '*soma* juice'

(IX.63.13), 'cow's milk' (I.37.5) and 'flavour' (V.44.13). *Atharvaveda* extended the sense to the "sap of the grain" (II.26.5) and 'taste' (III.13.15). Later, this sense became more common (*Rasa in Sanskrit Drama*, p. 197).

In the *Upaniṣads*, however, its use became less concrete. The *Upaniṣads* were works which were essentially metaphysical in content and symbolic in their use of words. Thus, all words here acquired a more filtered and ephemeral meaning than before. The concrete sense was very much there. But it only served to highlight the abstract. Hence, here *rasa* was used in an entirely new way. The concrete meaning existed, but a more abstract use was slowly making its presence felt.

The *Taittirīya Upaniṣad* said:

> *yad vai tat sukr̥tam, raso vai saḥ, rasaṁ hy evāyaṁ labdhvānandibhavati* . . . . (II.7.i)
>
> Only after perceiving the **essence** can one perceive bliss (emphasis supplied).
>
> — S. Radhakrishnan, *The Principal Upaniṣads*, p. 549

Though this expression came much later than *Ṛgveda*, it preceded *Naṭya Śāstra* by many centuries.

Whichever way *rasa* is seen — as flavour or as essence — the implication is that of something abstract which cannot be captured directly by the senses.

In the *Kauśitakī Brāhmaṇa Upaniṣad* it was said:

> *sa āgacchati śalajyam saṁsthānaṁ taṁ brahma-rasaḥ praviśati.* (I.5)
>
> He comes to the city of Salaja; the flavour of Brahman enters into him . . .
>
> — S. Radhakrishnan, *The Principal Upaniṣads*, p. 758

But even when this use 'flavour' is less connotative (unlike the earlier use which all the while implies 'essence') and more literal, the implication is abstract. In the context of the *Brahman* no word can be taken in its mere literal sense. Thus, in both these cases, the connotation generated is that of 'essence'.

Of the two illustrations above, the second one shows the use of the word *rasa* in a transition — in the process of transforming itself into an abstraction. The former shows the use as already having acquired its abstract/metaphysical implications.

In *Ṛgveda*, the use of *rasa* was almost always literal — meaning 'water', 'juice' or 'flavour'. Preceding (or contemporary to) *Nāṭya Śāstra*, the Āyurvedic science recognized six *rasa*s or chief constituents in any medicine. *Rasāyanaśāstra* (chemistry) also moved around the pivot of mercury or *rasa*. (*Rasa in Sanskrit Drama*, p. 198)

All these illustrations are relevant since, as we shall see later, the use of *rasa* in *Nāṭya Śāstra* retained all these meanings in its shadow; since in *Nāṭya Śāstra* we see *rasa* used both in a concrete culinary and an abstract aesthetic context.

So, it would not be a far-fetched supposition to say that *rasa* as a concept had a metaphysical past to link itself to. This is interesting because later, in the hands of Abhinavagupta, it again acquired metaphysical dimensions. Secondly, these illustrations show what kind of implications a concrete word like *rasa* generates when used in a metaphysical context. Finally, an interesting thing that is to be noted is that every connotative word (usually) has an essence that underlies its various uses. In case of *rasa* most of the meanings, 'flavour', 'juice' or 'mercury' (which is considered the primary ingredient of alchemy) presuppose that *rasa* is the most important or essential ingredient. Thus, the quintessential quality of *rasa* is **essence**.

In the above illustrations, in the *Upaniṣads*, *rasa* (flavour) was used in the context of *Brahman* in an attempt to capture the Ultimate in/through language. But what is the nature of this

Brahman?

The *Īśa Upaniṣad* says (V):

> It moves and It moves not; It is far and It is near; It is within all this and It is also outside all this.
>
> — *The Principal Upaniṣads*, p. 571

The entire passage is a series of contradictions which attempt to break any fixed frame of reference through which we might attempt to see 'It'. All that can be made out is that everything is relative; yet beyond this relative is the real — *Brahman.* In other words, it tries to break down our ordinary logic of perception and language.

This passage has been introduced here so that *rasa* can be understood in its proper context in the *Upaniṣad.* What is the nature of *rasa*? It is in a sense concrete — real — for it can be grasped by the sense. But its concreteness itself is effervescent. It cannot be rooted down in space. One cannot point and say, "this is it". It is perhaps the fact that it could not be rooted down like a tree or a spear that had made it eligible for use in the context of *Brahman.* It can be felt, apprehended by the sense of taste, and yet cannot be grasped as a totality. It is distinct, thus, as a **process**. Instead of being a thing that can be located, it is something that unfolds in time.

All sensory perceptions are in relation to space and time. But in each case, either space or time dominates. In the cases of vision and touch space dominates. In space, objects can be fixed, pointed to or grasped. But whereas (in these cases) space is determinate, time's perception is almost negligible. In this kind of sense-perception, our awareness of time comes only when there is movement (for movement makes time — a linearity — felt). Even so, the chronological manifestation of time makes itself felt **around** the object, rather than in it.

On the other hand, taste, smell and hearing are basically in terms of time. We are, in these instances, very keenly aware of time and its sequential movement, all these activities of perception being keenly felt as processes. But more important, there are no objects of perception — only processes that are felt. It is thus that in these instances time is in them. (True, seeing is also a sequence, but due to conceptualization we perceive units — trees, roads, cars etc., — and the perceptual process recedes to the background.) Here, space is vague. We are aware that they (smell, taste, sound) occur in space. But what exact space? We cannot define and say.

Rasa comes in this second category. As a very concrete word, in the sense of 'flavour' or 'taste', all the above-mentioned features are to be found in it. But have we not translated it earlier as 'essence?' Then why do we emphasize its sequential nature, its being a process?

By doing so, we will find out how the concrete and the abstract uses of *rasa* are related. We might also find out how diverse the two uses of the word are, i.e., if process (flavour is within a process of perception) and essence are inimical.

Essence is of **something**, be it an object or a process, and both object and process are in space-time. It is for this very reason that essence should not be confused with any object or any process. Essence cannot be said to have a frozen quality. In that case it can be located in space. Nor does it possess the quality of movement, in which case it can be traced in time. It is thus that essence cannot be said to be in the space-time continuum. We cannot also talk of locating it nor in terms of its duration. Hence, it cannot be grasped by the sense though it can be grasped through and beyond the senses. This clearly indicates that the two uses are inimical.

But are we justified in the claim that we have just made? Is *rasa* a process? Let us go back to the *Kauśitakī Brahmaṇa Upaniṣad* again: "The fragrance of *Brahman* enters (emphasis supplied) him." 'Enter' is the key word here. *Rasa* (flavour) is perceived only due to the process of entering. Thus, the perception of *rasa* is a process.

But in the *Taittirīya Upaniṣad*, it is said, " . . . only after perceiving the essence (or flavour) can one perceive bliss." What kind of perception is being referred to? In a metaphysical context, senses play only a subordinate role. Perception, as we have said before, can also be beyond the senses though through them. Let us take for instance the concept of truth. Though it might come to us through our hearing, reading or seeing of something, it is beyond any of the senses involved. Besides, in our daily life, often clarity of understanding comes suddenly — partly due to earlier cognition. But when such an understanding or insight comes in a moment, though it is through both conceptual and sense perceptions, it is not in them.

Rasa, as it is used in the *Taittirīya Upaniṣad*, comes at the end of a process; it is the result of a process but is itself beyond process. Its persistence is not as an object but as an essence.

Here, in a way, we see the movement of something beyond itself. In other words, there is the possibility of a transcendence. Undoubtedly, the perception of *rasa* is a **process**. But as we have seen, it can also be an **instant**. Beyond that (whatever it be, process or instant) it can still persist, for *Taittirīya Upaniṣad* says, in 'perceiving' it you perceive 'bliss'. This kind of perception cannot be located in space-time as bliss (in the context of *Brahman*) is beyond both space and time.

Let us list our findings. First, *rasa* is used in the sense of both process and essence before the time of *Nāṭya Śāstra*. Secondly, *rasa* perception is determinate, sequential and chronological in time as a sensory process. Thirdly, it is rooted in matter (here matter is whatever is directly apprehensible in space). It is exuded by matter but is not matter itself, i.e., its existence presupposes matter. Its source(s) is determinate in space, but it itself is indeterminate in space, i.e., it is pervasive in space. Fourthly, it is something which, when used directly in a metaphysical context, attains a new dimension — that of the essential. In this sense, *rasa* refers to a unique process that has the ability to elude space and time and become an essence. What this means is that the development of *rasa* as a concept has within itself the implications (and also the possibilities) of both process and essence.

To sum up, *rasa* is perceived in a process ('enter') which stretches to the edge where processes and products/objects disappear. Then there is a sudden leap into bliss. I use 'bliss' only to heighten the sense of space and time which are not there to the experience of a break in sequence.

Undoubtedly, in the pre-*Nāṭya Śāstra* context, *rasa* has only a secondary importance as a concept. But it is perhaps in its Upaniṣadic use that it can be related in any important way to the concept of *rasa* as it is to be found in *Nāṭya Śāstra*.

Hence, when we discuss *rasa* in *Nāṭya Śāstra*, we have to keep in mind these meanings of the concept which had already been in existence by then.

Rasa in Nāṭya Śāstra

Let us now look at *rasa* as it is used in *Nāṭya Śāstra*. Bharata, using it for the first time, says (*Nāṭya Śāstra*, I.17) :

> *rasānatharvāṇadapi*

> . . . he took . . . Sentiments from the *Atharvaveda*
> — Manmohan Ghosh, *The Nāṭya Śāstra*, p. 4

But between the *Vedas* and *Nāṭya Śāstra*, a fairly long gap (of at least five hundred years) is to be found. Even the Sanskrit used in *Nāṭya Śāstra* is distinctly different from that of the *Vedas*. It is much more likely that by the time *Nāṭya Śāstra* was written, the Vedic tradition had established itself so strongly that every new treatise tried to link itself to this tradition.

Be it so, this gives us one important clue. Bharata says these words when discussing the four primary constituents of drama — wisdom, dance, music and *rasa*. Thus, our supposition that *rasa*, though discussed briefly here, was still considered a very important constituent of drama is validated.

After this rather vague reference to *rasa* in the first chapter, Bharata deals elaborately with it in the sixth chapter of *Nāṭya Śāstra*:

> *tatra rasāneba tābadādāvabhivyākhyāsyāmaḥ. na hi rasādh kaścidārtṛta pravartate* . . . . (VI.31)
>
> Among these topics, we will first of all explain what are *rasas*. For without *rasa* no topic (of drama) can appeal (to the mind of the spectator)
>
> — Masson & Patwardhan, *Aesthetic Rapture*, Vol. I, p. 46

We immediately notice the great emphasis laid upon the relation of *rasa* to drama — it is indispensable, says Bharata, for without it nothing 'can appeal'.

What can be deemed one of the most important qualities of any literature, any work of art? That it attracts, it draws attention to itself. In Indian tradition, this is not enough. Beyond the mere act of drawing attention to itself a work of art must appeal. In other words, it should not contain mere shock-value. A lot of things come into vogue and then they are forgotten. Such things might immediately catch our attention. But they fail to sustain us for long. After the initial impact they may not have anything that touches us. Thus, a work of art is successful only when there is appeal. Without *rasa*, according to Bharata, there can be no appeal. Hence, without *rasa*, a work of art (here, drama) is incomplete, unfulfilled.

But to **whom** should it appeal? Obviously, to the spectator. And to appeal, the topic must have *rasa*. *Rasa*, in this sense, resides in the text. But a topic or a text will appeal to the audience only through an act of communication and if *rasa* is indispensable, it would imply that *rasa* must also be transmitted to the audience.

To sum up, *rasa* is indispensable to any work of art. Secondly, it must reside in the successful work of art. Thirdly, it is necessarily communicated to the audience or at least makes its presence felt — for unless it is communicated, how can one know that *rasa* resides in the work? Finally, its function is to make a work appealing. This is equivalent to saying that only *rasa* can make a work successful.

No doubt, when Bharata says that there can be no meaning without *rasa*, he is making a sweeping statement. True, literally, even without *rasa* (whatever it be) a work will remain meaningful. Then in what sense will a work become meaningless without *rasa*? It will become meaningless in that it will fail in its purpose — providing aesthetic delight. Thus, *rasa* makes a work appealing. In fact, as we shall see later, Abhinavagupta, speaking of beauty, says that the real essence of poetry is in the creation of beauty; that the perception of beauty is the soul of poetry (*Aesthetic Rapture*, Vol. I, p. 16). Thus, when *rasa* is considered as the soul of poetry, **meaning** and **appeal** become one and the same thing.

Coming to the word 'appeal' — *pravartate* — in its root sense it implies 'coming forth', 'manifestation', 'origin'. In *Chāndogya Upaniṣad*, it is used in the sense of 'circulated' or 'setting out'. In the *Mahābhārata*, it is used to mean 'coming from' or 'issuing forth' (*Monier-Williams Dictionary*). Thus, the key word is *pravartate*. It implies that *rasa* is the root, the origin, the cause. Bharata claims that without *rasa* nothing can 'issue forth'. It is as if this special something which infuses a work or is a very integral part of it is such that only it can make the work meaningful or appealing.

As mentioned earlier, a communication is indicated. Hence, unless *rasa* is communicated how can one talk of 'appeal'? Undoubtedly, Bharata is talking about the meaningfulness or appeal that the work produces in someone else other than the author. When he speaks in the context of drama he is talking about the audience. When *rasa* is savoured or tasted, it involves someone who takes in something and responds — the reader or the audience. Since the 'issuing forth' or the 'emergence' of *rasa* is being discussed, for whom does *rasa* 'issue'? Who sees or feels it 'issuing forth'? The perceiver, be it the reader, the audience or even the poet, is hence involved in a relation of response. Thus, this perception and the response are a reaction to a stimulus. Either a part of the stimuli is, or else the stimuli (text or drama) has some presence or essence which can be called *rasa*. This is successfully transmitted to the audience making the response more satisfying, more complete. This is all we can conclude safely at this point.

What is Rasa Made of?

But what is this *rasa* made of? What does it consist of? Bharata says in *Nāṭya Śāstra* (VI.31):

> *rasa* comes from a combination of *vibhāvas*, *anubhāvas* and *vyabhicāribhāvas*.
>
> — *Aesthetic Rapture*, Vol. I, p. 46

Giving an illustration, Bharata, in the same passage, says:

> Just as (flavour) comes from a combination of many spices, herbs and other substances, so *rasa*. . . from many *bhāvas*.
>
> — *Aesthetic Rapture*, Vol. I, p. 46

This passage is of great importance to us as it uses the word *rasa* in two different senses. In the first case, by *rasa* he means 'flavour' in the culinary context. In the second case, he uses *rasa* in its present aesthetic context. That both the uses are made together suggests the prevalence of the first (in the sense of flavour) and its popular currency. In other words, at that time, both the uses seem to have been favoured. Otherwise, Bharata would not have been able to use it so confidently without any fear of ambiguity since, at no point does he try to clarify that he is using the same words in two different contexts and with two different meanings.

Things can also be seen from another angle. Why does he use one *rasa* to illustrate the other? One, he must have been confident that he would create no ambiguity by such a use. Secondly, he could also have had a specific purpose in mind. A possibility is that the aesthetic concept of *rasa* at some point of time might possibly have been derived from the culinary concept. Such a possibility is very likely as we saw earlier in the context of the metaphysical use of the word. The other possibility is the similarity between the two uses, which might have made it easier for one to understand the more complex use.

Now, let us come back to our passage about taste and flavour. Flavour is derived from a combination of foodstuffs. Yet it is not present in them separately. If each is tasted in isolation, no particular flavour is experienced. It is only through a combination and a transmutation (for cooking involves a chemical change) that the flavour comes through. But how does it come through? Only through a process of tasting. This implies that a flavour cannot be known unless it is tasted. It is latent in food. In that state, its flavour is passive. Only when it is tasted does it become active. In other words, it is transmitted in a process. Two, the test of flavour is in its being tasted. Both point to the participation of the perceiver. Hence, the ultimate taste of *rasa* is in its being tasted or perceived.

Sthāyībhāvas

Coming to the various components or constituents that lead to *rasa*, we already know that it is made up of such constituents as *bhāvas*, (*sthāyībhāvas*, *sañcārībhāvas* or *vyabhicārībhāvas* and *sāttvikabhāvas*), *vibhāvas* and *anubhāvas*. But what is the relation among these? Bharata (*Nāṭya Śāstra*, VI.31) says:

> *Rasa* comes from a combination of *vibhāvas*, *anubhāvas* and *vyabhicārībhāvas*.
>
> — *Aesthetic Rapture*, Vol. I, 46

But here the *sthāyībhāvas* are not mentioned. A little later in the same verse he says:

> . . . the permanent emotions (*sthāyībhāvas*) attain the status of *rasas* when they are accompanied (*upagata*) by the various *bhāvas*.
>
> — *Aesthetic Rapture*, Vol. I, 46

In other words, what is suggested here is a certain relation between the *vyabhicārībhāvas* and the *sthāyibhāvas*. Elaborating their relation, Bharata (*Nāṭya Śāstra*, VII. 8) says:

> The permanent emotions are like kings, because many depend on them. So also the other *bhāvas*, being like servants that are subordinate to the person occupying the position of the king, resort to the *sthāyībhāvas* as being subordinate to them (or depending on them).
>
> — *Aesthetic Rapture*, Vol. I, p. 39

Let us, first of all, examine the *sthāyībhāvas*. Though Bharata does not discuss them in the sixth chapter of *Nāṭya Śāstra* (16-17), he gives the various *sthāyībhāvas* of the eight *rasas* as the following:

> Now I will list the *bhāvas* — those that are primary (*sthāyī*), those that (only) accompany the primary emotion (and are thus transitory) (*sañcārī*) . . . . The permanent emotions have been declared to be love (*rati*), amusement (or laughter) (*hāsya*), sorrow (*śoka*), anger (*krodha*), dynamic energy (*utsāha*), fear (*bhaya*), disgust (*jugupsā*) and wonder (*vismaya*).
>
> — *Aesthetic Rapture*, Vol. I, p. 44

'Love', 'amusement', 'sorrow', 'anger' etc. — what are they? Roughly they can be termed emotions or emotional states. Now what does *sthāyī* mean? In its root sense it means that which persists or stays; and these have been compared to kings.

In other words, they occupy a central position while the *vyabhicārībhāvas* or *sañcārībhāvas* occupy a secondary position. In *Nāṭya Śāstra* (IV.34), Bharata also compares them to an ocean which regains its composure even though it may now and then be disturbed (Kane, p. 361).

Both these examples, as well as the etymological meaning, point in the direction of durability or persistence or both. But next comes the question, can the *sthāyībhāvas* be directly perceived by the senses? Are they visible, audible or can they be touched? The answer is no. They can only be inferred.

VYABHICĀRĪBHĀVAS

Enumerated in *Nāṭya Śāstra* (VI.68) are the *vyabhicārībhāvas* of *bhayānaka* :

> . . . paralysis, sweating, stuttering, horripilation, trembling, a break in voice, change of colour, anxiety, confusion, depression, panic, rashness, lifelessness, fright, apoplexy, death and so forth.
>
> — *Aesthetic Rapture*, Vol. I, p. 54

'Confusion', 'panic', 'depression', 'rashness', 'fright' etc., are inward reactions while 'paralysis', 'trembling', 'change in colour', 'death' etc., are outward manifestations. Then, what exactly is the nature of the *vyabhicārībhāvas*? Certain possibilities can be seen here. One, Bharata, while talking of 'fright', 'rashness' etc., has seen them as totalities, that is, he has considers their emotional content as well as their outward manifestations. Secondly, in a similar way, 'change in colour' etc., suggest fright or even confusion. But fundamentaly, they indicate states that are fleeting.

We have already seen that Bharata compares the *vyabhicārībhāvas* to servants and the *sthāyībhāva* to a king. In the sixth chapter of *Nāṭya Śāstra* (18-20) Bharata lists thirty-three *vyābhicārībhāvas* : 'World-weariness', 'physical weakness', 'anxiety', 'envy', 'depression', 'laziness', . . . (*Aesthetic Rapture*, Vol. I, pp. 44-45). These are inward states. Among outward states are 'physical weakness', 'laziness', 'intoxication' etc. These suggest that Bharata, perhaps, refers to the **various states of the human organism** when he talks of the *bhāvas*. Let us not look so very keenly at the distinction between emotional and physical states. Instead, if we focus on the implication — states — in a broad way, we find that this organism (man) is indicated in various states such as 'laziness', 'anxiety', 'intoxication', 'envy' etc.

Analyzed this way, the earlier difficulty (of identifying emotions and their manifestations) vanishes. What comes out clear is the fact that they are **states**. The most remarkable quality of these states is their fleetness or that they are short lived. They are **transitory states** — both emotional and physiological — that accompany each **stable state** or *sthāyībhāva*.

Once the *bhāvas* are translated as **states** most of our difficulties vanish. We are now in a fairly good position to analyze the relation of *rasas* and *bhāvas*.

ANUBHĀVAS

How does one know about the various states? "He is afraid," one says. But on what basis does one say it? How can one know? There are two ways of knowing. One, when one verbally communicates that he is afraid. The other is when he shows outward signs of it. In *Nāṭya Śāstra* (VI.70) Bharata says:

> . . . violent changes (*bheda*) of the limbs, the face or the eyes, (such as) paralysis of the legs, looking about in panic, collapsing (*sanna*) (on the ground), drying of the mouth, palpitation of the heart, and horripilation.
>
> — *Aesthetic Rapture*, Vol. I, p. 55

These are the *anubhāvas* of the *bhayānaka* or **furious** *rasa* (or *rasa* of fear) that are listed here. Of course, his list is very rough and he sometimes confuses the manifestation for its implication..

For instance, 'palpitation' cannot be seen directly. But in literature (other that dramatic) it can be described, and this can indicate excitement (on account of fear). But basically, what are these? — a list of **signs** of different nature (auditory, visual etc.) which are generated by fear.

So, when one is in a state of fear, these are the outward manifestations or the effects. This is very essential for any kind of communication, for only on the basis of this (or verbal communication) can one know the inward emotional state of the person in a condition of fear. These are, in fact, tangible graspable proofs of a reaction to a specific stimulus.

When one is at the receiving end (a man in a given situation or even the audience), these are the possible outward manifestations. But more important, when one is at the giving end, (the actor, or even a person who want to communicate), these are the only outward signs (except language) through which he can communicate voluntarily or involuntarily. This implies (as we have hinted earlier) that communication is possible only through a **material** medium that can be perceived by the **senses**.

Here, an important point must be noted. In an enactment, we are not concerned with communication through verbalization or writing. Drama essentially means **action**. Its intimate relation to dance (in the Indian context) also made this essential for an aesthetic communication. But even otherwise, it is obvious (and must have been obvious then also) that there is a difference between showing a thing and telling a thing. A man telling that he is sad, and a man suggesting his sadness through certain indications are two different things. In any kind of art form, this difference becomes vital. It is, in fact, this possibility of using suggestion as a stimulus to evoke the intended emotional responses which seems to have influenced Ānandavardhana to propound the theory that **suggestion** is the soul of poetry (*Dhvanyāloka*).

Thus, in literature, a more effective way of telling an emotion is by showing its manifestation. Even otherwise, there is really no way of telling an emotion. By using the word 'sad' sadness cannot be communicated. In fact, there is no such concrete thing called sadness. The word 'sad' immediately brings to mind concrete instances and associations (sad situation, tears etc.) which are very much similar to the *anubhāvas* listed above.

Gnoli, among the modern critics, translates *anubhāvas* as **consequents** which are the results of **antecedents** (*vibhāvas*). S.K. De points out that *anubhāvas* are those that make the different kinds of representations capable of being sensed (De, p. 20). He defines the *vibhāvas* also in a similar way. Then what is it that separates them? The basic difference is that *anubhāvas* follow (as a consequence) the *vibhāvas*. Thus, here again, an intimate cause and effect relation is indicated. Kane also defines *anubhāvas* as those that convey the emotions through external manifestation (Kane, pp. 362-63). Here, once more, the quality of being perceived from outside (in a drama) is indicated. For him, *vibhāvas* are the determining and exciting elements (Kane, p. 362). But what is it that is determined or excited? Naturally, emotions. Hence, they come at the beginning of any emotional reaction (that is depicted in a work).

In a literary work, in this manner, the generation of emotions is indicated by the *anubhāvas*. But first of all, they must be generated. In order to be generated, they must have a reason, a cause and the nature of this cause is bound to be very complex, for this cause which stimulates an emotional state (in the subject in a work) can be both external and internal. A man can be unhappy without any apparent cause. He may think of something (pertaining to the past) and become unhappy. Again, an external event — a death or a theft — can make him unhappy. But if we look carefully, we find that all causes, in the long run, are born from outside. For instance, a man is unhappy for his past deeds. At present, the cause is internal. But at some point of time in the past, it was outside of him. Looking at this in another way, it can also be said that it is a certain absence of good (which can be considered as a negative stimulus) that makes him unhappy. It is thus in the case of *śṛṅgāra rasa* in *Nāṭya Śāstra* (VI.45) where the absence of the lover causes the beloved unhappiness. Absence of another person in a lonely house is the cause of fear (*Nāṭya Śāstra*, VI.68). It is also possible that some external object reminds one of some presence (of bad deeds) or some absence (of the lover) that makes one sad.

VIBHĀVAS

The *vibhāvas* listed under *bhayānaka rasa* in *Nāṭya Śāstra* are (for instance) the following:

> . . . ghastly noises, seeing of supernatural beings, fear or panic due to the cry of owls, jackals, going to an empty house or the forest . . . .
>
> — *Aesthetic Rapture*, Vol. I, p. 54

What is the nature of these *vibhāvas*? They are directly graspable by the sense and they are what generate an emotional state which in turn results in an emotion or state of mind (*bhāva*) and its consequences (*anubhāvas*).

Thus, the relation between the *vibhāvas* and the *anubhāvas* is now clear. First of all, they are not *bhāvas* (emotions or state) but those that **lead to** and indicate them. They are organically related to them. A *vibhāva* is that which leads to or causes the *bhāvas*. An *anubhāva* is one which outwardly manifests, necessarily follows, or is the effect of the *bhāvas* that can be noticed by the senses.

Rasa and Bhāva : Which One Came First?

About the relation of *rasa* and the *sthāyībhāva*, Bharata says in *Nāṭya Śāstra* (VI.31):

> . . . in the same way that beverages such as *sadava* (a combination of six flavours) are created . . . the permanent emotions attain the status of *rasa* when they are

> accompanied (*upagata*) by the various *bhāvas*.
>
> —*Aesthetic Rapture*, p. 46

Here, Bharata has made a distinction between *sthāyībhāvas* and the other kinds of *bhāvas* — *sañcārībhāvas* or *vyabhicārībhāvas* and *sāttvikabhāvas*.

Earlier, Bharata said:

> . . . the permanent emotions attain the status of *rasa* when they are accompanied (*upagata*) by the various *bhāvas*.
>
> —*Aesthetic Rapture*, Vol. I, p. 46

This stand is strengthened by what the later aestheticians say. For instance, according to Bhaṭṭa Lollaṭa, the determinants (*vibhāvas*) are the cause of the birth of feeling which constitute the *sthāyībhāva* (*Aesthetic Experience According to Abhinavagupta*, p. 25). For Śaṅkuka, *rasa* (which he identifies with the *sthāyībhāva* generated in the reader by his perception of *sthāyībhāva* in a work or play) is perceived by the audience by the *vibhāvas*, *anubhāvas* and the *sañcārībhāvas* (or *vyabhicārībhāvas*) (*Aesthetic Experience According to Abhinavagupta*, p. 31).

Now, by the various *bhāvas*, Bharata might be implying the *vyabhicārībhāvas*, the *sañcārībhāvas*, and even the *sāttvikabhāvas*, but he definitely cannot mean the *vibhāvas* and the *anubhāvas* which do not 'accompany' *bhāvas* — *vibhāvas* cause the *bhāvas*, and *anubhāvas* are the effects, indications or consequences.

A controversy rages in this context. Bharata says (though there are divergent views prior to him which he mentions in *Nāṭya Śāstra*) that *bhāvas* give rise to *rasa* and not *vice-versa* (*Nāṭya Śāstra*, VI.33):

> Do *bhāvas* come from , or does *rasa* come from *bhāvas*? Some hold that they arise from a relation of mutual

> dependence. But this is not true. Why? Because, we find that *rasas* come from *bhāvas*, but *bhāvas* do not come from *rasas*.
>
> — *Aesthetic Rapture*, Vol. I, p. 47

He justifies his claim by quoting some *ārya* stanzas — ancient stanza forms (*Nāṭya Śāstra*, VI.33-34):

> . . . *bhāvas* are so-called because they give rise to (*bhāvayanti*) . . . . As spicy (flavour) is created from many substances (*dravya*) of different kinds, in the same way the *bhāvas* along with (various kinds of) acting, create *rasa*.
>
> — *Aesthetic Rapture*, Vol. I, p. 47

This is justifiable for *rasa* itself is a heightened state achieved through emotions (in the perceiver). These emotions are the result of *bhāvas* suggested through the various indications such as *vibhāvas* and *anubhāvas*. Now, since *rasa* is the goal, once it is achieved, we cannot consider the possibility of anything beyond it. Simply put, *rasa* transcends *bhāvas* and hence cannot lead to them as it is itself the result of *bhāvas*. But as Abhinavagupta points out, the very concept of *bhāva* comes into existence only because of the concept of *rasa*. The very possibility of *bhāva* is contained in *rasa*. Hence, a relation of mutual dependence is to be perceived (*Aesthetic Rapture*, Vol. II, pp. 74-75). This justifies the *ārya* stanzas (the view opposed to that which Bharata quotes) (*Nāṭya Śāstra*, VI.38):

> . . . *rasas* are roots, and on them are founded the *bhāvas*.
>
> — *Aesthetic Rapture*, Vol. I, p. 47

From our above discussion of the *sthāyībhāva*, we know that it is indicated both in the work (Bharata, Bhaṭṭa Lollaṭa etc.) as well as in the perceiver (Śaṅkuka, Abhinavagupta etc.). Two kind of implications can be drawn from this. First, the *sthāyībhāvas* (the king among *bhāvas*) are what are generated in the work and lead to the *rasa* experience in the reader. Secondly, the *sthāyībhāvas* create a similar state in the perceiver which later gets heightened into *rasa*.

If we refer to our earlier discussion of the *vibhāvas* and *anubhāvas*, we find that they are apprehensible in nature, i.e., they can be grasped directly by the senses. Bharata has used *bhāvas* roughly in the sense of **states**. We have also seen the nature of the *vyabhicārībhāvas*. It seems, Bharata roughly categorizes them along with the *vibhāvas* and the *anubhāvas* — outward manifestations of emotional state or very fleeting inward states.

The World of Stimulus and Response

Rasa comes from a combination of the various *bhāvas*. What does this imply? Let us take the example of 'fear' to illustrate the point. A large empty house or darkness may give rise to fear and results in 'trembling' etc., on the part of the person concerned. The fleeting states that accompany this are 'paralysis', 'horripilation', 'trembling' and so on. All these are, in a dramatic context (and also in a literal one), detected by the audience. In turn, the *vibhāvas*, *anubhāvas*, *sancārībhāvas* etc. generate in the audience's mind a state that is **perceptive** to fear or a state of fear. This perception of fear is not necessarily that of feeling threatened, but that of experiencing that state of mind.

This implies that this state of fear is something induced by/ deduced from a totality (of *vibhāvas*, *anubhāvas* and *sañcārībhāvas*) and thus affects the audience. It (that which the audience feels) is not directly apprehensible by the senses. It is generated by a sequence, a combination and a totality of stimuli (which are all in a process). What can this state be called — the *sthāyībhāva* of *bhaya* or fear? *Bhaya* or fear, as such, cannot be located in a work of art or in a play. One cannot point and say, "there is *bhaya*". One may be able to talk of the signs of *bhaya*, but one cannot trace *bhaya* directly. Thus, the *sthāyībhāva* or the dominant emotional state that persists through a work is hidden in the work (is latent). Its nature is such that it can unfold only in time and thus manifest itself to its audience. But as such, it cannot be assigned to any one place in a work.

The other thing about *sthāyībhāva* is that it is the result of the various *bhāvas*. It is only because of them (*vibhāvas*, *anubhāvas* etc.) that it comes into existence. It is the result, in the audience, of a totality of stimuli; a response which persists throughout the performance; an awareness of a certain emotion which more or less persists throughout the work.

Let us now arrange our inferences. One, *sthāyībhāva* is not directly apprehensible or graspable by the senses, being a psycho-physiological state (most of which is unperceivable by another through the senses). By saying *bhaya*, fear cannot be generated in the audience.

Secondly, it is in the nature of a **response** to a stimulus. But the stimuli to which it is a response are of a very complex nature because these stimuli are not any direct kind of stimuli which we encounter in our daily life, but the kind that transform the reality. This creates a new problem. In real life, any response is the result of a stimulus. In drama (or any literary work), both the stimuli as well as the response have to be indicated. If one sees fear being enacted (or reads about it in a book), that fear must have a cause (definable or indefinable) that can be indicated. If this is not done, the work becomes incomplete and fails. Thus, in a sense, a world is being generated in a work. Diagrammatically, this can be represented thus:

Stimulus ——————— Response
(*vibhāva*) (*anubhāva*)

But for the audience, both the *vibhāvas* and the *anubhāvas*, the actors themselves and the totality upon the stage are the stimuli. Hence, diagrammatically:

Stimuli ———— actors ——— Response
(*vibhāva*) (*anubhāva*)

accompanying states
(*vyabhicārībhāvas*)

Stimuli ———— Response
(*sthāyībhāva*)

From this we can tentatively conclude that the *sthāyībhāva* is in the nature of a **response**, both within the work and also as one that is generated in the audience. It is, thus, not in the nature of a stimulus in itself.

But Bharata says that the *sthāyībhāva* attains the status of *rasa* in the long run. In other words, the process does not end only with the generation of the *sthāyībhāva*. What is the nature of a *sthāyībhāva* then, let us ask again? — a response which is the continuation of a process. One might ask, what process? We can answer, the process of enactment which takes place outside the audience (in the theatre or in a written work where the enactment is internalized) which generates a process of response in the audience. The process of response is heightened, as the performance continues, aided by the memory of what has already happened (the performance being in time, and so being an aesthetic act) so that a heightened state or mood of a certain durability slowly emerges — the *sthāyībhāva*. Diagrammatically:

Stimulus ———— Response ——— *sthāyībhāva*

But none of this, including the *sthāyībhāva*, is above **process** in itself. Nonetheless, *sthāyībhāva* is a process which is implicit and completely internalized in the sense that it is generated not in response (directly) to things outside, but to an **inner process of response**.

Then What is the Nature of Rasa?

We come to know from the above discussion that *sthāyībhāva* is not *rasa*. Then what is *rasa*? To this question Bharata replies (*Nāṭya Śāstra*, VI.31):

> . . . because it can be savoured.
>
> —*Aesthetic Rapture*, Vol. I, p. 46

This undoubtedly is a strange answer but an interesting one. Instead of saying, *rasa* is such and such, he so answers as to throw light upon one of its basic qualities—*rasa* can be savoured. Talking of time, one cannot point to it, "this is time". In the same way, one cannot point and say, this is *rasa*. We already know that it (even in the sense of flavour) cannot be located in space. It is perhaps for this reason that Bharata approaches the problem indirectly. In saying that it can be savoured, Bharata points to one of its qualities—just as when talking of time one says that change is one of its features.

Abhinavagupta discusses *rasa* elaborately in his *Abhinavabhāratī*. He also gives the views of other critics who preceded him. A brief discussion of those, here, would seem relevant. Briefly, the view of Bhaṭṭa Lollaṭa is that:

> the birth of *rasa* takes place out of the combination of the permanent emotional states. More precisely, the determinants (*vibhāvas*) are the cause of the birth of feeling, which constitutes the permanent state of mind.
>
> — *Aesthetic Experience According to Abhinavagupta*, pp. 25-26

Thus, according to Lollaṭa, feelings are generated by the *vibhāvas* and these feelings, when they persist, become *sthāyībhāvas*. Therefore *rasa* is simply a permanent state, intensified by determinants, consequents etc. (*Aesthetic Experience According to Abhinavagupta*, p. 26). This view, according to Abhinavagupta, is similar to that of Daṇḍin.

Śaṅkuka does not agree with this. For him, it is simply a permanent state of mind, and more precisely, the reproduction of the permanent state of mind proper to the person reproduced. This reproduced mental state (in the actor/stage) is perceived by the audience by the *vibhāvas*, *anubhāvas* and *sañcārībhāvas*.

"Thus, *rasas* are made up of the permanent feelings" (*Aesthetic Experience According to Abhinavagupta*, p. 31)

Here, the emphasis is on the actor — his various manifestations. *Sthāyībhāva* in him, when it is communicated to the audience, leads to *rasa*. Abhinavagupta, following his master Bhaṭṭa Tauta, criticized this theory. He points out that Bharata never said that *rasa* is the reproduction of a *sthāyībhāva* (*Aesthetic Experience According to Abhinavagupta*, p. 40).

According to Bhaṭṭa Nāyaka:

> it is neither perceived (*prati*), nor produced (*utpad*), nor manifested (*abhivyaj*).
>
> — *Aesthetic Experience According to Abhinavagupta*, p. 43

Abhinavagupta accepts one aspect of this theory, that *rasa* **cannot be created** (at will). More precisely, *rasa* cannot be born, has no beginning nor any end. He quotes *Nāṭya Śāstra* (VII) to justify that *rasa* is the aim of poetry — " (The mental states) are called *bhāvas* because they bring into existence (*bhāva*) the aim of poetry" (*Aesthetic Experience According to Abhinavagupta*, p. 50).

According to Abhinavagupta, in the ideal perceiver there occurs a perception transcending the words of the poem (*Aesthetic Experience According to Abhinavagupta*, pp. 52-53). In this perception, the emotion is perceived in its elementality, without any temporality or spatiality. For instance, fear (in this state) is perceived as an elemental fear, beyond what generates it, in whom and where (*Aesthetic Experience According to Abhinavagupta*, pp. 53-55). This is so, for according to Abhinavagupta, the real limiting causes (in everyday life — time, space, the particularized cognizing subject etc.) on one side, and those offered by the poem on the other, neutralize each other and then completely disappear (*Aesthetic Experience According to Abhinavagupta*, p. 58). Thus, the mind of the perceiver becomes free from obstructions and experiences the *rasa* untouched by any blemishes of the ego.

It is in this way that the mind becomes a generalized, neutral medium where *rasa* is fully manifest. He calls this state of mind *camatkāra.* It indicates a state in the enjoying subject (reader or audience) where he is immersed in the vibrations of a marvellous enjoyment — *adbhutabhoga* (*Aesthetic Experience According to Abhinavagupta,* pp. 59-69).

So, finally, Abhinavagupta concludes:

> From whichever point of view it is examined *rasa* is, in any case, simply and solely a mental state which is the matter of cognition on the part of a perceiver without obstacles and consisting in relish.
>
> — *Aesthetic Experience According to Abhinavagupta,* p. 62

Now comes the question, is *rasa* indeterminate in time as it is indeterminate in space? Raising this question is as good as asking whether *rasa* is a process or an essence. But we cannot go to this immediately. In using the illustration of 'flavour', Bharata acknowledges the growth (at least to some extent) of aesthetic *rasa* from culinary taste or relish (*rasa*). But this analogy confuses us. We are not in a position to infer from this whether *rasa* is a process or an essence. Even so, let us look at things closely. The Vedic use of *rasa* — as water, *soma* juice, or flavour — always implied a vital fluid. In ancient chemistry and medicine, again, *rasa* is used in the sense of the vital ingredient. Even in the culinary use of the word, *rasa* (flavour) is the most vital element and in fact the essence of food. Thus, in almost all these uses, the sense of 'vital' or 'essential' is carried connotatively — for 'vital' or 'essential' is that without which a thing loses its identity; without which a thing or a concept collapses. In other words, it is the essential quality. Let us stop here for a moment and go back to the analogy of flavour.

Savouring is a process; and what is savoured is a *rasa*. Hence, it is only through the savouring process that *rasa* can be known. But a knowing or experience cannot be possible as long as a process is dominant. It is only when a filtration or a transcendence occurs that an experience is achieved.

Thus, knowing of anything implies a transcendence of itself from its process quality or from time. When Abhinavagupta says that one is in a state of *camatkāra* (or when one is oblivious of time and space) he, perhaps, hints at this.

In saying that *rasa* can be savoured, Bharata acknowledges its tangibility. He emphasizes the process through which this savouring is possible. He also suggests the fact that *rasa* exists prior to its being savoured (if not *rasa* in an active form, at least *rasa* in a latent form). Thus, without any doubt, perception of *rasa*, very much like the perception of flavour, is through a process. The existence or even the finding of *rasa* is attached to the process of savouring. But the question is, can this **process of savouring** be identified with *rasa* or is *rasa* **beyond** this?

We already know that *sthāyībhāva* is the consequence of an inner process of perception — it is the generalization of emotions. But there must be a conscious or unconscious transcendence of these emotions within the mind of the audience. The relish is in that. One must be able to transcend one's ego and experience the *rasa* — this, according to Abhinavagupta, is known as *sādhāraṇīkaraṇa*. It implies a universalization of emotions. When our limiting emotions of daily life neutralize the particulars depicted in a work, what comes through is a transcendent elemental state (*Aesthetic Experience According to Abhinavagupta*, p. 58)

When seen this way, *rasa* is nothing but a heightened sequence of relishes generated by a stable and heightened state of emotion (*sthāyībhāva*). We have, earlier, seen that *sthāyībhāva* is considered (by most theorists) to be generated not only in the text or work, but also in the perceiver. This *sthāyībhāva*, in the perceiver, is the result of the *sthāyībhāva* in the work. This in turn is the result of the *vibhāvas* and *anubhāvas* (accompanied by the *sañcārībhāvas*) both in the work and also in the perceiver's mind (where the intensification of emotion results from and is similar to that depicted in a work). Thus, *rasa* comes to us through a series of processes.

But earlier, Bharata has acknowledged the prior existence of *rasa* (even before it is perceived), for he says that without *rasa* no work has any meaning. In this, what is implied is that *rasa* is already there in the work. In other words, its essential nature is hinted at, which is elaborated further by Abhinavagupta who compares *rasa* to a wondrous flower (*adbhutapuṣpavat*) which is self-created (*Aesthetic Rapture*, Vol. I, p. 32).

Abhinavagupta highlights this by suggesting that *rasa* is *alaukika* (not of this world, transcendent and sublime) — it is above and beyond its constituent parts. In a theatre, we neither live in the time and space of the original characters nor in that of the actors (and hence of the audience as well). We are thus, in a sense, outside both space and time. There is no parallel to what takes place in a literary experience, nor can we duplicate it. That is why Abhinavagupta compares it to a wondrous flower which has neither a beginning nor an end. It cannot also be experienced at will. It **simply happens** (*Aesthetic Rapture*, Vol. I, p. 37).

Two things are important here. One is the discussion of space-time. The other is the unusual nature of the *rasa* experience. We have already discussed the possibilities of space-time. Here, let it be mentioned that since *rasa* is the end (the goal to be achieved), once it is reached there is nowhere else to go. In this sense, *rasa* is beyond space-time. Earlier, in our discussion of Abhinavagupta, it has been emphasized that time and space in a work and in real life neutralize each other. Thus, *rasa* as an essence is also indicated by Abhinavagupta.

Finally, from the manner in which Abhinavagupta talks of *rasa* as beginningless and endless and the way he brings in man's latent emotions (*saṁskāras*), it can be said that *rasa* attains almost a mystical status in his hands. Bharata (we saw) claims that without *rasa* the essence of art is lost and the essence of art (according to him) is aesthetic delight. This is substantiated by the fact that he highlights dance which (as he also points out) has no (moral) function other than giving pleasure (*Nāṭya Śāstra*, I.164-65). In his comparison of *rasa* to flavour he says that the *sumana* (reader or audience) like the *sumana* (gourmet) attains pleasure by the act of savouring (*Nāṭya Śāstra*, VI.31).

Talking of *camatkāra* (which is the *rasa* experience in the perceiver), Abhinavagupta says that it is immersion in an enjoyment which can never be **satiated** (*Aesthetic Experience According to Abhinavagupta*, p. 59). In other words, it is an enjoyment that has no end. Thus, a transcendent delight (which is above the pleasures of the ordinary emotions) is indicated. It is an **act** which is also an **achievement** and hence outside of time. Again, discussing *camatkāra* a little later, he says, it "means the action of the tasting/enjoying subject, who is immersed in the vibrations of a marvellous enjoyment" (*Aesthetic Experience According to Abhinavagupta*, pp. 59-60).

Then he defines *rasa* as *alaukika*— out of this world. Thus, *rasa* is unique. He further adds that the experience of the poet and the spectator are (one and) the same (*Aesthetic Rapture*, Vol. I, p. 12). In other words, *rasa* is not only transcendent, wonderful and a miraculous delight that has no beginning nor end, but it is also such that it transcends individual ego, and goes beyond all differences into oneness.

Thus, the nature of *rasa* (the essential) indicated in its Upaniṣadic use comes very close to its use here as an aesthetic concept. In fact, the experience is compared to (and identified with) the experience of *Brahman* as we shall see below.

The Sympathetic Perceiver

A very basic question that must be asked prior to any discussion of an aesthetic possibility is, what is the purpose of art? One might say 'pleasure'. Another might reply, 'didactic'. But in whichever way it is answered, the underlying question is, whose pleasure, whose learning? In other words, there must be a **perceiver** who perceives it. But is that all? One perceives many things in his daily routine. Is the perception of an aesthetic object similar to that kind of perception? If it is, then it would no longer be categorized as or called an aesthetic object. Hence, once an object is considered an aesthetic object, its perception involves a specific kind of response.

Coming back to the point, a work (here, a literary work) of art is meant for a perceiver. Secondly, its perception does not remain a mere perception. It elicits a certain response. Thirdly, this response (whatever its didactic undertone) is one of enjoyment or relish. If this were not so, why would one take the trouble of going through the act of this kind of perception?

The moment it is said that aesthetic *rasa* is like culinary *rasa*, the analogy of food immediately brings in the possibility of relishing its taste. Thus, the extreme importance of the perceiver or the reader is noticeable.

This has, in fact, been emphasised and elaborated by Bharata in the sixth chapter of *Nāṭya Śāstra* (VI.31) where he says:

> As gourmets (*sumanas*) are able to savour the flavour of food prepared with many spices, and attain pleasure etc., so sensitive spectators (*sumanas*) savour the primary emotions suggested by the acting out of the various *bhāvas* and modulations of voice, movement of body and display of involuntary reactions, and attainment of pleasure, etc.
>
> — *Aesthetic Rapture*, Vol. I, pp. 46-47)

A new element, the *sumana* or the ideal perceiver is thus introduced. *Sumana*, in a culinary context, is one who is a specialist, a connoisseur. Hence the question, can *rasa* be perceived by all? If it can be, then there would be no need for the discussion of *sumana* — everyone would be an ideal reader. In other words, *rasa* perception needs an initiation and so, *rasa* cannot be perceived by all.

Who is a *sumana*? — The answer is one who has a pure (*śuddha*) mind (*mana*). Thus, a certain criteria is established. A *sumana* must be 'pure-minded'. Abhinavagupta in his *Abhinavabhāratī* (commenting on the word *sumana*) interprets pure-minded in this way:

> . . . with a mind that is completely free from any kind of obstructions from any sense-organ (i.e., completely concentrated) because they are completely absorbed in the thrill of imaginative experience . . .
>
> — *Aesthetic Rapture*, Vol. I, p. 47

Ānandavardhana uses another word, *sahṛdaya*, to imply the same — the responsive reader or one who is gifted with an alert sensibility (*Aesthetic Rapture*, Vol. I, p. 9). So, the perceiver must be one who must not have any personal biases. He must also be able to get completely involved in the aesthetic experience. This is what Abhinavagupta calls *sādhāraṇīkaraṇa.*

On the other hand, unless one is initiated, how can he be a *sumana* (in a culinary context)? Thus, certain specializations are needed, and training is necessary. In the context of language (be it verbal or gestural), certain conventions and manifestations (of responses) must be understood and certain states deduced — for *rasa* perception is not an automation. It is not a mere mechanical act as hearing or seeing. Abhinavagupta (referring to Daṇḍin's *Kāvyabhāratī*) says that when the reader is sensitive through former practice and merit, the meaning becomes clear (*Aesthetic Rapture*, Vol. II, pp. 66-67). It, thus, involves what Abhinavagupta calls *saṁskāra* (all experiences whether cognitive or emotional that are latent in the mind) and *vāsanā* (tendencies of past life) which can be compared to Carl Jung's 'Collective Unconscious'. Abhinavagupta, defining them, says that in the course of our ordinary life we acquire a certain proficiency through long practice in inferring people's mental moods and their basic emotions by observing certain signs consisting in causes, effects and accompanying elements. It is, thus, upon the reader's *saṁskāra* that a successful communication of *bhāvas* depends (*Aesthetic Rapture*, Vol. I, p. 26).

We come back, in this way, to the intricate relation of the perceiver with the *vibhāvas*, *anubhāvas* and *vyabhicārībhāvas* (antecedents, consequents and psycho-physiological states) that are to be observed in a work of art, and from which the *bhāva* (here in the sense of emotional state) is to be deduced.

When we roughly say that *rasa* was transmitted, what do we really mean? For, we have seen that *rasa* cannot be generated unless it is potentially there in the perceiver. Like emotions in man, they cannot be transmitted directly, but only stimulated in one who has the potential. When another's distress makes us feel distressed (in case of a simple emotion) what happens is that we are able to put ourselves in his position and identify with him. Hence, it is our participation, potential to share, to receive, that is important here.

Any work, be it a text, a performance or even a painting, in **itself** is inert. In itself, nothing is dynamic — not even man. As we have already seen, our entire discussion revolves around a relationship — between emotions, between stimulus and response, and between man and an aesthetic world. When we say — "he is angry", what do we mean? We definitely cannot enter his emotional state nor feel it directly. What are recognized are the physical or outward manifestations of his anger. Similarly, in a work, the various manifestations of emotions are co-related, combined and presented. In that, one can say that a certain work is **about** anger. But where is anger to be found in it? Anger is to be found in the work in the sense that the work has the potentials of anger, the outward signs of anger, the capacity to elicit the response of anger or its awareness in one. In this broad sense, *rasa* can be said to be innate in a work, in a latent form.

It is the same with *sthāyībhāva*. Where can one locate a *sthāyībhāva* in a work? It is not possible, since no emotion can be located outside man. Knowledge (of any kind) or information can be fed into man. It is something that can come from outside. But no emotion, no heightened state of mind can be borrowed — for they both involve an intimate inter-relation and are generated (owing to the presence of the inner potential) within one or else they are simply not generated. Thus, the perceiver is of fundamental importance in the discussion of *rasa*.

This reminds us of the *ārya* stanza in *Nāṭya Śāstra* that *rasa* and *bhāva* are mutually interdependent: for unless the *bhāvas* (through the indications or *anubhāvas*, *vibhāvas* etc.) are perceived, how can *rasa* be generated? It cannot be generated in response to emptiness and the *bhāvas* will have no function, no meaning, unless they are directed towards the generation of *rasa*.

Bharata says, "*rasa* comes from a combination of the various *bhāvas*" (*Nāṭya Śāstra*, VI.31). But unless *rasa* is already potential in that combination (to be stimulated in the perceiver), it cannot be generated. If a perceiver could generate it without any help or stimulation from outside, then the very discussion of aesthetics and *rasa* would not arise.

On the other hand, a work does not become manifest in or by itself. It is not self-created. There is always a man (or men) from whom it issues forth. It can even be said that the writer transforms his *rasa* experience into the correct combination of *bhāvas* through his *pratibhā* (genius/intuition) and hence *rasa* persists in a work, unseen, unmanifest. Abhinavagupta, highlighting this aspect, says that the "imaginative faculty" (here implying the *rasa* experience) is not only to be inferred by the sensitive reader as existing in the poet, but it is also to be directly experienced because the spectator himself is overcome with *rasa*. Quoting his master Bhaṭṭa Tauta, he says that, thus, the experience of the hero, the poet and the spectator is (one and) the same (*Aesthetic Rapture*, Vol. I, p. 12). In fact, elsewhere, talking of the aesthetic experience of poet Vālmiki (the writer of the

Rāmāyaṇa), he suggests that it is transmitted through the work to the reader.

When we talk of the **transmission** of *rasa*, we are referring to the relation of *rasa* with *bhāva*. The *rasa* experience of the writer gets translated into *bhāvas* (through the *vibhāvas*, *anubhāvas* and *sañcārībhāvas* indicated) which can be diagrammatically represented in this manner:

rasa — *bhāvas* — *rasa* stimulation/manifestation —
Pleasure (author) (Reader/perceiver)

The stimulus-response relation is all the more complicated, when this is taken into account. The author or the artist receives stimuli from outside which combines with his *pratibhā* (creativity) and gives rise to a different kind of response — the work of art. This work, in itself, contains a world (where we see both stimuli and response: *vibhāvas* and *anubhāvas*) that, as a totality, becomes a stimulus to which the audience or perceiver responds.

World — Artist — Work — Perceiver — *rasa* — Pleasure

Now, let us get back to the issue of the perception of the reader. Earlier, we had seen that *rasa* perception involves a series of stimuli and response relations. This involves sequentiality or *krama*, an interesting aspect of sense perception which was noticed as early as the AD tenth-century by Indian aestheticians. Abhinavagupta says that logically time must elapse between perception and response (in a work of art). This is called *krama* (sequentiality). But it passes so swiftly that one hardly notices it (*Aesthetic Rapture*, Vol. I, p. 21). This interesting observation not only applies to literature and music which unfold sequentially, but also to spatial arts since they also must be perceived first before one can respond to them.

Earlier, we had repeatedly emphasized relish or delight which is the **response** to the perception of good literature. Here, let it be mentioned briefly that in Indian aesthetics, the moral function of art has never been given a primary place as in the West (e.g., in Plato, Aristotle *et al.*). Bharata in *Nāṭya Śāstra* (I.164-65) justifies dance, which fulfils the simple function of being beautiful, for leading us to delight.

No doubt, the moral function of art has been given its due position. Bharata (*Nāṭya Śāstra*, pp. 60-64) points out that drama also fulfils a didactic function. Instructions are provided through a pleasurable medium. Even later aestheticians subscribe to the same view. But even so, morality has never been the main issue. One might find this strange. But if we look closely, we notice that what is called the *rasa* experience is a kind of delight that transcends ordinary levels of reality. It is thus that in such a state ego is effaced and a transcendence is achieved. Hence, morality, which is related to our day-to-day reality and to the ego (which does good or bad deeds), does not have a place in such an experience. Nonetheless, when we come to *śānta rasa* (which we shall discuss in the next section) we find that, since the ultimate goal of *rasa* is a state of bliss, *rasa* experience does serve a moral function — it helps one overcome one's worldly desires and achieve transcendence to a higher level.

We have briefly mentioned the concept of *sahr̥daya*. He is one who can be called (like *sumana*) the **ideal perceiver**. But what exactly does the word mean? *Sa* means 'identical' and *hr̥daya* stands for heart. In other words, this involves an identification as well as an identical inclination to understand the work in the sense in which a work is meant to be perceived.

Now, after Ānandavardhana, Abhinavagupta defines *sahr̥daya* as follows:

> . . . those people who are capable of identifying with the subject-matter, since the mirror of their hearts has been polished through constant recitation and study of poetry, and who sympathetically respond in their own hearts are known as sensitive readers.
>
> — *Aesthetic Rapture*, Vol. I, p. 6

Here, we have a description of all the necessary qualifications of a *sahṛdaya*. Like Bharata's *sumana* (pure-minded), the ideal reader's heart must be clear like a polished mirror. Personal biases must never come in the way. The reader's personality must never intrude. Bhaṭṭa Nāyaka highlights this when he says that *rasa* is revealed in poetry by the special power of words that suppress the thick layer of mental stupor (*moha*) occupying our own consciousness (*Aesthetic Experience According to Abhinavagupta*, p. 45). It is in this context that Abhinavagupta's concept of *sādhāraṇikaraṇa* must be discussed in detail.

Sādhāraṇīkaraṇa implies total identification of the perceiver with the work (which he perceives) (*Aesthetic Rapture*, Vol. I, p. 11). Thus, a great performance infuses the audience (by a process of universalization) resulting in the identification of the spectator with it (*Aesthetic Rapture*, Vol. II, pp. 61-62). In other words, it is not only necessary that the work must be infused with *rasa*, but the perceiver must also be ready for it. It is here that his training and study come into the picture. Besides, his *vāsanās* and *saṁskāras* (latent possibilities and earlier memory) help (in perceiving *rasa* from the *vibhāvas* and *anubhāvas*). In other words, training alone is not sufficient. It has to be complimented by the innate tendencies in man to experience (in oneself) and perceive (in others) emotions. This also holds the implication that *rasa* is not something that can be **acquired** but something that is and has only to be **revealed**.

Now, *rasa* involves total identification. But what does this state imply? It is a state when the personality or the ego does not intrude. In other words, *rasa* experience, as said earlier, is not something that can be perceived or relished by all. It is for this reason that Abhinavagupta says:

> *Rasa* is nothing less than the reader's reaction to, his personal involvement with, literature . . . .
>
> —*Aesthetic Rapture*, Vol. I, p. 25

Every reader, thus, is not the ideal reader. He must have training, inclination and the ability for total identification, which is possible only when there is no ego to intervene. This state of consciousness does not admit of experiences such as the desire to reject or accept (*Aesthetic Rapture*, Vol. II, pp. 61-62).

This is a very important aspect of the *rasa* theory for it gives a possible solution to the age-old question — how can painful things (sorrow, fear, disgust etc.) be relished in an aesthetic experience? Hence, Abhinavagupta reserves his greatest praise for the moment when the spectator is able to enter so deeply into the imaginative experience that he transcends his own personality (*Aesthetic Rapture*, Vol. I, p. 7). This is the state of **ultimate bliss** — *ānanda*.

Total identification implies the loss of a personal identity — for one is lost in the experience depicted in the work to the extent of forgetting himself. It is in this light that Bhaṭṭa Nāyaka differentiates the *rasa* experience of perceiving emotions from direct experience or memory which can also generate emotion (*Aesthetic Experience According to Abhinavagupta*, pp. 45-48). *Rasa* experience is, thus, an experience of a different order. Abhinavagupta also highlights the same aspect when he refers to Vālmiki's writing of the *Rāmāyaṇa*. The separation of the he-bird from his beloved (which is killed by a hunter) is what stimulates Vālmiki to write his epic. But Abhinavagupta is emphatic that the poet could not have composed the poem when he felt the emotion of sorrow himself. It is only when he had transcended his own grief could he possibly have universalized it. *Rasa* experience cannot hold the possibility of sorrow (*duḥkha*) since it is synonymous with bliss (*Aesthetic Rapture*, Vol. I, p. 47). Hence, this aesthetic experience is of a different order than ordinary experiences.

But if *rasa* implies total identification, then who is it that relishes? Abhinavagupta says that at the highest moment of aesthetic relish there is no subject or object (*Aesthetic Rapture*, Vol. I, p. 47). In the absence of an ego, an 'I', who is it that relishes the *rasa* experience? In the Indian context, the answer is relatively simple.

Now, since the *rasa* experience is *ānanda*, it is like the blossoming of a magic flower; it is essentially a thing of the present moment which does not depend on past or future time (*Aesthetic Rapture*, Vol. I, p. 18). Thus, through time, *rasa* transcends time. This state of consciousness, without any obstacles, is called *camatkāra*. It is thus, according to Abhinavagupta, an immersion in an enjoyment which can never be satiated (*Aesthetic Experience According to Abhinavagupta*, p. 59). It is **eternal** and hence transcends time. Since it has transcended the possibility of both a beginning and an end, it is a state akin to the experience of *Brahman* (the Absolute). Of course, once one comes out of the aesthetic state, the ego can recognize the fact that it had been submerged in a *rasa* experience of *ānanda*. This is akin to the *nirvikalpa samādhi* state in *yoga* (spiritual trance) and may be termed *rasa samādhi*. This also, interestingly, indicates that ordinary pains and pleasures do not affect one as they belong to the ego and to an ordinary state of perception.

Even if the mystical aspect is ignored, one cannot deny the fact that any deep aesthetic experience involves a forgetting of both ordinary time and space; and once one loses oneself in the experience, time and space (depicted) in the work are also forgotten. Both the 'times' and 'spaces' go to neutralize one another (*Aesthetic Rapture*, Vol. I, pp. 31-32), and one is only steeped in that unique heightened state of aesthetic enjoyment.

2

The Rasas and their Relationship

WHETHER *Nāṭya Śāstra* has listed eight *rasas* or nine *rasas* is controversial. But most scholars are of the opinion that the ninth *rasa*, i.e., *śānta rasa*, is a later addition. Nonetheless, Abhinavagupta highlights *śānta rasa*. He, in fact, suggests that all the other eight *rasas* lead to it. Therefore, it will be proper to discuss the eight *rasas* first and then discuss *śānta rasa* and its relationship with the other eight *rasas*.

The Eight Rasas

> In a drama there are the following eight *rasas*: erotic (*śṛṅgāra*), comic (*hāsya*), compassionate (*karuṇa*), furious (*raudra*), heroic (*vīra*), terrifying (*bhayānaka*), disgusting (*bībhatsa*) and awesome (*adbhuta*).
>
> — *Aesthetic Rapture*, Vol. I, p. 44

Bharata, in *Nāṭya Śāstra* (VI.15), classifies dramatic content on the basis of emotions. All these *rasas*, coming under a common class, must have something in common. The point of commonality is that they all have some emotional content. Yet they must also have their points of differences, on the basis of which they establish their own identities. These differences are the ways in which the various emotions are manifested.

Nāṭya Śāstra emphasizes the fact again and again that the

object of art is pleasure. No doubt, art can be didactic or full of philosophical speculations, but all of it must come through a medium that is pleasurable. In *Nāṭya Śāstra* (IV.164-65), Bharata justifies dance because it gives pleasure. In another instance, *Nāṭya Śāstra* tells the story of how a fight ensues when the demons are shown in a bad light (in the first dramatic performance). Hence, art should not hurt anyone. It should please all (*Nāṭya Śāstra*, I.64-68). Even in Aristotle, we find a grudging acknowledgement of this fact: "It is also natural for all to delight in works of imitation" (*Poetics*, p. 682). Thus, this ability to give pleasure or delight is another feature that brings the various *rasas* under a common category. They are primarily experiences that are rewarding. That the *rasas* like *bhayānaka*, *bībhatsa*, and *karuṇa* can also give delight has already been discussed.

Though all the *rasas* are pleasurable, the emotive content behind the pleasure is different. Thus, they can be compared to different roads that lead to the same goal or the same zone of pleasure. This categorization of emotions or even works of art is nothing strange to Indian aesthetics or poetics. In Aristotle's *Poetics* we find dramatic poetry broadly divided into tragedy and comedy (p. 683). Now, if we try to arrange Bharata's classification under these two heads, this is how it would look:

> *Tragedy*: Compassionate, furious, heroic, terrifying, disgusting, awesome or wonderful.
>
> *Comedy*: Erotic, comic, heroic and awesome or wonderful.

A number of elements overlap in these two categories: especially **heroic** and **awesome** (which I translate as **wonderful**). In other words, the basis of categorization in *Poetics* and *Nāṭya Śāstra* is different. Of course, later, Abhinavagupta categorizes *rasas* as *sukhātmaka* (which, in the work, lead to happiness) and *duḥkhātmaka* (those which lead to sorrow) [*Aesthetic Rapture*, Vol. II, p. 76]. But what I intend to point out here is that while in *Poetics* we have a binary division, in *Nāṭya Śāstra* we have nine different manifestations. Thus, while in Greek drama, tragedy does not admit of the possibility of comedy and the reverse, in Indian drama, the possibility of some of the elements being together in the same drama is admissible. Undoubtedly, the **comic** and the **terrifying** are not acceptable together, but in the erotic there is the possibility of separation (for some time), which leads to longing and sorrow. In longer works, especially in the Indian epics (the *Rāmāyaṇa* and the *Mahābhārata*) all the different *rasas* are to be found, though in the end, one of them might stand out most prominent.

But there are certain puzzling aspects of things that cannot be overlooked: for instance, why did the Indian aestheticians make the possibilities of love so narrow? *Śṛṅgāra rasa* or the erotic emotion focuses almost entirely upon manifestation of the love between man and woman. It ultimately leads to a physical union, and also suggests a union that transcends the physical. Abhinavagupta again and again emphasizes that mere lust is not to be considered *śṛṅgāra* (*Aesthetic Rapture*, Vol.II, p. 76). Rājā Bhoja, in later tradition, claims *śṛṅgāra* to be the only *rasa* and makes it too broad. Still later in the tradition, *śṛṅgāra* in the context of *bhakti* (spiritual devotion) leads to the possibility of a union with the Ultimate. This possibility is known as *bhakti śṛṅgāra*.

But what about the love between parents and children? What about the love among brothers and sisters? What about the love between two friends? True, these relations (roughly put) cannot lead to any union. But there can always be exceptions. A love between two friends might transcend physicality. Thus, this is an aspect that can be said to have been neglected. Now, what could have been the reasons for this?

For one thing, the essence of *rasa*, as we have discussed earlier, is in an intensification of a particular emotion to such a state where it gets transformed into something that cannot really be called an emotion in the ordinary sense. Since, the possibility of exploring the relation among parents and children, friends etc., is relatively rare, it could have led to their neglect. Besides, according to our tradition certain things are considered duties or *dharma*. *Dharma* has the following connotations: " . . . . that which is established or firm, steadfast, decree, statute, ordinance, statute, law; duty, right, justice . . ." (*Monier-Williams Dictionary*, p. 510).

Other than that, in Indian tradition, life has been divided into three *puruṣārthas* or broad sections: *dharma* (duty or profession), *artha* (commerce or wealth) and *kāma* (desire and pleasure). (A fourth was later added, *mokṣa*, but since this involves a transcendence of the world, it really cannot be considered a *puruṣārtha*.)

Thus, the love of parents for children, love among children etc., comes under the category of duties. Love between husband and wife also involves duty. But all the same, erotic love among (young) husband and wife are to be seen as *śṛṅgāra rasa*. But since, later in *Nāṭya Śāstra* we have the mention of three kinds of *śṛṅgāra* — *dharma śṛṅgāra*, *artha śṛṅgāra*, and *kāma śṛṅgāra*, this word, *śṛṅgāra*, need not necessarily mean only 'erotic'. It can roughly be translated as desire, that is, desire for righteousness, desire for wealth, and desire for love. But the various causes and manifestations of the *rasa* listed (namely, young men and women, flowers, laughter, games, shyness, smiling etc.) overrules the possibility of the other two *śṛṅgāras* being intended here (*Nāṭya Śāstra*, VI.45). So, what we have here is only *kāma śṛṅgāra*.

Nonetheless, it can be pointed out that the emotion of love or attachment figures in *karuṇa rasa* or the compassionate emotion as well. Interestingly, here we see love from a negative point of view, i.e., we see the negation, denial or blockage of love. When lovers are separated forever, when a father, a son, or a friend is killed, what is generated is sorrow at the death or separation of the object of love.

Coming back to the erotic or *śṛṅgāra rasa*, in *Nāṭya Śāstra* (VI.45), this *rasa* has been divided into two categories: love-in-union and love-in-separation. These are in fact the two possible conditions in which love can not only be felt, but will also thrive — for in the absence of the lover, one will realize how incomplete one's life is, and will also feel the anguish of separation and the desire for union. The first category depicts the intensification of love when the lover and the beloved are together. The second category depicts the reaction of the lover or the beloved in the absence of the loved object. Here, sadness, longing etc., are intermixed with the expectation of future union. Thus, the second category is close to *karuṇa rasa*. But while in *karuṇa* or the **compassionate** *rasa* there is no possibility of reunion, in love-in-separation, this possibility is not only present but it is also emphasized. *Karuṇa*, on the other hand, arises from the frustration of an attachment.

In Indian literature as well as poetics, it is *śṛṅgāra rasa* that is given maximum importance. Even otherwise, *karuṇa rasa* always occupies a secondary position wherever it is depicted in this tradition. The reason why this is so, and also why *bībhatsa* and *bhayānaka* do not figure very prominently, is not far to seek. In Indian tradition, there are two metaphysical possibilities that participate intensely in the lives of the common men: transmigration of the soul, and the consequences of one's *karma* or good/bad deeds. Thus, evil can never be rewarded. If not in this life, in the next life one will reap the consequences of one's evil acts. Similarly, good, if not now, will certainly be rewarded in the next life. It is thus that the very possibility of tragedy cannot be conceived here, for in a tragedy along with bad, good is also destroyed. So, here the scope for sorrow, horror, rage, etc., are minimal. Nonetheless, in the epics, especially in the *Mahābhārata*, all the *rasas* are to be found. But, since the Indian world-view is rather optimistic, the *rasas* such as *karuṇa*, *bībhatsa*, *bhayānaka*, etc., are not very visible.

Since *karuṇa rasa* involves a desire which is refuted, it is closely related to *śṛṅgāra* — for here we have the absence of the object of desire. Thus, between the two of them *śṛṅgāra* and *karuṇa* exhaust almost all the aspects of love. As, in this refutation, denial or separation there is the possibility of both violence and violation, it is related to both *bībhatsa* and *bhayānaka* where there is a violation or distortion of order and harmony.

Of the relation of *rasas*, *Nāṭya Śāstra* (VI.39) says:

> The comic aesthetic experience comes from the erotic. The compassionate comes from the furious. The awesome comes from the heroic and terrible from the disgusting.
>
> — *Aesthetic Rapture*, Vol. I, p. 48

Thus the *rasas* have been divided into two categories: primary and secondary. The primary *rasas* are those from which the secondary *rasas* are derived. Hence, the primary *rasas* are *śṛṅgāra*, *raudra*, *vīra* and *bībhatsa*. The secondary *rasas* are *hāsya*, *karuṇa*, *adbhuta* and *bhayānaka*.

The **comic** or *hāsya rasa* presupposes a state of well-being. Unless one is happy or in a positive state of mind, one cannot appreciate laughter or see anything funny. Since the *rasas* that show the absence of well-being are the following — *raudra*, *bhayānaka* and *bībhatsa* — the comic element is usually absent there. Even so, there is the possibility of the fusion of *karuṇa* and *hāsya rasa* — many examples of which we see in the West — that can lead to the 'comedy of the grotesque'. In *bhayānaka* and *bībhatsa* disgust and fear dominate. Hence, comedy does not find any scope in them.

But strikingly, the very structure of these *rasas* is similar to that of *hāsya rasa*. In all these three *rasas* there is an incongruity; something which is out of the ordinary, that is, unusual. Thus, all the three involve a break of harmony and order. But what determines the nature of the *rasas* is the nature of their response and their consequences. If they are harmless, it leads to *hāsya*. On the other hand, if they are such as destroy and deform permanently, the possibilities of *bhayānaka* and *bībhatsa rasas* arise.

Karuṇa rasa is the consequence of *raudra rasa*. *Raudra* or the **furious** *rasa* leads to damage and destruction. Thus, in its manifestation, it holds the potential of an intimate relation with *bhayānaka* and its consequences — destruction and devastation — hold the possibility of sorrow.

Adbhuta or the **awesome** *rasa* is considered a consequence of the action of *vīra* or the heroic. Heroic actions lead to an admiration for them. Since they are difficult, almost unbelievable, they lead to the experience of the awesome or the wonderful. Let it be said here that *adbhuta* indicates that which surprises in a delightful manner. But it also holds the possibility of seeing supernatural things that are almost frightening. In this way, the element of fear is also contained here. But as wonder dominates over fear, it is a positive *rasa*. For this reason, *bhayānaka* and *bībhatsa*, where fear and disgust are central, cannot lead to *adbhuta*. All these three *rasas* have the element of **surprise** in common. In *adbhuta*, it is of a positive kind. In *bhayānaka* and *bībhatsa*, it is of a negative kind.

In Indian tradition, *vīra* has always been an important *rasa*. In both the epics, where we see a lot of war and heroic action, it is manifest. Besides, in many of the plays of the Sanskrit dramatist, Bhāsa (fourth century AD), they prevail. *Vīra rasa* is not a very complex *rasa*. Here **dynamic energy** or *utsāha* is the most dominant emotion. Since, in response to it (upon the stage), *vismaya* or wonder can be shown, *vīra* is always accompanied by *adbhuta rasa*. Thus, if the focus is upon response, the central *rasa* can become *adbhuta*. But unfortunately, in Sanskrit literature, it has been rather neglected.

Raudra or the **furious** *rasa* is in most cases an accompaniment of *vīra*. This is so since *vīra rasa* is usually generated against some injustice, where there is the possibility of anger. In this regard, *raudra* and *karuṇa* are very similar, as both can be the result of some deprivation. At a physical level, there can be the deprivation of a hand or a leg or even of life. At a material level the deprivation of wealth (as in the case of the Pāṇḍavas in the *Mahābhārata*) and at an emotional level, the deprivation of love etc., can also lead to either of these *rasas*. Threatened deprivation and the trauma and insecurity following it can also lead to sorrow or rage. The difference is that, in *karuṇa*, the result of the deprivation is loss of hope and resignation. In *raudra* it is fury. The former involves a process of acceptance, while the latter involves a fierce reaction of protest and rejection.

Similarly, *raudra* is close to *bhayānaka* as, in both cases, the result is fear. The difference lies in the fact that in the former, the emphasis is on the element of anger, while in the latter, it is the resultant fear or fearsome atmosphere that is the focus of attention. Besides, *raudra* might have some just reason, in which case it fights for good and against evil. But in *bhayānaka* the atmosphere is always negative.

Bībhatsa and *bhayānaka* are the most neglected of the *rasas*, both in Indian poetics and in our ancient literature. It is only in some plays of Bhāsa (which take episodes from the *Mahābhārata*) that they are seen together with *vīra rasa*.

It is categorically stated in *Nāṭya Śāstra* (VI.39) that *bhayānaka* is the secondary *rasa* which has its source in *bībhatsa* or the **disgusting** *rasa*. In *bhayānaka* or the **terrifying** *rasa*, the immediate response (be it the response depicted in the work or the response of the audience) is fear. But in *bībhatsa* or the **disgusting** *rasa* there is an intermediary step. The first response here is lack of comprehension, for like *hāsya* it also arises from the incongruous. But as this incongruity is of a negative kind, it is more of a displacement, a substitution of the normal by the abnormal. It is this that strikes one first with surprise, a surprise which is of a negative kind and so cannot lead to *adbhuta rasa*. Only after that comes the possibility of fear. Thus, since *bībhatsa* precedes *bhayānaka* — before fear there has to be the possibility of an abnormality — *bībhatsa* is considered the primary *rasa*. It is usually the abnormality that is noticeable first. Only from that perception comes the possibility of fear. Even otherwise, many fears are the result of incomprehension, for instance, the fear of the dark. Here, darkness stands for the unknown. In it things lose their identity, and thus it indicates the possibility of disorder.

But the basic difference between these two *rasas* is that in *bhayānaka* fear is what is dominant. But in *bībhatsa* incomprehension lurks everywhere. Let us take the instance of a 'dead body'. It gives rise to disgust since it is something we do not understand. At the edge of life it lies like a question mark. It is a distortion of life, and hence disgusting. But the possibility of fear comes from many sources. Apart from the fear of ghosts etc., the other reason for fear is insecurity. A dead body implies that one can die — and is, thus, an implicit threat to existence. Besides, a dead body close by also suggests that whatever caused its death can also threaten one's life.

Bībhatsa and *bhayānaka* are both life negating. But if we look at any ancient literature closely, we find that it is *bībhatsa* that has been neglected everywhere. When Aristotle talks of tragedy ('pity' and 'fear') he is talking about two negative emotions. But disgust is an emotion that has never been emphasized until recently. It is perhaps with the two World Wars of the twentieth century, that *bībhatsa*, as a dominant force, emerged in literature.

The Greeks had always shown a stubborn optimism for life. This leads to tragedy, and disgust naturally takes the back-stage in such a situation. For instance, disgust is generated by the unnatural (son marrying the mother in *Oedipus Rex*), but even so the focus is upon the suffering that follows from it. Here again, we have ample evidence of how the disgusting can lead to the horrifying or the terrifying. But, in India, it is perhaps only in Buddhist literature that disgust or *bībhatsa* played an important role. Nonetheless, in the poetic works of Śaṅkarācārya we find that disgust plays an important function (*Mohamudgara, Bhaja Govindam* etc). Of course, the *Mahābhārata* is a literary work in which the element of the disgusting has been amply explored.

Before we end this discussion, one point needs to be highlighted: the response to the various *rasas* is two-fold — the response which is depicted inside the text and the response of the reader/perceiver.

In case of *śṛṅgāra*, there is an empathetic response in which the emotion of love is communicated to us. The sense of identification plays a very important role here. In case of *hāsya* the response of laughter is similar to what is being seen. But here, the cause is different. We are able to laugh only because we are able to alienate or separate ourselves from the object which is the source of mirth. Thus, a certain distancing is involved. Even so, we are not completely alienated since we are also aware of the possibility of ourselves sometimes becoming the object of laughter.

Karuṇa usually elicits the response of sorrow and compassion in the reader or the perceiver. Yet it can lead to anger if the cause of sorrow can be located and it is evil. Here, both distancing and identification are involved. 'Pity' is an emotion which comes when one can distance oneself from the victim. But if there is a feeling of identity, the sorrow will not only be felt but will also shared by the reader.

In *vīra*, the response is that of *adbhuta*. In the audience or reader, there can be a dual response of inspired courage and wonder. If the heroic acts are unachievable they lead to a response of wonder. This is a response where distancing is involved. But if it is the heroism of a common man (someone with whom we can identify) then both sympathy and identity will operate. Thus, here is the possibility of inspired courage.

Raudra is a *rasa* which depicts fury—death and devastation. Here, the response inside the text and outside will be similar. If one is involved in the perception of fury, he will respond with bewilderment. But at the end of fury, courage (to avenge some injustice), fear, disgust or sorrow at the waste can arise. *Raudra rasa* can be seen from a position of distance. But if the cause of *raudra* is some injustice, then there will be a sympathetic response of anger.

Adbhuta is a *rasa* where amazing or surprisingly delightful events occur. Here, both inside the text and for the reader, it will be a response of amazement, awe or delight. There is always a space across which one inspects the object of amazement; for amazement is shown when one is incapable of doing the same.

It is similar in case of *bībhatsa rasa*. The disgust generated will (or may) be manifest both inside the text and in the reader. Since disgust comes from disorder, incomprehension etc., it can only come from a sense of alienation from what is disgusting.

But in *bhayānaka*, though the perception of the terrifying comes from alienation, the response need not be that of fear. In the reader, the response can be that of fear or sadness or even retribution, depending on the nature of the object that is subjected to fear. If one can alienate oneself from the victim of terror (say, a bad man), the response will not be that of fear or sorrow. But one can perceive the terrifying element. If the victim is a man with whom one can sympathize, the response will be that of sorrow and if one can identify oneself with the victim, then he might even feel fear himself.

Śānta Rasa

Śānta rasa, it seems, was a later addition, though Abhinavagupta tries to show again and again that Bharata was aware of its possibilities. For instance, he quotes *Nāṭya Śāstra*, XVII.58:

> People devoid of passion (take delight) in mokṣa.
>
> — *Śānta Rasa*, p. 137

Mokṣa is the state of bliss when and where there is no distinction between joy and sorrow, where one has transcended the world of binaries and desires. Since Bharata points out that there are certain people who can take delight in *mokṣa*, it follows that they will take delight in the depiction of it in a fictitious form too. Hence, Abhinavagupta assumes that Bharata sees the possibility of *śānta rasa*, whether he lists it separately or not.

But why is it that *śānta* poses such a problem? What is its essence? According to *Nāṭya Śāstra* (the passages which come after VI.82 and which are possibly interpolations) it is defined in the following way:

> *Śānta rasa* has been taught as a means to the highest happiness (*naiḥśreyasa*). It arises from a desire to secure the knowledge of the Self and leads to knowledge of the Truth.
>
> — *Śānta Rasa*, p. 93

Now, the basic objections to its being called a *rasa* stem from the fact that it is difficult to locate an emotion here — for it is said that the experience of *śānta* is that of the "highest happiness" or of bliss. Bliss transcends the ordinary joys and pleasures (*śṛṅgāra, hāsya* or *adbhuta*) and refers to something that cannot exactly be called an emotion. On the other hand, since all the eight *rasas*, though they have their basis in emotions, cannot be called emotions proper but heightened aesthetic states caused by the respective emotions (*sthāyībhāvas* or the permanent states), *śānta* can also be considered within the category of the other eight *rasas*.

But certain theoreticians debate about its *sthāyībhāva* or its permanent emotion. In the passage from *Nāṭya Śāstra, sama* or calmness is listed as its *sthāyībhāva*. Yet, many have objected to this because it (depiction of calmness and inaction) cannot be shown upon the stage. In a passage of *Nāṭya Śāstra* it is said:

> *Śānta* should be known as that which brings happiness and welfare to all beings and which is accompanied by the stabilization (*samsthita*) in the Self that results from curbing the organs of perception and the organs of physical activity.
>
> — *Śānta Rasa*, p. 93

It is here that certain difficulties become obvious, difficulties which have been anticipated and refuted by Ānandavardhana, Abhinavagupta and others (***see*** *Śānta Rasa*, Masson and

Patwardhan, for further discussions). *Śānta* involves a state of stasis. For that matter, all the other eight *rasas* also involve this stasis. *Sthāyībhāva* or the permanent (stable) state persists in a work of art and then is both transformed and transcended in the response of the reader or perceiver to a heightened aesthetic state — *rasa*. *Śānta* also involves this stasis — but by the act of 'curbing the organs of perception' and of 'action'.

But as in the act of aesthetic perception all the five sense-organs are involved, this statement seems objectionable at first. Nonetheless, one can point out that a 'state of mind', is being emphasized; a way of looking at things, which still involves the five senses. Thus, 'curbing' here will not imply stopping the acts of perception, but it is stopping the act of being stimulated or affected emotionally by what is being perceived. This is substantiated in the next passage:

> *Śānta rasa* is that state wherein one feels the same towards all creatures, wherein there is no pain, no happiness, no hatred, no envy.
>
> — *Śānta Rasa*, p. 93

'Pain' and 'happiness', thus, are perceived (from a specific cause, the absence or the presence of which gives happiness or sorrow) but do not **affect** one.

Another interesting possibility, which has not been explored in *NāṭyaŚāstra*, can also be noticed here. If painful and pleasurable things do not affect one in the state of *śānta*, then the implication is that they did (or do) affect him at other times. Hence, prior to *śānta*, the possibility of the various emotions is to be seen and after the state of *śānta* is dispelled (being an aesthetic state, this is possible), the various other emotions can come flooding in. Remarkably, just the opposite possibility has been mentioned in the next passage of *Nāṭya Śāstra*:

> *Śānta* is one's natural state of mind (*prakṛti*). Other emotions such as love etc., are deformation (of the

> original state). The deformation arises out of this natural state of mind and in the end again merges back into it.
>
> — *Śānta Rasa*, p. 93

Even from a Freudian or Jungian context, a part of this argument seems reasonable. In the absence of any necessity or desire, the mind is neutral. When the desires are satisfied completely (which is improbable) or transcended, the state of mind gained is that of calm and neutrality. In fact, most of our efforts are directed to achieve a state of equilibrium or stasis. This is a desire for the refutation and transcendence of all desires.

> The emotions arise out of *śānta* depending on their particular respective causes. And when the specific causes cease to function, they all merge back into *śānta*.
>
> — *Śānta Rasa*, p. 93

It is thus that *śānta rasa* holds the possibility of the other eight *rasas*, and they all are, in this way, intimately interlinked with *śānta*.

From what we have seen about the other eight *rasas*, they are responses of either attraction or repulsion or of both. In *śānta*, we see a cessation of all these forces. *Śānta*, thus, is both similar and different from the other eight *rasas*. Some object that such a state as is suggested by *śānta* is indescribable and undefinable and as it involves the absence of desire (and hence of action) it cannot be depicted upon the stage or in literature. But we have to keep in mind the fact that (as Ānandavardhana has pointed out in *Dhvanyāloka*) the very essence of *rasa* is **suggestion**. Secondly, since all the other eight *rasas* can lead to *śānta*, this transformation can be depicted or shown, though the work might end in complete stasis.

Abhinavagupta, trying to locate the *sthāyībhāva* of *śānta rasa*, points out that the *sthāyībhāvas* of the other eight *rasas* can also be made *sthāyībhāvas* of *śānta*. He also shows the possible relations that the other eight *rasas* can have with *śānta*:

> . . . *rati* alone is the *sthāyin* in *śānta*. For it has been said:
>
> "The man whose love is centred in the Self, who is gratified in his Self, and who takes all delight in the Self — for such a man there is nothing any longer to be accomplished."
>
> In the same way, any of the *sthāyībhāvas* beginning with *rati* and *hāsya* and ending with *vismaya* can be explained as the *sthāyībhāva* of *śānta*, because we find that a person attains to liberation if he realises the oddity of everything in the world (*hāsa*); if he sees that the whole world is lamentable (*śoka*); if he perceives the happenings in the world as harmful to his spiritual well-being (and, angry with them, desires to conquer them) (*krodha*); if he resorts to extraordinary energy dominated by the absence of delusion (in order to overcome worldly temptations) (*utsāha*); if he feels afraid of all the objects of the senses (*bhaya*); if he feels disgust for young women etc., though they are desirable for all other people (*jugupsā*); if he feels astonished at his unprecedented realization of his own self (*vismaya*).
>
> — *Śānta Rasa*, p. 129

He indicates that all the eight *sthāyībhāvas* or permanent states hold the possibility of the "perception of truth" (about the real nature of the world) and thus, the possibility of a transcendence. In other words, they lead to the *sthāyībhāva* of *śānta* — *sama* (a state of calm which is the result of the perception of truth).

It is thus that the *rasa* experience of the eight *rasas*, when taken to their logical conclusion (in Indian tradition), lead to a transcendence of both that experience and of the self towards a self-realization. This, in fact, strengthens the hypothesis that *rasa* experience at its peak is similar to Self-realization.

Hence, once the various causes that lead to the various other *rasas* are transcended (overcome or dissolved) a state of bliss is achieved which is *śānta*. In this sense, the experience of *śānta* can be equated to that stage of the *rasa* experience where the self is transcended. For both the creator and the perceiver, thus, *śānta* holds the possibility of *mokṣa* or enlightenment where all the emotions and their causes dissolve.

Abhinavagupta implies this when he says:

> "What is the nature of true relish?" It is the following: The soul is tinged with *utsāha, rati* etc., which are capable of imparting their (peculiar) tinges to it. It is like a very white thread that shines through the interstices of sparsely threaded jewels. It assumes the forms of all the various feelings like love etc., (which are imposed on it), because all these feelings are capable of imparting their tinges to it. Even then (*tathābhāvenapi*) it shines (through them), according to the maxim, once this Atman shines, (it shines forever).
>
> — *Śānta Rasa*, p. 142

Thus, *śānta* shines through the other *rasas* (coloured jewels) like a "white thread" which is neutral and which can absorb the colours of the jewels, yet holds them together in a thread of continuity and is essentially capable of bringing about the realization of *mokṣa* where the *ātman* shines through.

3

Śṛṅgāra Rasa

WHEN one scans modern Western literature, one is surprised by the problematic nature of love or eroticism depicted in it. If we examine any Western love poetry of the seventeenth, the eighteenth or even the early nineteenth-century, be it English, French or Italian, we find that it almost always bears a striking similarity to ancient Indian or Chinese love poems. For instance the first stanza of Coleridge's "Recollections of Love" reads:

How warm this woodland wild recess!
Love surely hath been breathing here;
And this sweet bed of health, my dear!
Swells up,then sinks with faint caress,
As if to have you yet more near.

— *Norton Anthology*, Vol-II, pp. 381-82

Or any passage of John Keats's *Eve of Saint Agnes*:

"Ah, Prophyro!" said she, "but even now
Thy voice was at sweet tremble in mine ear,
. . . . .
How chang'd thou art! how pallid, chill, and drear!
Give me that voice again, my Prophyro, . . .

— *Norton Anthology*, Vol-II, p. 816,
lines: 306-312

The Sanskrit poetess Marula writes in "Meeting After Separation":

> When I said "You have grown thin"
> She came and clung to me.
> "Your clothes are bedraggled," I said
> And she hung down her head.
> When I said "I can hardly see you,"
> Her big breasts heaved, and she wept.
> When I embraced her
> She was troubled with indescribable love
> And in an instant the doe-eyed girl
> Was completely merged in my heart.
>
> — *India Love Poems*, p. 13

And the Chinese *Book of Songs* has a poem, "Here by the Wall-Gate":

> O, you with the blue collar,
> On and on I think of you.
> Even though I do not go to you . . .
> You might surely send me news?
> . . . .
> O, you with the blue collar,
> Always and ever I long for you.
> Even though I do not go to you . . .
> You might surely sometimes come?
>
> Here by the wall-gate I pace
> To and fro. One day when I do not see you
> Is like three months.
>
> — *Chinese Love Lyrics*, pp. 23-24

Perhaps, in the Indian poem the eroticism is more explicit, but so also in many English, French and Italian poems of old.

But in modern Western poetry we hardly see anything that can be compared with these illustrations. For that matter wherever we look — fiction, drama or poetry — what we see is violence, unnatural love (incest, homosexuality etc.) and unnatural separation. In other words, if we take a few straightforward and simple illustrations of love-in-union or love-in-separation, we will really be overlooking the real issues that confront us. For instance, Stephen Spender's poem "The Express" is a poem where we see love-in-union, but instead of a woman, the loved object is a train and for most part, in modern Western literature, love is celebrated in unusual ways and much of the best writings are about love-in-separation, namely, Gracia Lorca's *Blood Wedding* (which being a tragedy may also come under the category of *karuṇa rasa*), Antoine De Saint-Exupery's *The Little Prince* (a parable) or Vladimir Mayakovsky's long poem, *Cloud in Pants*. Unless such literature as is problematic is scanned and the ancient theory of *rasa* reinterpreted, criticized or even modified, justice can be done neither to the works under scrutiny nor to the theory which scrutinizes them (and is scrutinized in the process.)

Every interaction is also a series of modifications. When the ancient theory of *rasa* is brought face-to-face with modern literature, what we inevitably have is more in the nature of a confrontation than a meeting. In the process, both will lose or be modified to some extent by the interaction if they are both to co-exist. It is with this in mind that we must proceed.

Śṛṅgāra or the **erotic** *rasa* in *Nāṭya Śāstra* has been broadly divided into two categories : *sambhoga śṛṅgāra* or love-in-union and *vipralambha śṛṅgāra* or love-in-separation.

Love-in-Union

Let us discuss *sambhoga śṛṅgāra* or love-in-union first. In *Nāṭya Śāstra* it has been said that (VI.45):

> Of the various *rasas*, the erotic one arises from the *sthāyībhāva* of love. Whatever in the ordinary world is bright, pure (*medhya*), shining or beautiful is associated with love . . . .
>
> — *Aesthetic Rapture*, Vol. I, p. 49

In other words, the dominant emotion that is to be found in a work or the dominant response that it generates in a reader is what can broadly be called love. This is the key with which we must proceed to categorize the works that we shall take up for discussion here and in the other chapters.

The Permanent Emotion in Śṛṅgāra

Rati or love in Indian tradition has always been associated with optimism. In other words, love (to be more precise, love-in-union) leads to happiness. Since love according to this tradition is considered love only when it is mutual, and since *śṛṅgāra* is always supposed to lead to love-in-union, (for love-in-separation finally leads to reunion), 'bright', 'pure', 'shining' etc., are associated with it. The other implication is that love is always good as opposed to evil because the associations are that of 'pure', 'beautiful' etc. Abhinavagupta points out that the 'love' of Rāvaṇa for Sītā (in the *Rāmāyaṇa*) cannot be considered true love since there is mere lust involved there and no mutuality (*Aesthetic Rapture*, Vol. II, p. 77). In fact, this is usually to be found in all traditions — true love is always identified with purity.

The Causes of Śṛngāra

The sources of love are listed thus (*Nāṭya Śāstra*, VI.45):

> It has for its (*ālambana*)-*vibhāvas* young men and women who are noble born.
>
> — *Aesthetic Rapture*, Vol. I, p. 49

What gives rise to or causes love (the *vibhāvas*) is chiefly men and women. Man is the cause of love in woman and woman is the cause of love in man. In other words, they are both the source and manifestation of *rati*. Youth is emphasized since it is the age where passion rules. But does this mean that old men and women are not included? In Indian tradition man goes through four stages in his life — *bramhacārya*, *gṛhasthya*, *vāṇaprastha* and *sanyāsa*. The second period that starts from the age of twenty-five is the age for getting married. Since after marriage (due to togetherness) love loses its insecurity, uncertainty and thus much of its interesting possibilities, this has not been mentioned. And as deviant love (love for someone else's wife etc.,) is considered immoral, it does not get much scope here. But when we look at Sanskrit literature, we have many examples of deviant love. In fact, in the *Nāṭya Śāstra* itself, a kind of heroine is mentioned whose moral position is questionable. Besides, the famous love of Rādhā for Kṛṣṇa which has been used again and again (say in *Gītagovinda*) is an instance of deviant love since Rādhā is both older than Kṛṣṇa and married. Hence, even though some later aestheticians object (especially Abhinavagupta), illicit love is to be found both in literary theory as well as Sanskrit literature. But to sum up, even though there is a lot of illicit love in our traditional literature, our theories are relatively silent about them.

Does this mean that evil, disgusting, lowly etc., cannot be associated with love? For one thing, if love is one-sided and forcible, it will give rise to disgust: and if two evil persons are truly in love, then there is nothing evil **in that** love. The same applies to the love between persons of low birth — love raises them.

Hence, what is important here is the emphasis on mutual response. Abhinavagupta emphasizes the aspect of union where two become one (*Aesthetic Rapture*, Vol. II, p. 77). If one's love is pure (in one-sided love) it will lead to sacrifice which has a chance of manifesting sorrow (at least in the reader). This will naturally lead to *karuṇa rasa* rather than *śṛṅgāra*. Let us keep this in mind and look at the passage on love-in-union in the *Nāṭya Śāstra* (VI.45):

> It arises from (*uddīpana*)-*vibhāvas* such as a (representation) of the seasons, garlands, ointments, ornaments, people dear to one, objects of the senses, fine homes, love-making, going to gardens (and there) experiencing, listening to and seeing games, sexual play and so forth.
>
> — *Aesthetic Rapture*, Vol. I, p. 49

Here, the emphasis is on the congenial climate for love. Śakuntalā and Duṣyanta in *Abhijñānaśākuntalam* meet under such a congenial climate — spring, blossoms, sweet air, festivity etc. But what has not been emphasized here is the fact that love can also blossom in the desert or inside a prison. But if we overlook the *vibhāvas* or **causes** listed and look at the essence, what is actually being said is that the environment must be congenial. If we look at things in this way, the problem disappears — for if a man and a woman meet in a storm, it might be the ideal condition for bringing them together. The main thing is that the causes must be such that they make a path for mutual attraction. Thus, in *Blood Wedding*, which we shall discuss shortly, which is cast in the background of a bleak Mexican village, that earth is congenial for passion (both love and violence).

The Effects and Consequences of Śṛṅgāra

The *anubhāvas* or effects (consequences) of *śṛṅgāra* are as follows (*Nāṭya Śāstra*, VI.45):

> It should be acted out by such *anubhāvas* as a skilful (use) of the eyes, frowning, side-glances, flirtatious movements (*lalita*), gentle bodily movements (*aṅgahāra*), and soft speech.
>
> — *Aesthetic Rapture*, Vol. I, p. 49

These are the usual and age-old tools for the expression of love in almost all cultures in the world. The four poems quoted above (English, Sanskrit and Chinese) are pointers to the fact. But it is more important to note that (*Nāṭya Śāstra*, VI.45):

> The accompanying transitory emotions that do not belong to love are laziness, violence, disgust.
>
> — *Aesthetic Rapture*, Vol. I, p. 49

'Laziness' can be ruled out in all cases of love. It is without doubt inimical to love. 'Disgust' is also inimical to love. But hatred (not mentioned here) is very closely associated with love — in Lorca where the central characters hate their own passions. Besides, where pride comes in the way of love, hatred is a defence mechanism. But 'violence' is not necessarily inimical. We have to understand that violence is being used here in the negative sense — where it does some damage and does not give any pleasure. Similarly, repulsion must not also be confused with disgust — what repels may have an undercurrent of attraction. It might be a manifestation of one's resistance to get into a relation which intermixes both pleasure and pain. In other words, a repulsion may actually be an attraction that is hidden and of which one is afraid.

Violence looks a little problematic. In both Lorca and D.H. Lawrence, love and violence are intermixed. But it is the kind of violence that gives pleasure rather than unmixed pain. On the other hand, anger and hatred (whether real or feigned) have the potential for violence — and they are very intimately related to love; and for that matter violence is not unassociated with love even in the Indian tradition — when it is used for furthering or intensifying love. For instance, this poem by Kālidāsa:

> Proud one be not proud; what you have heard, is false, dear,
>
> Why be angry with your server? If you believe it,
>
> Chain me quickly with your arms, bruise me with your teeth, bruise me with your pointed breasts,
>
> And if you think the fault mine pierce me with the arrows of your side-glances.
>
> — *India Love Poems*, p. 59

Obviously, it is the girl's anger (caused by jealousy) that the speaker is countering through his words. Though breasts and feminine hands cannot do much violence, nails and teeth can inflict (pleasurable) injuries. Thus, there is the possibility of violence in love arising out of jealousy, anger and sexual excitement.

Love-in-union, as we have mentioned earlier, is not a very striking feature of modern Western literature. But we have to keep in mind the fact that this possibility has been relentlessly explored since the time of the ancient Greeks. Besides, anti-romanic stance, scepticism, rejection, unnaturalness, rebellion etc., that are at the root of this difference in attitude, are also the basic features of modern literature. Not that love has not been explored, but the intellectual and the metaphysical overtones have dominated. Yet it does not mean that love has not been very positively explored as we find in Lawrence's works or the works of Gabriel Garcia Marquez (especially in *Love in the Time of Cholera*). In fact, Lawrence's attitude is very similar to the Tāntric attitude. Both hold the potentials of a transcendence (one aesthetically, and the other through a sexual-spiritual exploration) and hence of *śānta rasa.*

Violence, Terror and Love

The poem of Lawrence that we take up for examination has the basic features of any Lawrencian writing — the exploration of the complex psychology of love. Here, we have an interesting work where we see the exploration of fear and violence in love.

"Love on the Firm" has a woman as its narrator. Technically speaking, we have here all the things (mentioned in *Nāṭya Śāstra*) necessary for love. The initiating causes or the *uddīpana-vibhāva* are the woman and the man whom she describes. The *ālambana-vibhāvas* or the accompanying causes are the beautiful evening, a lonely house in the woods, birds etc. But a more remarkable feature is the suggestion of 'fear' and 'violence' everywhere in the poem. The poem begins:

> What large, dark hands are those at the window
> Grasping in the golden light
> Which weaves its way through the evening wind
> At my heart's delight?
>
> Ah, only the leaves! But in the west

I see a redness suddenly come
Into the evening's anxious breast —
'Tis the wound of love goes home!
— *Norton Anthology*, Vol. II, p. 2228

Already fear and love, both, are suggested: fear by *vibhāvas* like 'what large hands', 'grasping', 'redness', 'anxious breast' etc., and love by *vibhāvas* like 'the evening wind', 'love goes home' etc.

The love in the air and in nature are suggested by the following lines:

The woodbine creeper abroad
Calling low to her lover:
The sunlit flirt who all the day
Has poised above her lips in play
And stolen kisses, shallow and gay
Of pollen, now has gone away —
She woos the moth with her sweet, low word;
— *Norton Anthology*, Vol. II, p. 2228

Into such an environment — and we already know that the speaker has thoughts of love in her mind — comes the man from the farmhouse, for whom (it seems) the woman has been waiting. Already we see the suggestion of fear everywhere — a kind of fear that is both attractive and attracted to what it fears:

Into the yellow, evening glow
Saunters a man from the farm below;
Leans, and looks in at low-built shed
Where the swallow has hung her marriage bed.
— *Norton Anthology*, Vol. II, p. 2228

Yet, interwoven into this is the suggestion of terror:

Whose plaintive cry is heard as she flies
In one blue stoop . . .
Into twilights' empty hall.
— *Norton Anthology*, Vol. II, p. 2228

Then the man opens the latch and gets in. Everything suggests that she knows he is coming; in fact she is waiting with fear and attraction, like a helpless bird, like a rabbit caught in a snare. Yet she is (fatally) drawn to him:

> I hear his hands on the latch, and rise from my chair
> Watching the door open; he flashes bare
> His strong teeth in smile . . . .
> . . . . With his hand he turns my face to him
> And caresses me with his fingers that still smell grim
> Of the rabbit's fur! God I am caught in a snare!
>
> — *Norton Anthology*, Vol. II, p. 2229

Attraction and terror merge in a climactic intensity:

> . . . . then his mouth came to my mouth! and down
> His bright dark eyes came over me, like a hood
> Upon my mind! His lips met mine and a flood
> Of sweet fire sweeps across me, so I drown
> Against him, die, and find death good.
>
> — *Norton Anthology*, Vol. II, p. 2229

The **accompanying states** of emotion that the woman experiences (and that are communicated to us) are those of fear, anxiety and agitation. Besides, violence (which is considered inimical to love in *Nāṭya Śāstra*) is suggested: the dead 'rabbit', 'snare', the woman's feeling that she is a victim etc.

But we must keep in mind that violence has never been depicted though suggested. More important (as in Kālidāsa), violence is hidden behind attraction in more than one way. Underlying sexuality there is always the possibility of violence. Besides, since attraction and attachment involve the fear of losing or of not getting, the fear of pain is there. The fear of being made a victim is always there. So, when attraction overcomes this fear, there is a violence against the self. This is to be seen in Lorca's *Blood Wedding*. Thus, in a sense, in love, each is the victim of the other's attraction.

In the last line of Lawrence's poem, we find the woman a victim — but a victim who relishes her 'killing' and finds "death good".

This poem also raises another question in our mind — are *bhayānaka rasa* and *śṛṅgāra rasa* inimical? Though nothing is mentioned explicitly in *Nāṭya Śāstra*, it seems more likely that they are incompatible: love being positive and terror (terrifying) being negative. But the *vyabhicāribhāvas* or the accompanying states of *bhayānaka* like fear, anxiety and agitation are not inimical to *śṛṅgāra rasa*. Hence, even in *Nāṭya Śāstra* the possibilities of these — though not explicated — have not been overlooked. 'Trembling', 'perspiration' and 'fainting' are mentioned among the *vyabhicāribhāvas* of *śṛṅgāra*. Thus, that kind of fear which is not tinged with disgust (*jugupsā*) can be manifest in *śṛṅgāra rasa*. It is the same with the violence in this poem: it is not inimical to love. It rather heightens pleasure and pleasure is the primary feature of love or *rati*.

Inanimate Objects and Love

"The Express", by the British poet Stephen Spender is about an intense relation of the speaker with a train. It is another poem, like "Love on the Firm", where violence, power, grace, cruelty, sexuality etc., are latent. Can it be a love poem when there is no woman involved? Secondly, what are the causes or *vibhāvas* that generate the emotion of love-in-union?

The first objection can be answered by pointing out that since time immemorial, non-human objects like the sun (male), the moon (female) etc., have been attributed with masculine/feminine qualities. Dawn in *Ṛgveda* — *uṣā* — is considered a female and we have many verses addressed to her (*Ṛgveda*, V.80.5-6):

As conscious that her limbs are bright with bathing,
she stands, as 'twere, erect that we may see her.

Driving away malignity and darkness, Dawn, child of
Heaven, hath come to us with lustre.

The daughter of the sky, like some chaste woman,
bends, opposite to men, her forehead down.
— *History of Indian Literature*, Vol. I, p. 83

But one might again argue that in modern literature, traditional symbolisms are not necessarily used. What about a train which is only a modern creation? We can answer by saying that the poem first of all makes a woman of the train, i.e., shows the womanly qualities in the train:

. . . But gliding like a queen, she leaves the station.
Without bowing and with restrained unconcern.

She passes the houses which humbly crowd
outside . . .
— *The Golden Quill*, p. 59

The train's pride, cruel beauty etc., are suggested here. Besides, it is personified and described as a woman — 'she'.

Beyond the town there lies the open country
Where gathering speed, she acquires mystery . . .
— *The Golden Quill*, p. 29

Here, it is the admiration of a man for a beautiful woman.

It is now she begins to sing — at first quite low
Then loud, and at last with a jazzy madness
— *The Golden Quill*, p. 59

Along with her feminine qualities, the cruelty and the sexual violence within her are also being hinted at.

Coming to the *vibhāvas* or the **causes** again, the world through which the poet and the train travel and which affects them is congenial for the intensification of love: 'town', 'open countries', 'metal landscape', 'new eras of wild happiness' etc.

But the consummation comes in the second part of the poem — where the train's response to the poet is suggested and where they both transcend the ordinary world:

Lying with your eyes shut, together, secretly,
You and she are flung into a darkness beyond the
    waters of her mouth,
Where no hand can clutch and all identity is lost.

— *The Golden Quill*, p. 60, lines: 28-30

It is thus, unusually, the possibility of *śānta rasa* (which is also there in devotional love — *madhura-bhakti* poetry) is hinted at.

In both Lawrence and in Spender there is a consummation which almost leads to a complete loss of identity. If we look at Lawrence's poem, we find an experience which is a dissolution of identity in love (and thus both attractive and frightening). The implication is that of death, but of a beautiful, pleasurable death. In Spender, the transcendence, this time by a man (the poetic speaker), is more smooth.

Union in Love

Abhinavagupta comments as follows on the relation between man and woman in *śṛṅgāra* (in *Abhinavabhāratī*):

> The words 'man' and 'woman' convey the idea of mutual love culminating in the desire for sexual enjoyment . . . The love which is a *sthāyībhāva* progressing continuously from its faint beginning up to its final realization and its end in the attainment of complete happiness (in sexual union).
>
> — *Aesthetic Rapture*, Vol. II, p. 79

The important ideas contained herein are of mutual enjoyment and complete happiness in union. We have already discussed the possibilities of one-sided love. Now, let us see what could possibly be meant by 'union'. Union is where two things merge into one. 'Complete happiness' is also a very significant term, for 'complete' means where there are no imperfections or deficiencies. A man and a woman can be completely happy only when there is nothing dividing them, nothing separating them — when what they share is whole. Thus, the possibility of reaching *śānta rasa* (which Abhinavagupta feels is what the eight *rasas* lead/can lead to) is indicated here.

The following lines of Rainer Maria Rilke's "Love Song", for instance:

> How shall I hold my soul, that it may not
> be touching yours? How shall I lift it then
> above you to where other things are waiting?
> Ah, gladly would I lodge it, all-forgot,
> with some lost thing the dark is isolating
> on some remote and silent spot that, when
> your depths vibrate, not itself vibrating.
> You and me — all that lights upon us, though,
> brings us together like a fiddle-bow
> drawing one voice from two strings it glides along.
> Across what instrument have we been spanned?
> And what violin holds us in his hand?
> O sweetest song.
>
> — *Collected Poems*, Vol. II, p. 114

The poem, even at its beginning, transcends physical love. Thus, it holds the possibility of transcending *śṛṅgāra* through itself, towards *śānta rasa*. The originating causes are the two identities. The accompanying causes though not specified — "all that lights upon us" — are of a mysterious and metaphysical nature. The manifestation and the result are "drawing **one** voice from two strings" and consummation in the loss of identity when they become one "sweet song".

The poem, nonetheless, raises problems. Nothing physical is mentioned or involved. It is a metaphysical poem about souls. Yet, since Abhinavagupta suggests possibilities of transcendence into *śānta rasa*, the case remains open. Besides, this kind of writing is well-known in religious poems in Hindu, Hebrew and Christian cultures.

Deviant Relations, Incomplete Relations and Other Problems

Before we discuss love-in-separation, let us discuss certain other problems that we face in modern literature like the intervention of intellect, and the depictions of abnormal relations, unusual consummations or relations that are not complete.

Let us take Pablo Neruda's poem "Adonic Angela" to illustrate the first problem:

> Today I stretched out next to a pure young woman
> as if at the shore of a white ocean,
> as if at the centre of a burning star
> of slow space.
>
> From her lengthily green gaze
> the light fell like dry water,
> in transparent and deep circles
> of fresh force.
>
> Her bosom like a two-flamed fire
> burned raised in two regions,
> and in a double river reached
> her large, clear feet.
>
> A climate of gold scarcely ripened
> the diurnal lengths of her body
> filling it with extended fruits
> and hidden fire.
>
> — *Residence on Earth*, p. 50

The basic difficulty that faces us here is that of comprehension. What does he mean by "lengthily green gaze"? Do we understand what he means by the expression "dry water"?

A reader of Sanskrit literature would be left dumbfounded. But does this mean that such works as these do not hold the possibility of the *rasa* experience?

But then, we have to remember that understanding is to a

very great extent a matter of convention. In India, the convention has always been respected, valued and followed. Even when there has been a break or a movement away from the convention, it has been so in an articulate and comprehensive way. Hence, in such a literature, all the variations and deviations can be understood. But if we look at modern Western literature, the first thing that confronts us is the use of a kind of **private language** — where the convention created is (to some extent) private and an arbitrary one of the artist's creation. Hence, only when the artist's use of language is grasped (more or less) at an intellectual level, an emotional enjoyment of the work is possible.

The present poem is about the interaction of a man and a woman. Here again, the man (as in many traditional Sanskrit poems) celebrates the woman's body. What at first hampers our perception is the **use of language**. The description is unusual, true, but even so the possibilities of consummation are clearly discernible: "filling it with extended fruits/and hidden fire". The ripeness of the body and the fire, which attract the man, rather invite him, are clearly noticeable. Here again, one might ask, is this love mutual? This can be answered by pointing out that the poem endows the body with a thinking, philosophical/ philosophizing quality. Nowhere is the mind of the woman even mentioned. It is in the body that we perceive all the indications of love, and it is the body that responds, reciprocates.

Coming to the second point, love, in modern literature, to say the least, is intriguing. There is a lot of unnaturalness in it if we look at things from a traditional point of view. In Indian tradition, if an incestuous relation is explored, it cannot lead to the fulfilment of *śṛṅgāra rasa*. This, for the simple reason that the unnatural aspect will get highlighted and it will give rise to disgust. But since we are looking at modern literature, we must also look at what is meant by tradition in a broader way. If some 'abnormality' is incorporated into a tradition and becomes a part of it, from then on the element of the unnatural becomes less noticeable.

On the othcr hand, it must be asked, what kind of delight is it when an unnatural relationship is being explored? To a great extent, the delight will be of a sensational kind — pleasure at relishing the forbidden. But once the inhibitions are quietened, once the excitement for the forbidden vanishes (and it is accepted in the convention), the aesthetic qualities can be more clearly noticed. The issue will be whether the manifestation of love has been successfully handled or not. For instance the last two stanzas of Charles Boudelair's poem "Jewels" reads:

As if a new Genesis had been at work,
I saw a boy's torso joined to Antilope's hips,
belying that lithe waist by those wide loins . . .
O the pride of rogue upon that tawny skin!

And then, the lamp having given up the ghost,
the dying coals made the only light in the room:
each time they heaved another flamboyant sigh,
they flushed that amber-coloured flesh with blood!

— *The Flower of Evil*, pp. 26-27

The speaker's words suggest that his beloved is making love to another person and that too, a boy. Two unnatural things — betrayal, and perversion (a woman making love to a boy with all its suggestions of incest). But what is more surprising is the poet's mixed reaction of grudging revulsion and admiration at this sight.

The poem also raises more complexities since the poet's reaction (which is an awareness of convention and its rejection) is again a part of the aesthetic experience both for him and for us. To a certain extent we can understand that the admiration comes from the transcendence of ego which is possible due to what the aesthetic aspect of the sight generates in him. In that, he himself becomes a partly detached observer — who vicariously participates in an act of consummation as a voyeur. It is in that detached participation that *śṛṅgāra* is to some extent generated. But even so, we are left with a certain sense of incompletion —

perhaps an experience that the poet **intends** to generate in us.

This is thus a key problem that will again and again confront us when we analyse things from the point of view of the *rasa* theory. For the essence of *rasa* experience is an **intensification**. But much of modern literature has the tendency to abandon things in the middle — questioning the very possibility of completion. Does this undermine the quality of a good Western work? This, as we have seen before, is debatable.

Love-in-Separation

Let us now come to the possibilities of **love-in-separation**. Though, even here, the final act is that of consummation, it might throw some light on the possibilities of incompletion in love or even final separation.

Effects and Consequences of Separation

In *Nāṭya Śāstra* (VI.45) it is said:

> As for love in separation, it should be acted out by *anubhāvas* such as world-weariness, physical weakness, anxiety, envy, fatigue, worry, longing, dreaming, awakening, sickness, insanity, apoplexy, lifelessness, and death.
>
> — *Aesthetic Rapture*, Vol. I, p. 49

Some of the consequences (*anubhāvas*) listed here have been problematic for some later aestheticians as weli. For instance, the case of 'world-weariness' or *nirveda*. As Masson and Patwardhan comment, "to be separated from the woman one loves is only a reason to find ways to be reunited, and not an occasion to give way to disgust with the world" (*Aesthetic Rapture*, Vol-II, p. 82). But we can point out that when one is separated from one's beloved, hope and despair (born of fear) alternate and when despair becomes too intense, one is likely to slide into an attitude of abandon, of renunciation, in order to get relief from the agonizing pain of separation. This docs not last. But this possibility undoubtedly exists. It is here that the possibility of *śānta rasa* can be discerned.

Similarly 'death' poses another problem. And this possibility is very important for understanding *vipralambha śṛṅgāra* in a Western context. Abhinavagupta, commenting on this, says that death should not be shown upon the stage but suggested (*Aesthetic Rapture*,Vol. II, p. 83) in *śṛṅgāra rasa.* What this implies (as he also says elsewhere) is that the moment death is shown it becomes the focus of attention and hence leads towards the *karuṇa* or the **compassionate** *rasa.* In Indian tradition, since there is a strong belief in rebirth and in a heaven, what is always indicated (in such cases) is that the lovers are united in the next birth or in heaven. In the modern context, this can be suggested if we are made to feel that even death could not separate the lovers, or if the central focus is upon the manifestation of love and death is made secondary. Even so, the sorrow generated from love is very distinct (as we shall see in chapter on the *karuṇa rasa*) and hence needs special attention. On the other hand, love-in-separation is very distinct from love-in-union where, even apart from union, the very possibility of any negative factor is removed from the air as we saw from the *vibhāvas* listed: spring, garlands, festivity etc. In *vipralambha* or love-in-separation the same *vibhāvas* no longer look appealing in the absence of the lover. They rather add to the pain; and the manifestations of this are very much closer to *karuṇa*—listlessness, worrying, longing etc. In contrast, the *anubhāvas* or consequences of love-in-union are coyness, shyness, a faint smile etc. (*Nāṭya Śāstra,* VI.45).

The issues we have raised here will figure prominently in the works we will take up for discussion now, viz., *The Little Prince* and *Blood Wedding.*

Separation and Longing

Before we discuss these texts, let us emphasize an important aspect of love-in-separation—longing and its associated emotions.

Abhinavagupta, commenting on love-in-separation in *Abhinavabhāratī* points out that in love-in-union there is always the fear of separation and in separation the hope of union (*Aesthetic Rapture*, Vol. II, p. 80). He, in fact, quotes *Amaru 23* to show that "the mixture of both these states . . . in effect gives rise to an extraordinary aesthetic delight" (*Aesthetic Rapture*, Vol. II, p. 82). Whatever else it does, this passage points to the opposition of *śṛṅgāra* to *śānta rasa*. Even when the fear of separation is transcended in a moment of union, the state is precarious. The moment consummation is achieved, all the worldly fears come in again. But in *śānta rasa* the world itself is transcended and there is no fear as there is nothing to lose.

Hope and Despair

Another aspect of *śṛṅgāra rasa* that comes to light here is the immense importance of hope-despair which co-exist in love. This is particularly noticeable in *vipralambha śṛṅgāra*. In love-in-union fear intensifies love. In love-in-separation fear of losing and longing, both get intensified in the absence of the loved object.

In Saint-Exupery's *The Little Prince*, both longing and the fear of losing persist throughout. This little book can be looked at as a parable or even as a kind of simple tale. A pilot with an engine trouble finds himself in the middle of a desert. There he meets a little man — the little prince who is from a planet not bigger than a small hut. The pilot and the little prince become friends and slowly we come to know of the antecedents of his journey to the earth. As the narrative proceeds, we are told that the little prince is suffering from some secret sorrow: "I am very fond of sunsets", (*The Little Prince*, p. 22) tells the little prince at the end of the fourth day of their meeting. On the fifth day the little prince looks very worried and asks the pilot who talks of sheep, "A sheep — if it eats little bushes, does it eat flowers too" (*The Little Prince*, p. 23). And when he realizes that a sheep eats anything, even a flower with four little thorns, the little prince is very sad. This intrigues both the pilot and the reader; and so, when the little prince seems very hurt to hear that "... flowers have thorns just for spite" (*The Little Prince*, p. 24) we do not know what to think.

Soon, we come to know that there is a little flower in the planet of the little prince and that he is actually in love with her. We need not emphasize here that a flower can be considered a woman (like the train in Spender's poem). But with its little thorns the cruel little flower — which is actually not so cruel — is a real woman:

> "Somewhere my flower is there . . ." But if the sheep eats the flower, in one moment all his stars will be darkened . . . .
>
> I did not know what to say to him. I felt awkward and blundering. I did not know how I could reach him, where I could overtake him and go on hand in hand with him once more.
>
> It is such a secret place, the land of tears.
>
> — *The Little Prince*, p. 26

In this way, the narrator tells us of the little prince's sorrow.

Here we have *vipralambha śṛṅgāra* or love-in-separation. 'Anxiety', 'worrying', 'lifelessness', 'death' — these are the manifestations in love-in-separation. But it is so very close to *karuṇa rasa*! How does one really distinguish between them? The problem has been resolved by Bharata by pointing out that there is no hope of reunion in *karuṇa* (*Nāṭya Śāstra*, VI.45).

In *The Little Prince*, the flower, like the Yakṣī in Kālidāsa's *Meghadūtam*, is in some way responsible for the little prince's exile. In *Meghadūtam*, the Yakṣa disregarded his duties owing to his excessive love for his beloved. And here it is the flower's cruelty that makes the little prince leave. But it is not really cruelty. In fact, the little prince has misinterpreted her indirect expression of love for cruelty. The flower is a delicate one (or acts as if she is) and likes to be pampered a lot by her little prince. But she never shows her gratitude for what he does for her:

> So the little prince, in spite of all the good will that was inseparable from his love, had soon come to doubt her. He had taken seriously words which were without importance, and it had made him very unhappy.
>
> — *The Little Prince*, p. 30

He decides to take leave of her, first by cleaning up his little planet, putting her under a jar for protection, and then by taking formal leave:

> "Goodbye," he said to the flower
> But she made no answer.
> "Goodbye," he said again.
> The flower coughed. But it was not because she
> had a cold.
> "I have been silly," she said to him at last. "I ask
> you forgiveness. Try to be happy . . ."
>
> — *The Little Prince*, p. 32

A little later, when the little prince is about to go, she says:

> "Of course I love you" . . . . "It is my fault that you did not know it all the while."
>
> — *The Little Prince*, p. 32

The little prince's pride stops him from staying back and the flower is too haughty to call him back. That is how his journey starts.

In the end, after his various adventures — all the while pining for her — the little prince finally goes back to his planet with the help of a poisonous snake. This is very important: as his body is too heavy, he feels he has to go without it. He asks the snake to bite him. But here death is of no consequence since it only makes it easier for him to reach his beloved.

The Problem of Interpretation

But another problem confronts us here. The narrator tells us towards the end:

> But there is one extraordinary thing . . . when I drew the muzzle for the little prince, I forgot to add the leather strap to it. He will never be able to fasten it on his sheep now. So now I keep wondering: what is happening on his planet? Perhaps the sheep has eaten the flower . . .
>
> At one time I say to myself; "surely not! The little prince shuts his flower under her glass globe . . .
>
> — *The Little Prince*, p. 87

This leaves us poised on a very critical position. In fact we are reminded of Abhinavagupta's comment that hope and despair enhance the element of love in *śṛṅgāra rasa*. But since there is no resolution, how does the reader look at things? If one is in a hopeful mood, he says, no, surely the flower is safe and happy with the little prince. But if one is a little low, he asks what if . . . ? In fact the narrator's position and ours are very much similar. Thus, it is the reader's **participation** here that is of key importance. What this tells us is that even though the *rasa* experience is derived from a work, its very manifestation and the way it is perceived will depend to a very great extent upon the perceiver and the way he participates in the work.

Love Between Friends

Another point that has not been made until now but which also cannot be overlooked here is the fact that a friend is being separated from a friend. To console the pilot the little prince tells him:

> In one of the stars I shall be living. In one of them I shall be laughing. And so it will be as if all the stars were laughing, when you look at the sky at night . . . .
>
> — *The Little Prince*, p. 83

Again, there is hope. At least by looking at the sky each will know that the other is there in one of the stars; and in the end, the pilot keeps on hoping that the little prince might some day come back again. Thus, it is this sustained hope that averts the manifestation of *karuṇa* (sorrow) though it constantly hovers around.

One last point should be made. In *The Little Prince* we also have a story about the friendship and love between two men. But unfortunately, in Indian critical tradition, friendship between two men or between women has never been emphasized even though there is ample evidence of it in ancient Sanskrit literature — the friendship between Kṛṣṇa and Arjuna in the *Mahābhārata*, Rāma and Sugrīva in the *Rāmāyaṇa*, Śakuntalā and Priyamvadā in *Abhijñānaśākuntalam*, Cārudatta and Maitreya in *Mṛcchakaṭikam* and the hero and *vidūṣaka* (an entertaining companion) in general in ancient plays.

One-Sided Love

We have already considered the possibility of one person being in love while the other is not responsive. Since it is not mutual, this, according to *Nāṭya Śāstra*, cannot lead to *śṛṅgāra rasa*. But if we look closely at this one-sided love, an important ingredient that we discover is **hope**. If this hope is not unfounded, and if as perceivers, we feel that it has possibilities of reciprocation, then *karuṇa* or the emotions and states associated with sorrow will not dominate. Besides, the sorrow generated by love is very distinctly different from other kinds of sorrows. It is perhaps for this reason that, in *Nāṭya Śāstra*, so much of emphasis has been give to love-in-separation and to the possibilities of sorrow which it can generate.

The essence of *śṛṅgāra* is fulfilment — mutual. Even in *vipralambha śṛṅgāra*, after a delay that causes suffering, there is union. But what can be said about a work that shows all the causes and effects of unrequited love. The consequence, both for the subject experiencing it and for the reader, is painful. This is especially so for the reader, who can distance himself and thus sympathise. But it is sometimes possible that a work demands and manages to elicit empathy — a sharing of the emotion that the character undergoes. It is so in Mayakovsky's long poem, *Cloud in Pants*. From a Western perspective, this poem would be called a love poem. True, here we find a mind agonized and tormented by love. But what should we call it if we look at it from the framework of *rasa*?

Let us look at it here for its content of love, longing and unhappiness, and especially their inter-relationship. The first section of the poem is about the agony of waiting. While the narrator waits for Maria, Maria does not come:

> "I will come at four" said Maria
> Eight.
> Nine.
> Ten.
>
> — *Longer Poems*, p. 10

The waiting is tormenting:

> . . . my heart's steel and ice.
> At night one wants to hide one's metal
> in something feminine,
> soft and nice.
>
> — *Longer Poems*, p. 10

So much so that:

> Nerves,
> barmy,
> gallop and stampede,
> little,
> big
> single and in pairs,
> race till, exhausted,
> they fall off their feet.
>
> — *Longer Poems*, pp. 11-12

And when Maria finally arrives:

> You entered,
> curt as a knife-thrust unparried
> torturing the kid of your glove.
> "You know,
> I'm getting married!"
> There now, talk about love!
>
> — *Longer Poems*, p. 14

But even then, after a thousand nameless affairs, the speaker cannot forget Maria:

> Maria!
> One poet sings sonnets to Tiana
> while I,
> all human,
> flesh all the way,
> just beg for your body
> like Christians for manna:
> "Lord, give us
> our daily bread . . . .
>
> Maria!
> Your body
> I'll love and tend
> the way a soldier,
> chopped short by war,
> cherishes his only leg.
>
> — *Longer Poems*, p. 24

Two things draw our attention — the agony and the violence. But as we shall also see in Lorca's *Blood Wedding*, this is a kind of violence which is not inimical to love — it comes out of too much tenderness. Besides, since this agony is due to cruelty (a kind of violence), it is not out of place here.

The Problems of View-Point

Nothing in itself is either ugly or beautiful — what really

determine them are the connotations. As we have already seen in Neruda, connotations and new relations can also be generated in a work of art. Even otherwise, it is the framework through which we look that is very important. Let us take the instance of a dead body. In itself it simply is. But its connotations are many. If the dead body is of a dear person, it gives rise to sorrow. A decaying body or a bloody body gives rise to fear or disgust. But if it is handled in such a way (in literature) that one forgets the usual associations of a dead body, then it can even generate laughter or love. It is thus with Mayakovsky's 'nerves'. The way they are portrayed, they almost become miniatures of the narrator in his agony.

But how do we look at this poem? Does it manifest *vipralambha śṛṅgāra* (love-in-separation) or does it generate *karuṇa rasa*? We can answer these by asking, what does the poem focus on? It focuses on the agonies that are born out of love. Hence, though the *vibhāva* or the cause is love, the consequence is that of agony. The *anubhāvas* or the consequences are those of *karuṇa rasa* (anguish, desperation, lamentation etc.). Another element is the element of hope. There is virtually no hope here — or at the most, a hope against hope.

Again, it is possible that the girl's cruelty will generate in us disgust. This, of course, depends upon the treatment. But what we notice more acutely is the pain. So, the *anubhāvas* or **consequences** common to both *śṛṅgāra* and *karuṇa* are present.

Now let us look at Lorca's *Blood Wedding* from the perspective of *śṛṅgāra*. The reasons we might do so are manifold. For one thing this play is what in the Western terminology will be called a 'tragedy'. And a tragedy is problematic for us since in practice we hardly have anything corresponding (exactly) to it in ancient Indian literature. For another thing, there is a lot of violence in the play, and this generates the possibilities of *raudra* or even *bhayānaka rasa*.

The mood of the play is sombre and there is always the smell of death everywhere. The Mexican setting is dry and hot and there is poverty all around. In fact, the lovers in this play have not been able to marry because the man is poor and the girl's father is rich. These look inimical to *śṛṅgāra*. But as we have discussed earlier, the environment should be considered congenial and here it is congenial for the blossoming of love. And, one thing that we must remember is that when the play starts, the man (Leonardo) and the woman (bride) have already been in love. We are made to understand that it is all over between them. But in the play, we realize that in one another's absence it has only intensified. Thus, the element of love-in-separation is beautifully depicted here. Leonardo is already married and even has a child; and the Bride is about to be married off. While dressing up the Bride the servant says:

> Oh, lucky you — going to put your arms around a man; and kiss him; and feel his weight.
>
> BRIDE : Hush.
>
> — *Three Tragedies*, p. 53: Act I.i

This only heightens the Bride's longing for Leornado and when, just before the wedding they meet at the Bride's house she says:

> BRIDE : Don't come near me!
>
> LEONARDO : To burn with desire and keep quiet about it is the greatest punishment we can bring to ourselves. What good was pride to me — and not seeing you, and letting you lie awake night after night? . . . . You think that time heals and walls hide things, but it isn't true . . . .
>
> BRIDE (*trembling*): I can't listen to you. I can't listen to your voice. It's as if I'd drunk a bottle of anise and fallen asleep wrapped in a quilt of rose. It pulls me along, and I know I'm drowning — but I go on down.
>
> — *Three Tragedies*, pp. 57-58: Act II.i

All the *anubhāvas* of *vipralambha śṛṅgāra* are present here — longing, burning, trembling, agony. The drive for union is so strong that they decide to fly. They know that the odds are against them and what they are doing will lead to disaster, yet they cannot help it:

> BRIDE : . . . . I love you! I love you! But leave me!
> For if I were able to kill you
> I'd wrap you round in shroud
> with the edges bordered in violets.
> Oh, what lamenting, what fire,
> sweeps upward through my head!
>
> LEONARDO : What glass splinters are stuck in my tongue
> Because I tried to forget you . . . .
> But I was riding a horse
> and the horse went straight to your door.
> And the silver pins of your wedding
> turned my red blood black . . . .
> Oh, it isn't my fault —
> the fault is the earth's —
> and this fragrance that you exhale
> from your breasts and your braids.
>
> — *Three Tragedies*, p. 83: Act III.i

This is when they are away inside the jungle. But a search party (with the Bridegroom at the lead) is drawing near:

> LEONARDO (*embracing her*):
> Any way you want!
> If they separate us, it will be
> because I am dead.
>
> BRIDE : And I dead too.
>
> — *Three Tragedies*, p. 86: Act III.i

Since what is emphasized here is their unification, even after all their efforts to the opposite, we have a union after a period of separation. But certain things again trouble us. First, since this love (as we shall see in the chapter on *karuṇa*) leads to a lot of bloodshed and death, is it evil? Secondly, in the play, what inevitably follows is tragic. In that case (if we consider this a union) what is it that comes through — *śṛṅgāra* or *karuṇa rasa*?

The solution to the first objection can be found by looking at the treatment. How is love treated? True, there is destruction, but does it suggest evil? The answer will be relevant. Here, against all odds, even in the nearness of death, love brings them together. Thus, the power of love is suggested. In that, the lovers transcend death — death becomes secondary. Seen this way it is pure union that is highlighted.

More Than One Rasas

As regards the second problem, it has remained controversial even among the ancient theoreticians. But when Ānandavardhana and Abhinavagupta (in *Dhvanyāloka*, *Locana* and *Abhinavabhāratī*) discuss the *mahākāvyas* (the epics) like the *Rāmāyaṇa* and the *Mahābhārata*, they point out that these have all the eight *rasas* in them. This means that at some point of time each of this possibility is heightened into an intensification to produce the *rasa* experience in the reader.

Thus, though it might be said that the *Mahābhārata* has *karuṇa* or *śānta rasa*, it is to be noted that the other *rasas* also manifest themselves in the work. It is so with *Blood Wedding*. In Act III, scene one, it is love that is consummated and in Act III, scene two, it is sorrow that reaches its highest intensity.

So, in a long work, it is always possible that two or even more *rasas* reach their peaks. Though it can be broadly said that finally *karuna* is the outcome, *śṛṅgāra* can have its moment of intensity even in a tragic work.

4

Hāsya Rasa

WHAT is it that makes us laugh? Something **funny** or **amusing**. But what does anything funny or amusing consist of? It is this that is very important if we are to understand what *hāsya* or the **comic** *rasa* is all about. Someone falls down and we laugh. The **unexpected** happens here. An order is broken by accident. An ironic remark makes us laugh. Here, language is used in an unexpected way — some unusual or incongruent relation is discovered. It is different from what can be called **joy**, generated when lost friends meet or something pleasing or wonderful is achieved. This, joy, can be found in *rasas* like *śṛṅgāra, vīra* or *adbhuta*, but it is not essential to *hāsya*.

The *Nāṭya Śāstra* (VI.48) expresses the following views where the *hāsya* or comic *rasa* is concerned:

> As for the comic (*rasa*), it consists of (or is based on) the primary emotion of laughter. It arises from such *vibhāvas* as wearing clothes and ornaments that belong to someone else or do not fit (*vikṛta*), shamelessness (*dhṛṣṭya*), greed, tickling sensitive parts of the body, telling fantastic tales, seeing some (comic) deformity (*vyaṅga*), and describing faults (*doṣodāharaṇa*).
>
> — *Aesthetic Rapture*, Vol. I, p. 50

The *sthāyībhāva* or the **stable state** — *hasa* or laughter — is generated by things that "do not fit". As we saw above, the 'not fitting' aspect brings in the element of incongruity into the order of things. It is so with the possibilities of 'deformity' as well which can lead to the comic, and again can give rise to disgust or fear.

One of the Oldest Emotions

The key element of the **comic** must have been discovered earlier than *Nāṭya Śāstra* to have been listed in it, though it was manifest even as early as in the *Vedas*. This is not surprising since the depiction of the comic or the humorous can be traced back in the West to the Greeks — even as early as Aristrophanes, comedy had developed immensely. In the East, the comic is an undercurrent in much of ancient Chinese and Japanese literature. There is a story about the famous Taoist Chuang Tzu:

> When Chuang Tzu was about to die, his disciples expressed a wish to give him a splendid funeral
>
> . . . . "We fear," argued the disciples, "lest the carrion kite should eat the body of our master"; to which Chuang Tzu replied: "Above the ground I shall be food for kites; below I shall be food for mole-crickets and ants. Why rob one to feed the other?
>
> — *The Wisdom of China*, p. 55

The Chinese poet Han-Shan always manages to find something funny about his poverty:

> In the house east of here lives an old woman.
> Three or four years ago, she got rich.
> In the old days she was poorer than I;
> now she always laughs at me for not having a penny.
> She laughs at me for being behind;
> I laugh at her for getting ahead.
> We laugh as though we'd never stop,

she from the east and I from the west!
— *Cold Mountain*, p. 26

Similarly, the sixteenth-century Japanese poet Basho writes playfully:

A male cat
Passed through the hole
In the broken hearth
To meet his mistress.
— *The Narrow Road to the North*, p. 25

or with surprised delight:

In a way
It was fun
Not seeing Mount Fuji
In foggy rain.
— *The Narrow Road to the North*, p. 51

And in India, among the ten types of plays discussed in *Nāṭya Śāstra*, *prahasana* (roughly translated as humorous/farce comedy) deals almost entirely with wit, humour and satire.

Disorder, Cruelty and Laughter

The very moment that man conceived of the possibility of order he also perceived the possibility of disorder, and it was this disorder—when it was of a relatively harmless kind—that could give rise to laughter. The psychological reasons behind this are manifold and complex and it is not our intention to elaborate upon them. But let it be said that in laughter the element of cruelty can never be ruled out completely; and so also the possibility of the grotesque.

Even in the verses that we have quoted, a certain amount of cruelty is perceivable. The laughter of the rich woman at Han-Shan's condition is cruel. But what could have given rise to it? Perhaps the woman overlooked the cruel ways of fate (making a poor man rich and leaving the other as he is) and saw only the incongruent — she gets rich while the poet is as poor as before. The other possibility is a laughter born out of pride (about which we are not talking here). It is possible for Han-Shan to laugh only when he also overlooks the cruel and manages to see the funny side of things. He suggests this in his other poems where in his poor man's dress he looks like a scare-crow or a joker. In the same way, he is also able to see the poverty of the old woman's mind since the old woman is deceived when she thinks herself rich. Han-Shan finds this funny. This also holds the element of the incongruent.

In the first poem by Basho about the cat, the hole in the hearth suggests the possibility of poverty. But the poet looks at this hole, not from the point of view of poverty, but from that of a romantic adventurer and so finds it funny. In the second poem, the delight is partly due to the fact that the proud mountain, Fuji, because of the fog, cannot show itself off. Cheating it of showing off gives the poet delight. But since the proud is cheated, the element of cruelty is modified and even justified. And in the Chinese parable that we cited at the beginning, it is the incongruent way of thinking that has been pointed out.

So many possibilities are noticeable here: laughter is related to cruelty, sadness, to defect, to disorder and so on. Now coming back to *Nāṭya Śāstra*, we do find that all these possibilities exist here — some have been suggested and certain others explicitly mentioned.

The Nature of the Disorder

What is the nature of disorder in *hāsya rasa*? Let us go back to the passage from *Nāṭya Śāstra* that we have cited above. We have already discussed that laughter is generated when 'clothes' or 'ornaments' "do not fit". Here, the key term is "do not fit". Clothes and ornaments are only examples of not fitting. But they also suggest the fact that what does not fit must be innocuous, harmless and temporary. Thus, if a lip does not fit, this deformity will give rise to either a sense of sorrow or the grotesque. But if the lips are twisted and made to look grotesque, this is both harmless and temporary. Even so, we see cruel laughter when a tramp dresses funnily. Here, laughter is possible only because the elements of sadness in the object and cruelty in oneself are being overlooked. In the same way, when one talks of the laughter arising out of seeing or imitating some deformity (*vyangya*), in the first instance, laughter will be disturbed when the imitation is being presented and the object of imitation is present. For one thing, if the imitated object does not participate in the fun, it will lead to the possibilities of hurt and cruelty. But in its absence (say, a tramp), the humorous angle (and not the cruel one) can be brought to focus.

So, when one sees some deformity, as we said, it must be harmless, i.e., the laughter arising from it should not lead to cruelty. But if the object of laughter participates, this fear is ruled out completely, as in the instance of clowns who know they are funny and find it (or act as if it is) funny.

'Shamelessness' has been listed as another of its element. This, at first, looks a little confusing. If one is shameless it might lead to disgust — a man going about naked in the streets, for instance. But shamelessness can lead to laughter when it does not threaten the order of things or the conventions and norms when creating some minor disorder. Baudelaire's book, *The Flower of Evil*, which was considered 'shameless', led to court litigations instead of laughter. Hence, the reader or the perceiver should not feel threatened by the shamelessness that he perceives. Let us for instance take the last stanza of W.S. Gilbert's poem, "When I, Good Friends, Was Called to Bar":

> At length I became rich as the Gurneys —
> And incubus then I thought her,
> So I threw over that rich attorney's
> Elderly, ugly daughter . . . .
> And now, if you please, I'm ready to try
> This Breach of Promise of Marriage!
>
> — *Norton Anthology*, Vol. II, pp. 1614-15

Here, the lawyer who has himself made a "breach of promise of marriage" tries out a case of Breach of Promise of Marriage. Two possibilities suggest themselves. One, that the lawyer is himself not aware of his own incongruous situation. The other is that he is shameless.

'Greed' is associated with shamelessness, and when greed leads to no major disaster but to some minor mishap (either for the greedy man or for another person who is either a fool or as greedy) it is funny. For instance, the lawyer's greed — he ditches the rich lawyer, who has sponsored him, the first chance he gets in his efforts to rise in life. But all lawyers being considered greedy, we find it funny that one lawyer manages to cheat another lawyer (for only a lawyer can cheat a lawyer). Greed can also lead to funny behaviour — stuffing oneself with food or gold, or trying to steal too many things and stumbling and falling etc.

"Tickling sensitive parts of the body" leads to a laughter that is generated by direct contact. In the perceiver, this can lead to **sympathetic** laughter. Abhinavagupta comments in *Abhinavabhāratī* that a certain kind of laughter is contagious. Even if one does not see the cause, one laughs because everyone else is laughing (*Aesthetic Rapture*, Vol. II, p. 86). This can be shown to be happening within a text for in real life, in an environment of laughter, one finds oneself laughing without any cause. But how far is this practicable for the reader/perceiver, who is aesthetically distanced? This is debatable.

"Telling fantastic tales" can lead to either the **comic** or the **absurd**. For instance, George Luis Borge's stories (which will be discussed in the sections on *bībhatsa* and *bhayānaka rasas*) lead to the latter. But Mayakovsky's play, *Bed Bug* or H.E. Bates's story, "An Improbable Tale" (about fooling someone or incongruous situations) can lead to laughter.

'Deformity', as we have already discussed, can be comic. We need not go into that again. But let it be said that deformity is also related to other emotions like sorrow (amputation of hands or legs), fear and disgust (when the deformity looks terrible). Deformity when temporary, harmless or simulated is funny, but as mentioned earlier, the element of cruelty lurks in the shadow.

Cruelty Beyond the Laugh

The element of **cruelty** lurks behind everything in *hāsya rasa*. But unfortunately, not much has been said about this aspect by the Indian aestheticians. If we look closely, laughter can at any moment lead to cruelty. All that is needed is a slight twist of perspective — as we saw in Han-Shan's poem. But if the element of cruelty is brought into focus, the same thing or situation will look very different, i.e., it might generate disgust or sadness. Thus, in *hāsya* or **laughter**, cruelty is either **overlooked** or **undermined**.

For instance, in Lewis Carroll's verse, "The Walrus and the Carpenter", the situation holds the possibility of humour, sadness and cruelty. The element of the comic arises from the way that the Walrus and the Carpenter cheat the Oysters. It also arises from the way Carroll narrates the episode:

> "O Oyster," said the Carpenter,
> "You've had a pleasant run!
> Shall we be trotting home again?"
> But answer came there none —
> And this was scarcely odd, because
> They'd eaten every one.
>
> — *Norton Anthology*, Vol. II, p. 1611

The Walrus and the Carpenter promise a fine walk to the Oysters and take them out by guile and eat them. Here, the key to the generation of humour is the **treatment**. But even so the elements of the cruel and the sad persist to such an extent that the response is not complete. In other words, one does not manage to forget everything in laughter. This is potent with what in the West is known as the "comedy of the grotesque" (J. Wilson Knight: *The Wheel of Fire*). What happens in such a situation is that the comic and the sad are juxtaposed in such a way that the reader's response is **undecided** and incomplete. Here, the *rasas* are mixed up and ambiguous, resulting in an unusual kind of aesthetic sensation.

Satire and Hāsya Rasa

Doṣodāharṇa or 'describing faults', can lead to satire. Literally, *doṣodāharṇa* means "citing or giving examples of faults". What is the usual response to the citing of faults? In the person whose faults are being cited, it may lead to unhappiness, anger, or even disgust (at the constant nagging or at oneself). In other words, even when the faults are being cited, they should be clothed in such a manner that a certain incongruity, a certain distortion (which is not too harsh) is noticeable. Besides, in a reader, the faults of an evil man will undermine the element of the possibilities of cruelty in the criticism so that he can look without any other disturbance at the comic side of things. Thus, a satire focuses on the relatively less serious defects (which a perceiver shares and so can find funny) or it makes relatively serious problems look much less serious. Thus, it is again the **treatment** that is important. It is the way that 'faults' are seen and made to be seen in a work that determine the nature of a satire. Even so, a satire can become grotesque, and so serious (e.g., the last sections of Swift's *Gulliver's Travels*) that the comic element no longer emerges prominent. What we have instead is the "comedy of the grotesque". This is especially to be seen in the works of T.S. Eliot discussed in the section of *bībhatsa rasa*.

But in Mayakovsky, it is the comic, in fact, the farcical element, that rules. His *Bed Bug* has for its central character an ex-party worker (who is an opportunist, a shameless rogue) who is attempting to become a bourgeois. He, for instance, in the first scene is not able to distinguish between a brassier and a bonnet:

WOMAN SELLING HABERDASHERY :
Fur-lined . . .
PRISYPKIN (*gushingly*): What posh little bonnets!

ROZALIA PAVLONA : They're not bonnets!
PRISYPKIN : I've got eyes, haven't I? Say we have twins . . .

— *Vladimir Mayakovsky: Plays/ Articles / Essays*, Vol. III, p. 79

The various accompanying states or *vyabhicārībhāvas* of *hāsya rasa* are (*Nāṭya Śāstra*, VI.48):

> Dissimulation, laziness, drowsiness (*tandrā*), sleep, dreaming, awakening, envy etc.
>
> — *Aesthetic Rapture*, Vol. I, p. 50

'Dissimulation', always holds the potential of mirth as we saw in the cheating of one lawyer by another or the cheating of the Oysters by the Walrus and the Carpenter. For instance, in H.E. Bates' story "The Flying Goat", the man telling the story (a fantastic tale at that) is bluffing outright, to which the narrator listens for a long time almost believing it. At the end:

> "How many times did you see the flying goat?" I said. "I mean you, yourself."
>
> "Well, he said . . . . I heard all about it, but I never got a chance to see it . . . .
>
> Don't you believe it? he said.
> "Oh! Yes," I said, "I believe it."
>
> After all, he said, it takes no more believing than the feeding of five thousand people with two loaves of bread and five small fishes, does it?
>
> — *Humour*, p. 5

This, the other man says, referring to **faith** in Biblical terms, immediately after which he prepares to leave. The narrator by now knows what he had been listening to.

> "No, you don't" I said. "Wait a minute. Just sit down. It is my turn to tell you something. I'd like to tell you about

> my uncle Walter's musical pig . . .
>
> — *Humour*, p. 5

Here, first the deception gives rise to comedy. Next comes the realization on the part of the reader that the other man will now have to listen to one big long lie (tit for tat).

Deception may also indicate self-deception. For instance, the narrator of Paul Jenning's short story "UB" says, celebrating the great advantages of his UB jalopy (car) over the modern car and its complications:

> You couldn't have left one of the rubber-mounted cars at the bottom of the garden through the whole war, as I did UB, and found it ready to drive again after fitting a new hood, new plugs, new windscreen wiper (and, come to think of it, a new windscreen), two new tires, new king-pins, new front spring, new cylinder head, new battery, re-wiring, re-painting, drying out the magneto in the oven, getting the dynamo re-wound and mending the leaks in the radiator.
>
> You would have found the rubber (*he is referring to the new cars*) had perished.
>
> — *Humour*, p. 56

This self-deception is not the cause of the comic to the narrator, but to the one who responds. Hence, it is not really laughter caused by **oneself**, for the narrator is not aware (apparently) that he is the victim who is being laughed at.

'Laziness' and 'dreaming' have comic potentials without doubt. But one might ask, what about 'drowsiness'? When drowsiness is caused by drinking etc., it holds comic potentials. The sudden 'awakening' of a lazy man, or a foolish man, or even a sleepy man can lead to his incomprehension of things and thus might generate laughter — he might say funny things or act incongruently.

But more problematic is 'envy'. This brings us back to the problem of the relation between cruelty and humour. A cruel man, when he sees disorder in the enemy camp, will find it funny. Even in the reader, when envy results in disaster (tit for tat), laughter might be generated. This may be called 'cruel laughter'. But it is justified by the antecedents and it is only when (thus) the cruel aspect is subverted that laughter dominates. It is similar when one laughs at one's own disaster — manages to see the funny side of things. In Gilbert's poem, the young lawyer's cheating of the rich lawyer is a cruel act. But since lawyers by tradition are considered cheats their disasters generate mirth. Another such instance is the Russian writer Nikolai Gogol's *The Government Inspector* where a scoundrel (posing as a government inspector) cheats the corrupt officials of a small Russian town. In such instances, the comic rules supreme in a satire. Besides, usually when a thing is satirized, first of all it is shown in a bad light before being satirized. This distances us or rather puts us (the readers) in opposition to the object being satirized and thus makes us see the comic element along with the narrator (or narrative angle) within the framework of the text.

In *Nāṭya Śāstra* (VI.48) the **comic** emotion has been divided into six categories: arising in the noble born or the high, arising in the ordinary people, and arising in the lowly in two different ways — out of one's **own** actions and from seeing someone else's actions (*Aesthetic Rapture*, Vol. I, pp. 50-51).

The division in terms of dignity of the individual can be roughly equated to what in the West is known as 'high' and 'low' or farcical comedies. Sometimes the laughter is witty and gentle and gives rise to humour (a smile). At other times it is boisterous, more physical (funny action) and gives rise to violent laughter (in the text as well as in the reader).

Causes of Laughter

The categorization of the causes of laughter is very interesting: that which is born and discovered (the *vibhāvas* or the **causes** and the *anubhāvas* or the **effects** can be located) in the same person, and that where there is a subject (inside the text) and an object of laughter — one's funny act causes the other to laugh. In *Nāṭya Śāstra* (VI.48) it is said:

> When one laughs on one's own, that laughter is said to be existing in oneself. When one causes another person to laugh, the laughter is said to be existing in another person.
>
> — *Aesthetic Rapture*, Vol. I, p. 50

This aspect has not been much dealt with by Bharata or the later aestheticians. But for a contemporary mind, this subtle division is important. If one refers back to Han-Shan's poem, one finds the first kind of laughter — at oneself. This helps us explain a very fine psychological aspect behind laughter. No comic emotion is possible as long as a thing is considered with **seriousness**. If a donkey becomes the object of intense contemplation (as in the Spanish poet Juan Ramon Jimenez's prose poem *Platero and I*) it becomes poetry of a different kind. Similarly, God, treated with enough lightness becomes a fit subject for comedy. Laughing at oneself presupposes this psychological conditioning, "I am funny", and one can be funny only when one does not take oneself too seriously. This attitude makes life (when too difficult) tolerable.

The other kind of laughter, at another, also involves trivializing the subject. If one sees evil too seriously, one is horrified. Hence, in a satire, there is a trivialization of all things. When the satire is about the entire mankind, it also involves the reader as well as the narrative voice, and hence here we find laughter at **oneself**.

But coming back to the second kind of laughter, two new possibilities present themselves. The object or the **source** of laughter is either aware of it or not aware of it. Here, we find that if the cause of laughter is not aware of it, this very possibility (as in fools) generates incongruity and hence laughter. In the hero of *Bed Bug*, Prisypkin, we find this aspect highlighted.

The play starts with the preparations for a marriage — between Prisypkin, formerly a worker and Party member and Elzevia, a manicurist and a bourgeois. At the beginning of the play we find Prisypkin gradually betraying Party ethics for a comfortable life. All through the play his shamelessness and complete unawareness of what kind of a figure he cuts heightens the comic element. For instance, we are informed by the Youth With the Broom, just before the marriage:

> The rubbish he leaves is more high-class these days. Before it was beer bottles and fish tails, now it's scent bottles and coloured ribbons.
>
> — *Plays/Articles/Essays*, p. 82: Scene 3

Here, the source of mirth is the second person (Prisypkin) about whom the first person is speaking. As the play progresses, in the marriage scene, everyone gets drunk and there is a brawl in which, by accident, the place catches fire and everything is burnt down. Only, it is possible that some bodies are intact since the firemen flooded the cellar and the water froze. Now, one would object, here is death and this is inimical to *hāsya rasa*. But we can point out that it is the treatment that is important. Here, first, death has been trivialized. Secondly, the emphasis is on other things — the focus is on the comic possibilities only. For instance, after the fire, the firemen talk:

> FOURTH FIREMAN : One charred corpse of unknown gender with a fork in its head.
>
> FIRST FIREMAN : A former woman with a wire crown on her head has been found under the stove.
>
> THIRD FIREMAN : An unknown person of pre-war built has been found holding the cash register. Must have been a bandit.
>
> — *Plays/Articles/Essays*, p. 92: Scene 4

This is a key passage which shows how death has been undermined. The firemen's description is full of comic elements: for the attention is on the comic consequences of the brawl on the bodies. This passage also makes us aware of the close relation of *hāsya* and *bībhatsa* (the comic and the grotesque). This corresponds to what is called **black humour** or **gallows humour** in contemporary Western literature.

We quickly move away (without hovering over corpses) into a fantastic world fifty years hence where the world has undergone a sea-change, and where Prisypkin (whose body had frozen) is about to be resurrected. This (resurrection is so simple) also undermines the seriousness of death. In the absurd, scientific (anti)-Utopia that is depicted in the rest of the play, emotions like love, tenderness, sadness etc., do not hold any value. The incongruent (which is also trivialised) is heightened by the entry of the foreign element—Prisypkin. The moment he is resurrected, he creates havoc everywhere by spreading contagious diseases like love, drunkenness, dancing, giggling etc. Strangely enough, along with Prisypkin a bed bug (which always made him scratch himself earlier) has also survived. In fact, it once escapes causing a lot of panic, and a number of volunteers are involved in its capture.

Meanwhile, the new world finds this human-like creature (Prisypkin) a fraud and imposter, which looks like a man, but is actually not one. It also discovers that the bed bug (which for them is extremely valuable) needs human blood to survive and hence is restored to Prisypkin (for whom the bed bug is the only friend). The Director declares:

> In accordance with the principles of the Zoological Gardens, a live human body is required for the continuous biting by a recently acquired insect and for the maintenance and development of the latter in the conditions to which it is accustomed.
>
> —*Plays/Articles/Essays*, p. 115: Scene 9

Then Prisypkin, who is considered an animal, shouts from behind his bars:

> Citizens! Brothers! Friends! Mates! Where did you come from? There are so many of you! When did they defreeze you? Why am I alone? Brothers, mates, come up here with me!
>
> —*Plays/Articles/Essays*, p. 115: Scene 9

Since he is kept under security, he does not know that there are so many people outside. So when he sees them outside, he bursts out in surprise.

The Need for Distancing

Distancing is a most important component of any kind of aesthetic appreciation. In *hāsya rasa*, its role is all the more significant. In most cases a satire, behind the laughter, hides something very serious. But man can live with all the problems surrounding him without going mad only when relieved by laughter.

Hence, it is very important that **pity** is never given a scope to emerge. This is done by putting the reader in opposition (and not in sympathy with) to the object that causes laughter. In fact, when a person laughs at **himself** he manages to distance himself from himself, i.e., see himself from outside. The reader or the *sahṛdaya* must also be able to do so.

High and Low Comedy

When we look at *hāsya rasa* in Sanskrit drama, the earliest examples are to be found in plays known as *prahasanas*. In *Nāṭya Śāstra* they have been divided into two categories: *śuddha* (pure) and *saṅkīrṇa* (mixed). In the first kind we have the humorous speeches of the rich, the hermits etc. The second has hetaerae, servants, eunuchs, parasites, cunning persons etc (*Rasa in Sanskrit Drama*, p. 189). We mention these here just to point out that even in India, comic plays were roughly divided into two kinds — high and low.

In the three classes of people — noble characters, common character and low class characters — the manifestations and the possibilities are different. It is specified in *Nāṭya Śāstra* that in noble characters, it should be depicted or suggested by the manifestation of 'smiles', 'slight laughter' and 'suggestive glances'. In common characters it should be enacted by 'mocking laughter', and 'open laughter'. In the low class characters it should be depicted in 'loud' and 'excessive laughter' (VI.52-56).

Thus, here we have the possibilities of wit and repartee (as in Restoration Comedies), of gentle humour as well as farce. It is the element of the farcical that we find in the Italian writer Italo Calvino's short story, "The Adventure of a Crook". While running from the police the crook gets into the room of an old prostitute (with whom he is familiar.) The prostitute is about to go to bed with her husband. So, the husband has to take his pillow and move to the corridor to make room for the crook on the bed. The narrative brings in and emphasizes the element of the "comically grotesque":

> In Armanda's huge bed, her body, in great mounds under the sheets, seemed to take up all the space .... Beyond, as if in a fold of the blanket, on the far side of the bed, her husband Lilin was lying; and he seemed to want to bury his little bluish face in the pillow, to recover his interrupted sleep.
>
> — *Difficult Loves*, p. 14

Once Jim (the crook) is inside and is just preparing to go to bed, there is a loud knock. This time it is the police man searching for the crook. The prostitute tells him that Jim is not inside. (He is actually hiding in the bathroom.) But the police man seems to be in no mood to leave. Meanwhile, inside the bathroom, Jim's basic instincts surface:

> He . . . . stole a box of tablets, then continued his tour of the toilet . . . . He opened a closet . . . . Inside it Armanda's clothes were hanging. Jim stuck his revolver into the pocket of the fur coat.
>
> — *Difficult Loves*, p. 18

Now that he has got rid of the revolver he had stolen, he does not like the proposition of spending the rest of the night in a damp bathroom. So, when the policeman is just into the bed, he comes out and hands himself over to Sodder, the policeman, who:

> . . . got up, mumbling, and slipped on his trousers. "What a lousy job . . . Never a moment's peace."
>
> — *Difficult Loves*, p. 18

Reluctantly he takes Jim and goes out and when they are all gone Armanda (the prostitute) calls out to her husband:

> "Lilin," she called, "come on, Lilin, come to bed, come on, Lilin honey, come."
>
> Lilin was already gathering up the pillows, the ashtray.
>
> — *Difficult Loves*, p. 19

The description of the prostitute is grotesque and the characters are all of the lower order. Most important, the plot is farcical —revolving around a prostitute's bed.

The Comedy of the Grotesque

In the above story, if we look closely, we find a lot of potential for the **compassionate** or *karuṇa rasa*. But, though all the possible interrelations between the two *rasas* are suggested (or at least implied) nothing is said clearly in *Nāṭya Śāstra*. In Shakespeare's *King Lear*, the fool points out the possibility of mirth in Lear's situation to Lear. The key to the comic, the Fool's message seems to be, is to look for it. Here, the relation of the husband and the wife (the prostitute) holds both the potentials. But it is the comic element that has been explored though the darker side has been just hinted at. Thus, here is not unmixed mirth, but a mirth mixed with a little sadness, as in Han-Shan's poem:

> Lilin has to wait till the last customer has gone before he can get into the bed and sleep off the weariness that accumulates during his lazy days. There is nothing in the world that Lilin knows how to do or wants to do; if he has his smoke, he's content. Armanda can't say Lilin costs her much, except for the packets of cigarettes . . . .
>
> — *Difficult Loves*, p. 14

After a drink, when in the evening he comes out of the pub, his wife is still on her beat:

> Without looking at him, on the steps of the sidewalk as if on a stage, her bosom compressed in the armature of wires and elastic, her old woman's body in her young girl's dress, nervously twitching her purse in her hand . . . she tells him no, people are still around, he must go off and wait. They woo each other like this, every night.
>
> — *Difficult Loves*, pp. 14-15

The element of the incongruous gives rise to the funny — the strange, 'lazy' husband, the strange kind of wooing! But in the second passage, the grotesque is poised on tears. Their poverty, their insecurity and their ageing — these lurk in the shadows. Thus, the grotesque need not necessarily lead only to *hāsya* or *bībhatsa rasa.* It can also lead to *karuṇa.* It is unfortunately true that in Indian aesthetics, this has not been highlighted. But we can also say (as we have elaborated earlier), that it is the **treatment**, the way of looking at things (even a corpse) that will decide the *rasa.* Here, undoubtedly, the sad and the comic co-exist. But if the comic element comes through, it is only because the negative, though everyone (including the characters in the story) is aware of it, is forgotten in those moments of hilarity.

Hāsya vs Śṛṅgāra

Before we conclude this discussion, it must be pointed out that in *Nāṭya Śāstra* (VI.39-40) the relation between *hāsya* and *śṛṅgāra* has been specified. It is said that the **imitation** of *śṛṅgāra* leads to *hāsya*. It is also said that *hāsya* is derived from *śṛṅgāra* (*Aesthetic Rapture*, Vol. I, p. 48). In Greek mythology, interestingly, there is only one goddess, Aphrodite, for both love and laughter.

In *śṛṅgāra*, *harṣa* (humour) is latent. Both the *rasas* refer to positive states of mind. Whereas *vīra rasa*, which is also considered a positive emotion, can lead to negative consequences (death, sorrow, etc.), the end of *hāsya* and *śṛṅgāra* can never be negative. But what poses a problem is how can *hāsya* come from *śṛṅgāra*, and how can the first be an imitation of the second?

It is a noticeable fact that where laughter (not happiness) and love are found together, the comic element will blend into the general atmosphere of fun and festivity. The imitation (aping) of harmless things, if shown in a particular way, leads to humour. It is thus with the imitation or enactment of love in Calvino's passage. But it holds, at the same time, the complex possibility of the pathetic. We may not be able to resolve the issue, but this must be pointed out.

Abhinavagupta emphasizes that mere sexual desire is not real love. Hence, the mere depiction of sexual consummation will not lead to the generation of *śṛṅgāra*. It might lead to lust. It can also lead to disgust and terror (in case of molestation or violation) (*Aesthetic Rapture*, Vol. II, p. 76). But what has not been highlighted in *Nāṭya Śāstra* is that it may lead to mirth, as we find in another of Calvino's stories, "The Adventure of a Soldier".

Wherever love or even lust is emphasized, the comic element will move to the background. But humour can be discovered almost anywhere. One has to have the eyes for it. For that the basic ingredients — incongruity, a mild disorder, deceptions, dissimulations etc. (discussed in *Nāṭya Śāstra*), should be discernible.

In "The Adventure of a Soldier", the private soldier is a small and timid creature. Sexual advance is not something to be expected of him — especially towards an elderly widow and in a train, when they are both strangers:

> Tomagra, a young infantry private on his first leave . . . huddled down in his seat for fear that the lady, so ample and shapely, might not fit; and immediately found himself in the aura of her perfume.
>
> — *Difficult Loves*, p. 3

The language that describes this event is grand and almost heroic. There is an incongruence between language and matter:

> It was still a very light contact, which every jolt of the train could break off and recreate; the lady had strong, fat knees, and Tomagra's bones could sense at every jolt the lazy bump of the knee cap.
>
> — *Difficult Loves*, p. 4

The emphasis is not on the element of lust, but upon the way it is manifest — timidly and with a lot of dissimulation. The mirth also arises from the soldier's timid uncertainty:

> Tomagra decided to transmit, somehow, a message to her: he contracted the muscles of his calf into a kind of hard, square fist, and . . . quickly knocked at the calf of the widow.
>
> — *Difficult Loves*, p. 5

He cannot be sure if the widow knows of his intentions and efforts. Here, parts of their limbs become characters enacting the parts of the soldier and the widow in a miniature scale. This is **comically grotesque**. But these efforts at contact are sometimes lost and he has to begin again:

> Now he had to begin all over again; that patient and

> prudently established contact had been lost. Tomagra decided to be more courageous.
>
> — *Difficult Loves*, p. 5

And there is an absolute sincerity in Tomagra's efforts, as if he is having a spiritual experience. Thus, again the element of the incongruent:

> Indeed, the hand groped around. There:like a butterfly's lighting, the fingers already sensed her presence . . . and the widow's gaze beneath the veil was impregnable . . . But no! Tomagra had already withdrawn his hand, like a mouse scurrying off.
>
> — *Difficult Loves*, p. 7

And even after their sexual consummation:

> . . . the widow remained with her clear, stern gaze (she had blue eyes), with her hat and veil squarely on her head, and . . . he had again a brief spurt of fear , thinking how he, Private Tomagra, had been so daring.
>
> — *Difficult Loves*, p. 12

An interesting thing is the element of 'dissimulation' that dominates throughout. Here is a funny play-acting (on the widow's part) of dignity. This gives rise to the ridiculous. Behind it is a mild kind of irony — a smile at the 'puritanical' widow's hypocrisy. In Tomagra, eroticism is enacted in the face of 'impassivity' with timidity. It is these that suggest displacement (of a harmless kind) and therefore mirth.

5

Karuṇa Rasa

In Indian tradition, the exploration of sorrow usually has a relatively small role to play in literature. This is so, for as we have said, there is hardly any scope for tragedy in our world-view. Still, *karuṇa rasa*, though it has for its central emotion **sorrow** or **pathos**, is a very important *rasa* which is found very markedly both in the *Mahābhārata* and the *Rāmāyaṇa.*

The Causes of Karuṇa

According to *Nāṭya Śāstra* (VI.40) *karuṇa*, the **compassionate** or the **pathetic** *rasa*, comes from the **primary** *rasa* of *raudra* or the **furious**:

> The result (*karma*) of the furious should be known as the aesthetic experience of compassion.
>
> — *Aesthetic Rapture*, p. 48

Karma is a very important word here. Apart from meaning 'result', it has also a string of other connotations like 'deed', 'consequence' etc. What this implies is that *raudra* is the cause which results in or leads to *karuṇa.*

What does *raudra* do? How does it manifest itself? It does so through violence, displacement etc., irrespective of good or evil. In other words, *karuṇa* is generated from certain causes or *vibhāvas* which are the consequences or the *anubhāvas* of *raudra*. Thus, *raudra* is the source of *karuṇa* and hence the primary *rasa* to which *karuṇa* can be related.

The features of *karuṇa rasa* are listed in *Nāṭya Śāstra*, (VI.61) as follows:

> Now (the *rasa*) known as *karuṇa* arises from the permanent emotion of sorrow. It proceeds from *vibhāvas* such as curse, affliction (*kleśa* or affliction of curse), separation from those who are dear, (their) downfall, loss of wealth, death and imprisonment, or from contact with misfortune (*vyasana*), destruction (*upaghāta*), and calamity (*vidrava*).
>
> — *Aesthetic Rapture*, Vol. I, p. 52

The *sthāyībhāva* of *karuṇa* is *śoka* or sorrow. In other words, the emotion or the mood that is generated and which persists throughout is that of unhappiness.

Its causes or the *vibhāvas* are such as can be related to the *anubhāvas* or the effects of *raudra rasa*: 'curses' 'affliction (from curse)', 'death', 'imprisonment', 'destruction' etc. But one might ask, what about 'separation from dear ones', 'downfall', 'loss of wealth', 'calamity' etc.? The answer lies in the last-mentioned cause—calamity. This is so for a calamity is an aggression which is not caused by man, but (in all literatures) by gods, the mother earth or simply by an impersonal nature. For instance, Śiva's *tāṇḍava* dance or the anger of Indra (thunder and rain) can lead to *raudra rasa*. Hence, these are also the manifestation or the consequences (effects) of *raudra rasa*.

Who is the Aggressor?

'Who is the aggressor', is an important question to ask in *raudra rasa*. The disaster can be caused by an external agent. But then, what about a man's own mistakes which lead to disaster (the way the Greek furies chase a man for his mistakes in Greek tragedies)? In the first place, such a disaster is of his own creation—in which case we normally cannot sympathise with him. But if his disaster far exceeds his mistakes (as happens with king Oedipus in *Oedipus Rex*—the punishment for pride is immensely more than it should be) we feel compassion. But such an effect of a disaster cannot be caused by any aggression or violence (from outside). So where is the possibility of *raudra* here?

This can be answered (at least partly) by replying that the aggression here is the aggression of fate against one. Man is not in control of his life and thus, this is an aggression that is a creation of the interaction of himself and his surrounding.

For instance, the lament of the gambler in the *Ṛgveda* (X.34):

> She wrangles not with me, nor is she angry:
> To me and comrades she was ever kindly.
> For dice that only luckless throws affected
> I have driven away from home a wife devoted.
>
> — *History of Indian Literature*, Vol. I, p. 103

In this passage, sorrow or *śoka* can be felt for the man, but more so for the wife. In fact, sorrow for the man can be felt only because at one point he realizes his mistakes. But when he is in the gambling mood, he is the cause of the sorrow inflicted upon his wife, i.e., he is the source of *raudra*. Yet, what when he himself suffers? Who is the cause now? If we feel sorry for him now it is only because we separate him from the person who gambles like a demon. And what is it that makes the two men different?

> And those brown nuts, thrown down, have raised their voices,
> I go, like wench, straight to the place of meeting.
>
> — *Indian Literature*, Vol. I, p. 103

It is the dice (the call of the dice) that makes him a different person. Thus, the dice here is the monster, the cause of sorrow in him and the source of *raudra*.

Tragedy and Karuṇa Rasa

A man's mistakes can at any moment lead to disasters. It is in fact this possibility that, in the West (especially in Greek and Renaissance literature), leads to tragedy. In the Indian context, the source of *raudra* can be traced back to that flaw which leads to the disaster.

In fact, a discussion of tragedy is essential for any discussion of *karuṇa rasa.* If we look closely we find that tragedy can be included within the categorization of *karuṇa.* But not necessarily in all cases — for though, in a tragedy, the waste of good leads to sorrow, there is also a spirit of resolution in it, for the very essence of tragedy is **hope** (not in modern tragedy, of course, where there is nothing glorious, nor any hope). And it is the loss of hope which is the essence of *karuṇa,* for in *Nāṭya Śāstra* (VI.38) it is said:

> The compassionate (*rasa*), on the other hand, consists in all loss of hope of ever meeting again.
>
> *Aesthetic Rapture,* Vol. I, p. 50

This is where *karuṇa* differs from *vipralambha śṛṅgāra* where there is reunion again.

But a question creeps up, does it mean that in all cases of *karuṇa* there is complete loss of hope? When a man loses his wealth, he might get it back again. When a man goes to jail, he might come back again. Yet, is the suffering felt here (both by the source of suffering and by the reader) made null and void when the original position is restored? It can be pointed out that, in *vipralambha śṛṅgāra* the separation is temporary. Most important, the separated lovers know it. They live in uncertainty reliving their past — which is the source of both pleasure (when they think of the good times) and pain (since at that time they are separated). For their pain they also have certain pleasures. And the audience or the reader knows it. But in *karuṇa* there is no hope of ever meeting again.

In a tragedy, the possibility of some achievement, some glory, some retribution is to be seen. When, in the end, good is destroyed, some evil is also destroyed along with it. But in *karuṇa rasa* what is emphasized is the aspect of sorrow. In a tragedy (at least according to the traditional concept of it) at the end there is hope and the establishment of order. Thus, whether a tragedy is in the *karuṇa rasa* or not will be decided by what dominates at the end — the sense of waste or something positive. It is in this context that we can take up Lorca's *Blood Wedding* again. Right at the beginning of the play we have the foreboding of an impending disaster as well as the fresh memory of old sorrows. When the bridegroom (he has just fixed up his marriage) asks his mother for a knife, the word 'knife' immediately brings into the mother's mind memories of past bloodshed as well as fresh apprehensions:

> Knives, knives. Cursed be all knives, and the scoundrel who invented them . . . . Everything that can slice a man's body. A handsome man, full of young life, who goes out . . . . and then that man doesn't come back. Or if he does come back it's only for someone to cover him up . . .
>
> — *Three Tragedies*, p. 33: Act I, Scene 1

That was the way her husband had gone and that was also the way that her elder son had died and all that is left her is this younger son for whom she is afraid. She has reasons for it, for the girl he has decided to marry has had an old lover and she fears a clash:

> They told me the girl had a sweetheart some time ago.
>
> NEIGHBOUR : She was about fifteen. He's been married two years now . . .
>
> — *Three Tragedies*, p. 38: Act I, Scene 1

The Mother's hunch is correct. Even as the wedding preparations are being made, the Bride flies with her past lover, Leonardo. In

Spain, in that time, it could only mean one thing — bloodshed. Death is not shown upon the stage, but we know that the bridegroom, who had gone chasing after the lovers, has finally caught up with them. We hear of the outcome.

LEONARDO'S WIFE : I want to go back and find all about it.
MOTHER-IN-LAW (sternly):
You, back to your house.
Brave and alone in your house.
To grow old and weep . . .
LEONARDO'S WIFE : What could have happened?
MOTHER-IN-LAW:
It doesn't matter what.
Put a veil over your face.

— *Three Tragedies*, p. 89: Act III, Scene 2

In this instance, we see the separation of the husband from the wife. On the other hand there is the agony of the bridegroom's mother:

MOTHER:
Neighbours: with a knife,
with a little knife,
on their appointed day, between two and three,
these two men killed each other for love.
With a knife,
with a tiny knife
that barely fits the hand,
but that slides in clean
through the astonished flesh
and stops at the place
where trembles, enmeshed,
the dark root of a scream.

— *Three Tragedies*, p. 94: Act III, Scene 2

In the chapter on *śṛṅgāra rasa* we discussed the possibility of love-in-separation in this play. There, we found that (Act III:

Scene 1) we have a celebration of love even in the face of death. True, death and destruction lurk in the background; but in the moment of intensity towards the end of the scene it is love that is central.

In the same way, here it is *karuṇa* that predominates. We see a widowed wife who, once she has gone home, will for the rest of her life 'weep'. The mother sees only the waste of youth and blood for love. Her attitude towards love is not negative. But it is as if she knew that it is not only powerful and pervasive, it is also fatal. This is suggested when she says "on their appointed day" they "killed each other for love". Here, it is love which (unusually) manifests itself as the source of *raudra* that leads to destruction and sorrow. But, remarkably, love has been treated in such a way that (though it is ferocious) nowhere is it felt to be disgusting or a sheer waste.

Is there any hope in the play? True, Leonardo's wife has a child. But what future will he have in a place where every young man's blood is hot and where passion reigns supreme! Needless to say, as the source of *karuṇa* is *raudra*, there is a lot of violence in the play.

Karuṇa vs. Vipralambha Śṛṅgāra

Another point has to be briefly made. Though in *Nāṭya Śāstra* (VI.45), the relation of *karuṇa* and *vipralambha śṛṅgāra* has been pointed out, the element of *karuṇa* in love-in-separation has never really been elucidated. Save the differentiating element of **hope**, the two *rasas* are very close — distress, pain, agony etc., are the manifestations in both cases. But in love-in-separation we have two kinds of pain — one that is pleasurable, and the other that is not. The first kind of pain is caused by the attraction of the beloved object against which the lover fights (for fear that he/she will be imprisoned or bound by that love, and for fear of the dissolution of the ego). But the second kind of pain, which is caused by the fear of separation from the beloved object, is never pleasurable. It is this kind of pain which has great affinity to (in fact, can be categorized under) *karuṇa.*

But then one might ask, what about this element of hope? How does it really operate? Again, two possibilities open themselves up. In a text, there might be no foreboding and love-in-separation might be depicted with all the suggestions of reunion, but then in the end, suddenly disaster strikes. In this case, what about the major body of the text — does it generate *śṛṅgāra* or is most of it affected by the *karuṇa* which is the result of the final separation at the end? Here, the participation of the *sahṛdaya* (or the sympathetic reader) is very important. When the reader participates in the text for the first time, since he does not know of the outcome **yet**, he relishes the possibilities of love-in-separation until (towards the end) disaster strikes. But if the same text is read a second time, since he now knows the outcome, the *sthāyībhāva* or the stable state of *śoka* or sorrow will persist.

Subjectivity

What we have again and again emphasized earlier is the perspective or the point of view from which things are seen. Thus, in itself, nothing is the subject of love or of sorrow. Every situation has the potential of all the *rasas*. Even in objects and unlikely people, beggars or old men (as in Marquez's *Love in the Time of Cholera*), love can be depicted. In the same way, a situation of love might be depicted, but the focus may be upon something else — sorrow, anger or even disgust, as we will see in Mayakovsky's *Cloud in Pants*. Thus, in a text, apart from what is being shown, a **way** of **seeing** things is being generated. It is as if the text also has five senses that filter the world in a particular way.

A similar thing can also be said about the perceiver or the *sahṛdaya*. Each reader has his own *saṁskāra* or mental disposition. It is this that determines to a great extent how he sees, not only the world, but even a text or a work of art. Thus, a Marxist reader might find the Marxist Ideology everywhere or a Feminist might see things in another specific way. But if we are to go by the Indian concept of the *sahṛdaya* (the sympathetic perceiver) we must remember that the work has been written in a specific way and is supposed to be read in a certain manner. Here, we are not talking about the writer's intention, but of what is to be found in the work, in the way it is written. When these two perspectives meet (the text and the reader) and make a rapprochement (according to the Indian theorists), a reading can be more or less productive. When saying this, we must remember that in the Indian aesthetic tradition, texts might have been difficult, even rigorous, but never obscure. This can be said about all imaginative texts that intend to say something beyond themselves; which link themselves to some real or assumed world outside themselves.

Coming back to our point, in *Cloud in Pants*, though the situation is generated by (deprived) love, the emphasis is on something else—the tenderness, the longing, the disillusionment etc. Thus, our thesis that the same kind of situation can generate different kinds of emotions or states is substantiated. In Calvino, it gives rise to love. In Boudelaire and Bhartṛhari (we will discuss them in the chapter on *bībhatsa rasa*) it gives rise to disgust.

Pity

Coming back to the concept of tragedy, we find that in his *Poetics* Aristotle tells us that in tragedy, there is the "purgation of emotions through pity and fear" (p. 1451). Thus, here 'pity' at the waste of good has the potential of sorrow. But, much more important, 'fear' is also being emphasized, i.e., horror (*bībhatsa*) and terror (*bhayānaka*).

It is these associations of *karuṇa* that are found in Franz Kafka's *Metamorphosis*. Now, in the Indian context, let us look at the various associative implications that the *vibhāvas* or **causes** of *karuṇa* have. For one thing, since most of them are the manifestation of *raudra*, they are the result of violence, anger, fury etc. This was illustrated in *Blood Wedding* where the fury of knives in the young flesh sprout blood. For another, they are to be found in the mood when sorrow is being generated. But the relation of *raudra* and *karuṇa* are irreversible and not reciprocal. *Raudra* can lead to *karuṇa*, but the reverse is not possible. One might, of course, object and ask, what happens when a son takes revenge for his father's death? But we can reply that the moment one takes up arms, sorrow is blocked, and all the energy is directed in the direction of a destruction. Thus, the perspective shifts.

The *vibhāvas* or causes of *karuṇa* are 'death', 'calamity' and 'destruction' (*Nāṭya Śāstra*, VI.61). Death implies separation, and hence sorrow. Destruction and calamity lead to loss (of wealth, life etc.) and hence sorrow. But all these have other associations as well. Death holds the possibility of the repulsive and the grotesque, and destruction and calamity are fierce, awesome. It is thus that these emotions hover around *śoka* or sorrow.

Bībhatsa vs. Karuṇa

Kafka's *Metamorphosis* is a problematic and complex novella — for here, *bībhatsa* and *karuṇa* are juxtaposed. One might object that the two *rasas* are inimical. He may say, the moment the son's body is seen as rotting flesh (or, here, seen as an alien thing) the dominant state will be disgust. Thus, a mere shift in looking at an object will transform things: for as long as one looks at it as the son's body, *karuṇa* will be manifest, but the moment one is unable to recognize the son in it, disgust will surface.

If we keep this in mind, Kafka's work will not pose to be a problem — for here, the narrative (for the most part) is from the point of view of the narrator, Gregory Samsa, who is transformed into a giant bug. Besides, the emphasis is more upon the transformation of relationships among the family members rather than the physical transformation itself. Thus, the disgust (it is undoubtedly there), instead of being directed towards the narrator, is directed towards the other people — father, sister and mother. Even so, they cannot be really blamed if they cannot believe that the metamorphosed insect still thinks like a man or has any semblance of humanity left. It is this blocking off (partially) of the possibility of disgust that heightens the element of sorrow. Here, interestingly, there is "separation from dear ones" (*Nāṭya Śāstra*, VI.61), but in the form of an **alienation**. Thus, one of the causes of sadness is the mental or emotional separation.

On a routine, working day:

> Gregory Samsa woke from uneasy dreams one morning to find himself transformed into a giant bug. He was lying on his back, which was of a shell like hardness, and . . . . His many legs, pitifully thin in relation to the rest of the body, thrashed ineffectually before his eyes.
>
> — *Franz Kafka: Stories*, p. 91

This description at the beginning of *Metamorphosis* makes us notice two things that are considered inimical to *karuṇa*. The element of *bībhatsa* in the description of the body, and the element of 'fantasy' — an incredible happening. And we must remember that fantasy is an element which is more congenial to humour, wonder or even to the grotesque than it is to sorrow.

But we can counter these objections by saying that here the element of fantasy is only a **tool** and not the end. It is used to create an unusual and striking situation where human misery and alienation can be successfully explored. Besides, the first objection can be tackled by pointing out that we are looking at the world basically from Gregory's point of view:

> "What is happening to me?" he thought. This was no dream . . . . Try as he might to throw himself over to the right, he always rocked back into his previous position.
>
> — *Franz Kafka*, p. 91

He faces a serious difficulty in the very act of getting up. Since he does not want to frighten his family which is frantically knocking at the door, his condition generates more of compassion or pity than disgust. But the parents who are not ready for this transformation are horrified:

> His mother, looked first with clasped hands at his father, then took two steps towards Gregory and sank down . . . . His father looked hostile and clenched his fist as if to force Gregory back into his room.
>
> — *Franz Kafka*, p. 103

Here, the responses are those of horror and disgust, but they are the tool (or the manifest states, *vyabhicārībhāvas*, inside the text) that heighten this drama of alienation. This unjust alienation (who is it that is unjust — God?) gives rise to sorrow, especially in the face of Gregory's great concern that he should create no inconvenience in the family. The mother at first attempts to overcome this alienation. But her son's grotesque shape is so disquieting that she is no longer able to recognize him as her son.

All through the text, the element of the grotesque is treated (used as a tool) in such a way that it becomes a part of the ordinary reality — Gregory never questions why he has been transformed. He simply accepts the fact that he has been turned into a dung beetle. It is this which, when it suddenly clashes with the ordinary reality, shows the grotesque in a more poignant light:

> "Don't let me keep you, sir; I'll be in the office directly . . . ." Unfortunately it seemed he had no proper teeth — how was he to grip the key? . . . he actually managed to move the key, ignoring the fact that in doing so he was clearly damaging himself in some way.
>
> — *Franz Kafka*, pp. 100-102

What he is doing (he has not yet opened the door) is trying his best to save his job. Since he is late for the office, the head clerk has himself come to look into the matter. Thus, the element of the grotesque is forgotten both by Gregory and the reader. What surfaces is the urgency to save the job which cannot be saved. For a few moments the grotesque stops becoming grotesque and becomes poignant. It is this transformation that gives rise to sorrow; for the grotesque is nothing but the seed of an alienation. Here the alienation is one-sided and the attempt to close the gap is also one-sided:

> In the morning, with the door locked, everyone had wanted to come in; now that he had opened one door . . . the key had been taken away and put back in the locks from outside.
>
> — *Franz Kafka*, p. 109

Alienation

In *Metamorphosis*, it is alienation that plays a most critical role. The alienation grows and even when contact is established, it is a displaced kind of contact. And it is this disjunction that heightens the element of *karuṇa* :

> She [Gregory's sister] did not spot Gregory straight away, but once she noticed him under the couch . . . she got such a fright that she involuntarily slammed the door shut again. But thinking better of her action she opened it again immediately and tiptoed into the room, rather as if she was in the presence of a chronic invalid or even a stranger.
>
> — *Franz Kafka*, p. 110

This new relation increases the alienation. But once the family adjusts itself to thc transformation, and Gregory more or less adjusts to his new condition, it is the interaction and (ironically) the gradual alienation of a different kind that makes us sad. Here is unhappiness along with shock on the part of the parents and the sister in the first few days of the transformation. But once they get used to it, they slowly stop feeling that it is Gregory. Thus, for them the relation between the Gregory they knew and this creature grows dim, while for Gregory the past becomes more poignant and the present more painful.

In fact, Gregory more or less gets used to this new life until he marks a gradual change in his sister's attitude. Since he is now out of work, all the other members of the family do some work or the other. They, in fact, keep three paying-guests in the house. Gregory had (earlier) always had a secret ambition to send his sister to a good institute for learning violin. One evening, in front of the paying-guests she plays violin. They don't seem very impressed or interested. But it is Gregory in his dark room who is drawn to the sweet sound of the violin. In his love for his sister, hypnotized by the music, he drags his body from the dark room and reveals himself. The three gentlemen behave violently and declare that they would leave immediately. After the episode his sister reacts very suddenly:

> "My dear parents" said Gregory's sister, banging her hand down on the table by way of an introduction. "We can't go on like this . . . . I refuse to utter my brother's name in front of this creature, so all I say is: we must try to get rid of it . . . "
>
> — *Franz Kafka*, p. 138

It is in this that Gregory's alienation is complete. But we really cannot blame his sister. She is young and for how long can she take this nightmare! They have no way of knowing that even though he cannot speak, he can understand them — is still human under his shell. It is after this episode that Gregory loses what little will he had that sustained his body:

> He recalled his family with sympathy and love. His own belief that he must go was even firmer that his sister's. He remained in this state of vacant and peaceable reflection until the church clock struck three in the morning . . . . Then, independently of his will, his head sank to the floor and his last breath streamed feebly from his nostrils.
>
> — *Franz Kafka*, p. 141

What is interesting in this passage is Gregory's transcendence of his misery. His dying moments read like a spiritual experience. Thus, the possibility of *śānta rasa* is discernible here.

The moment Gregory is dead, the family is relieved. When they are just preparing to take a day off (with him alive, someone had constantly to be in the house) the servant woman tells them gloatingly that she has disposed of the body. This immediately puts them in a black mood. But they soon overcome it, and as the story ends we find that:

> Mr and Mrs Samsa . . . were struck almost simultaneously by the realization that in recent months . . . she had blossomed into a beautiful, full-bossomed girl . . . . at the end of the journey, their daughter was the first to stand up, stretching her young body.
>
> — *Franz Kafka*, pp. 145-46

For a reader, interestingly, the possibility of disgust at the family's attitude, if explored (in the story) could lead to "world-weariness" and hence to *śānta rasa*.

But can we really call the family selfish? Enough hint is given in the story to make us realize that the sister is growing into her maidenhood and there is a world open before her. But this strange creature stands in the way to her happiness. The parents cannot feel this as acutely for they are nearing their end. Thus, a **source** is denied which **causes** *śoka* or sorrow. No effort is made in the story to point to a cause responsible for this metamorphosis, nor is a reason for the metamorphosis visible. This poses an interesting problem. In such a story (as with the 'comedy of the grotesque'), where is the scope for the 'purgation' of emotions? Does this heighten things into a state of *rasa*?

The reader is poised very delicately upon two possibilities. If he reads the story without questioning, he is initiated into sorrow. But if this question, why did it happen to Gregory, comes up and dominates his reading (which is very likely), it will leave him with a sense of incomprehension — he will be bewildered by the displacement, and this can lead to disgust (in a metaphysical sense) and to terror.

Karuṇa and the Other Rasas

A nightmare can lead to *karuṇa* as well as to *bhayānaka rasa*. We saw an instance of it in Kafka's work. And this depends upon the nature of the object. For instance, in Eugene O'Neill's, *The Emperor Jones*, the play generates no sympathy from the reader for Jones, for he is a cruel tyrant and his suffering is justified. But the destruction and devastation of war leads to *karuṇa* along with *bhayānaka* and *bībhatsa rasas*. The British war poet, Wilfred Owen (who himself died in the First World War) writes in his poem, "Futility":

> Move him into the sun —
> Gently its touch awoke him once,
> At home, whispering of fields unsown.
> Always it woke him, even in France,
> Until this morning and this snow.
> If anything might rouse him now
> The kindly old sun will know.
>
> — *Golden Treasury*, p. 450

Or in "Strange Meeting" Owen describes his meeting with an enemy soldier in Hell, where the enemy soldier tells him:

> I am the enemy you killed my friend.
> I knew you in this dark; for so you frowned
> Yesterday through me as you jabbed and killed.
> I parried; but my hands were loath and cold.
> Let us sleep now . . .
>
> — *Golden Treasury*, p. 453

The possibilities of *bībhatsa* and *bhayānaka* exist here. But the focus is upon the great waste caused by the war. Thus, the consequences of the fury of the heartless monster — War — are pity and sorrow. But even here, in the last line of the second poem, the possibility of *śānta rasa*, of peace, is evoked — "let us sleep now . . . ."

Another interesting relation is the relation between *vīra rasa* and *karuṇa rasa*. In *vīra rasa*, the consequence of heroic action leads to bereavement and separation, especially when the heroism is a sheer waste. What purpose did the killing by the narrator (in "Strange Meeting") serve? His enemy was only a frightened, young lad like himself who would have gladly made friends with him at any other time.

Now, what about the relation of *hāsya* to *karuṇa rasa*? What about the possibility of hope in *karuṇa*? How intimately are *karuṇa* and *śānta rasa* related? Most important, how can *karuṇa*, which shows unhappiness and pain, generate in the audience an emotion which is tolerable, even pleasurable?

We shall deal with these problems sequentially. As we found in the chapter on *hāsya rasa*, in the West, there is such a concept as the "comedy of the grotesque". What this consists of is a juxtaposition of the tragic and the comic in such a way that neither is realised fully in the work. Since (as we also saw in *Nāṭya Śāstra*), the grotesque is associated both with *hāsya* and *bībhatsa*, we should not be surprised if they are combined. This possibility does exist, though no Indian aesthetician has affirmed it. On the other hand, what is much more interesting is the fact that their combination holds this possibility — manifest or choked. This we have already noticed while discussing *Metamorphosis*. Whether it will lead to the realisation of any *rasa* or not is debatable. But let it be pointed out here that in modern Western literature, the Theatre of the Absurd juxtaposes farcical elements with the inability to locate Man in a metaphysical sense.

Hope and Karuṇa Rasa

We have already discussed the relation between hope and sorrow. *Karuṇa* will surface where man has not only lost hope, but even the will to fight. But here a finer distinction of hope can be made. A character hopes inside a work. But we as readers know the case to be hopeless. In other words, a work might show the manifestation of hope, but if it does not **indicate** hope it will lead to the perception of sorrow.

In Gabriel Garcia Marquez's *No One Writes to the Colonel*, the colonel waits for ages for his pension papers. In a small decadent Spanish town, he and his wife live in abject poverty and wait:

> For nearly sixty years — since the end of the last civil war — the colonel has done nothing else but wait. October was one of the few things which arrived.
>
> — *No One Writes to the Colonel*, p. 3

What was the colonel waiting for? His son was dead. He was seventy-five. What was there for him, except perhaps the very act of living itself:

> Fifteen years of waiting had sharpened his intuitions. The rooster sharpened his anxiety.
>
> — *No One Writes to the Colonel*, p. 12

The fighting rooster holds the only promise of money for him, but it might lose the fight as well. In fact, what sustains them is a mystery:

> "This is a miracle of the multiplying loves," the colonel repeated every time they sat down at the table during the following week. With her astonishing capacity for darning, sewing, and mending, she seemed to have discovered the key to sustaining the household economy with no money.
>
> — *No One Writes to the Colonel*, p. 19

What generates the element of pity and sadness all through is the hope of the old colonel. In fact the old couple survive only upon the old man's hope.

The colonel's wife wants that they should sell the cock and

take whatever money they get for it. She is afraid it might lose. But the old man refuses to part with it at any cost:

> Now go to sleep. If we can't sell anything tomorrow, we'll think of something else . . . .
>
> — *No One Writes to the Colonel*, p. 62

But the old woman keeps on pestering the old man. What if they cannot sell anything? The old man replies that when the cock wins the fight they will get some money. When the old woman says that she fears it might lose, the old man answers:

> "There are forty-four days left to begin thinking about that."
> The woman lost her patience.
> "And meanwhile what do we eat?"

It had taken the colonel seventy-five years — the seventy-five years of his life, minute by minute — to reach this moment. He felt pure, explicit, invincible at the moment when he replied:

> "Shit."
>
> — *No One Writes to the Colonel*, p. 62

What generates *karuṇa* is the fact that the reader knows that the only thing they have is hope. Their inconveniences, their pathetic plight (by sympathy) generate sorrow. But when we reach the end, we start empathising with the old colonel. We participate in his courage to face life, and it is this optimism which makes the work transcend the limitations imposed by sorrow on it. Thus, here sorrow and its accompaniments are the *vyabhicārībhāvas* or the accompanying states that lead to the realization of the heroic.

The States That Accompany Karuṇa

Talking of *karuṇa* and *śānta rasa*, the list of accompanying states of *karuṇa* that we find in *Nāṭya Śāstra* (VI.61) mentions the following:

> world weariness, worry, longing, panic, mental aberration (*bhrama*), confusion, weariness, fear, dejection, depression, sickness, lifelessness, insanity, apoplexy, fright, laziness, death, paralysis, trembling, change of colour, tears, change in voice and the like.
>
> *Aesthetic Rapture*, p. 52

Briefly, it can be said that the accompanying states and effects of *bhayānaka* and *bībhatsa rasas* are to be found here — 'fear', 'trembling', 'change in colour', 'insanity', 'confusion', 'death' etc.

But three things in particular are important. One, 'laziness' is inimical to sadness and we do not see how it can be related to *karuṇa rasa.* But it is perhaps due to an inaccurate translation. The Sanskrit word *nirveda* indicates 'resignation' or 'indifference' (as a result of resignation) rather than 'laziness'. An instance to the point is Ernest Hemingway's story "The Victim" where the central character waits in a lonely room for his killers to come and kill him. He has been running from them for so long that now he is tired and even as Nick Adam (who sees the killers) warns him, he simply waits resignedly.

Secondly, what has been translated as "mental aberration" — *bhraman* — is much more connotative and also suggests 'illusion'. This is poignant because it gives rise to hope which collapses immediately — say, a father's illusion of seeing his dead son alive. When this illusion is broken, sorrow is heightened.

Thirdly and most important for our purpose here is the possibility of 'world-weariness'. This is also one of the *vibhāvas* or causes of *śānta rasa.* We have seen earlier, in Owen's poem and also in *Metamorphosis*, that this is possible. Here, we can add that in the *Mahābhārata*, the destruction and the grief ultimately leads to 'worldly-weariness', and renunciation on the part of the Pāṇḍavas.

How Can Karuṇa be Relished?

The most problematic issue that confronts us is, how can the depiction of sorrow be relished? We have already discussed this in the context of *sahṛdaya*. But let us discuss it briefly again.

Aristotle pointed a way out in his theory of **purgation** — the negative emotions in the perceiver are purged out by sympathetic participation. In India, Abhinavagupta commenting on *Dhvanyāloka* in his *Locana* says that sorrow which is the *sthāyī* of *karuṇa* has been capable of being aesthetically appreciated through sympathy and identity. Once it is aesthetically enjoyable it is *karuṇa rasa* — when the sorrow (felt) is different from the ordinary sorrow we feel in everyday life (*Aesthetic Rapture*, Vol. II, p. 82)

What can we deduce from this? First, the sorrow experienced in ordinary life is different from the sorrow experienced in a work of art. But in what way? The first is painful while the second is a pleasurable experience? But what is it that makes the latter so distinctly different. Abhinavagupta, referring to the writing of the *Rāmāyaṇa* (which was inspired when poet Vālmikī saw the cruel killing of the she-bird when two birds were making love) says that "Vālmikī, who felt the sorrow of the male bird, at the *moment* (emphasis supplied) of grief, burdened by grief could not have written a thing which gives pleasure" [*Aesthetic Rapture*, Vol. II, pp. 83-84]. So, what is involved here is an aesthetic distancing which is equally applicable to the reader: for a writer, unless he puts himself in the position of a reader (the sympathetic reader or the *sahṛdaya*), cannot know what his work will be like. Hence, the reader is both distanced and intensely participating, since he is objective, seeing things in more than one way (as I. A. Richards points out in his "Imagination"). In this ways, he is capable of relishing even the negative emotions or states which, aesthetically transmuted, can no longer be recognized as negative any more.

6

Raudra Rasa

ABOUT *raudra rasa* the first question that must be raised is, what kind of a *rasa* is *raudra*—positive or negative? *Nāṭya Śāstra* tells us (VI.63):

> Now (the *rasa*) called *raudra* has anger for its permanent emotion. Demons, monsters and violent men are its characters. It is caused by battles. It arises from (*sic*) such *vibhāvas* as anger, provocative actions (*ādharṣana*), insult (*adhikṣepa*), lies, assaults (*upaghāta*), harsh words, oppression (*abhidroha*, or according to Abhinava, "murderous intent") and envy.
>
> —*Aesthetic Rapture*, Vol. I, p. 53

Abhinavagupta classifies *rasas* into *sukhātmaka* (causing happiness) and *duḥkhātmaka* (causing unhappiness) [*Aesthetic Rapture*, Vol. II, p. 76]. *Raudra*, then, would come under the category of negative states as it causes pain. But if we look at it from the angle of good and evil, what is to be found here? Since it is associated with *vīra rasa* (we will discuss their relation below) it can lead to good or the destruction of evil even as *vīra* can lead to *karuṇa* or sorrow and pathos.

The Stable and Accompanying States in Raudra

If we look closely at the passage quoted above, the most

important thing that we notice is its *sthāyībhāva* or stable state of anger or *krodha*. This anger can be generated by 'harsh words' and 'oppression'. Here, it is a just anger and can be considered an emotion which might lead to the end of evil. But anger can also be generated by 'demons' and 'monsters', and these are evil. Thus, what follows will be *karuṇa* as well as *bhayānaka*. 'Anger', 'provocative action' etc., are neutral terms which can be applied to both good and evil.

The accompanying states or *vyabhicārībhāvas* of *raudra* are (*Nāṭya Śāstra*, VI.63):

> beating, splitting, crushing, ripping open, breaking, brandishing of weapons, ...
>
> — *Aesthetic Rapture*, Vol. II, p. 53

Here, the very basic manifestation of anger has been suggested — violence. But what is more noticeable in modern Western literature is an anger that is impotent — which does not get an outlet and which has to make do with the fury of words. Let it be mentioned here that when anger does not have a cause that can be located (for instance, a metaphysical position like the Absurd) and at which it can direct itself, after some time it might lead to despair and fear as in Absurd Literature.

Anger Through Words

In modern literature, *raudra* or the furious is manifest more in words that in deeds. Of course Bharata has also listed this possibility in *Nāṭya Śāstra* (VI.66):

> Such is *raudra rasa* in which **words** and actions are terrifying (emphasis supplied).
>
> — *Aesthetic Rapture*, Vol. I, p. 54

Thus, words can both manifest anger as well as inflict pain. Even otherwise, words communicate an (furious) intention, whether it is carried out in action or not. This is enough indication of *raudra*.

Injustice and Raudra

Raudra can usually be associated, when justly felt, with 'injustice', and 'oppression'. In fact, in modern literature, this kind of injustice, oppression and cruelty is very much felt; especially in a literature (a movement) which is considered outcast, as with the decadent French writers (Rimbaud, Verlaine etc.) and also in the Beat writers like Allen Ginsberg and others. But anger, if in excess of its cause (**fury** suggests this), can inflict pain and cause sorrow. On the other hand, if choked, it might lead to incomprehension, disjunction, and holds the possibility of *bībhatsa*. Ahab, in *Moby Dick*, acts with fury against the whale. But his metaphysical position holds an uncertainty which suggests both sadness and the grotesque.

The Accompanying States

The various accompanying states of *raudra* are (*Nāṭya Śāstra*, VI.63):

> Correct perception (*asammoha*), dynamic energy (*utsāha*), panic, resentment, rashness, violence, pride, sweat, trembling, horripilation, stuttering (*gadgada*) and so forth.
>
> *Aesthetic Rapture*, Vol. I, p. 53

"Correct perception" poses certain problems. As we shall see a little later, it is the cause of *vīra rasa*. Here, it can mean that when injustice, oppression etc., are perceived there might be the need for fury. Hence, it is indicated here that "correct perception" leads not only to heroic action but also to anger. *Raudra* is also related to *vīra rasa* in other ways. In heroic actions, the element of fury is perceivable, if not always, at least sometimes. It is for this reason that Abhinavagupta has related *utsāha* or dynamic energy, which is the primary state or the *sthāyībhāva* of *vīra*, to anger or *krodha* (*Aesthetic Rapture*, Vol. II, p. 89). This can be justified by the fact that even a meek man, furious at some injustice, can act courageously. Both the *rasas* involve action, 'dynamic energy', 'correct perception' etc.

'Panic' and 'violence' side-by-side may look strange. But we must remember that here we are talking about the accompanying states, and hence in a work of literature violence can lead to panic.

Raudra and Other Rasas

One might ask, if *vīra* and *raudra rasas* are so similar, what is it that differentiates them? A close look shows that the primary states (*sthāyībhāvas*) of the two are different, i.e., dynamic energy and anger respectively. Anger is a state which is more or less blind. In other words, 'correct perception' might get blocked by anger. Hence, there is the possibility of some wrong action. Besides, anger need not necessarily be correctly channellised. Fury might lead to a lot of words, but no action. But in case of *vīra*, the energy will either be reserved or correctly channellised. It is thus, always, a positive state or emotion.

Raudra is very closely associated with *bhayānaka* as well. We have seen that the manifestations of the **furious** are the following: 'beating', 'splitting', 'crushing', 'ripping open' etc. All these have suggestions of blood and mutilation. Such actions give rise to fear, and also to disgust. Thus, *raudra* is also related to *bībhatsa*.

One might ask, since *raudra* leads to these two *rasas* it might become subsidiary, especially if too much of attention is given to the manifestation and the consequences of *raudra*. This need not be the case. It depends to a great extent upon the treatment. Besides, if, for instance, the object of *raudra* is not frightened, *bhayānaka* cannot get manifested. Similarly, if the fury is at some injustice or some unjust person, the element of fear will be shown (by the unjust person), but the reader (alienated from him) will not participate in his fears.

Raudra and Vīra

Nāṭya Śāstra (VI.39-40) says about the relation of *vīra* with the other *rasas*:

> The awesome aesthetic experience comes from the heroic . . . . The result of the furious should be known to be an aesthetic experience of compassion.
>
> — *Aesthetic Rapture*, Vol. I, p. 48

What the first part of the passage suggests is that wherever heroism is manifest, *raudra* will accompany as an accessory. Besides, the heroic emotion is the source of the **awesome**. This need not always be true. In *No One Writes to the Colonel* (in the chapter on *karuṇa*), we found that what effuses the work is the old man's courage to face and live life. But there is no scope for *raudra* there. Yet it indicates a very profound psychological aspect hidden behind the **furious** emotion: that of a courageous state of mind. A man burdened by sorrow cannot become furious; he might whimper. This is so, for the moment one gives vent to sorrow, he has lost his positive frame of mind, his strength to fight back. Similarly, a man who is afraid cannot at the same time become furious. Thus, even with a bad man or with a monster, the important thing is a courageous frame of mind. Even though the actions of a bad man or a monster are not heroic, the frame of mind is one that is ready to take up any challenge. The passage, understood in that way, makes sense.

Raudra and Karuṇa

Raudra is always associated with violence and destruction. But it is not necessarily productive. The moment it is channellised in a positive direction, it becomes *vīra*. Hence, in *raudra*, the central emphasis is upon the turmoil, the fury, and its consequences. It is thus that *raudra* will invariably lead to *karuṇa rasa*. So, it is not surprising that the effects or *anubhāvas* of *raudra* are also similar to the *anubhāvas* of *karuṇa*, i.e., tears, fear, trembling etc. But, as pointed out earlier, this need not always be the case, especially if the fury of man, God, or nature is against an oppressor.

On the other hand, a reversibility is noticeable in the relation of *raudra* and *karuṇa*. Injustice can lead to suffering and hence to *karuṇa*. But if one does not give vent to sorrow and suppresses it or fights it, anger and fury will be manifested. Hence, *karuṇa*, choked or suppressed, will lead to *raudra*. If we look again at Mayakovsky's poem *Cloud in Pants* from this angle, we notice this blockage. After a long waiting, when his beloved finally arrives, it is only to inform him that she is getting married to someone else. This cruel and unjust act hurts the narrator and the narrator fights back his tears with fury. Thus, *karuṇa* is blocked off by a process of transformation of the emotions:

"Hullo!
Who is speaking?"
Who can it be —
Mother?
Mother!
Your son is beautifully sick . . . .
His heart is on fire
. . . . Mother,
leaps like a naked whore through the smoke
out of a burning brothel . . . .
Look out with your boots, Messers, firemen,
hearts on fire should be handled with caresses!

— *Longer Poems*, p. 13

In the fourth section of the poem when he begs Maria (his cruel beloved) to open the door, *raudra* and *karuṇa* alternate:

Dear, don't be afraid . . .
Dear, never fear
if in fits of dishonesty
I'll cling to a thousand pretty faces again . . . .
Maria! come nearer!

— *Longer Poems*, p. 25

and towards the end of the poem he lets off his steam at God:

> You omnipotent? Deal out death and life?
> You're just an ignoramus, a petty brute . . .
> — *Longer Poems*, p. 25

and at the angels:

> Let your feather shiver in St. Vitus' dance:
> couch in heaven,
> lip-serving
> wing-flapping rascals!
> I'll rip you all up, stinking with incense,
> from here right down to Alaska!
> — *Longer Poems*, p. 25

But as he himself notices at the end of his outburst:

> The Universe
> sleeps, its huge ear
> dotted with star-ticks
> laid on its paw.
> — *Longer Poems*, p. 26

Here, one might ask, who is the victim in this kind of rage? Who is the subject of *karuṇa* here? The answer will be, the narrator himself. Since, his rage has no victim, it ends in impotence. Thus, the very impotence of his rage, manifest in his rage, leads to *karuṇa*. So again, at the end of rage (though not as a consequence) there is sadness.

Impotent Rage and Suffering

This illustration of impotent rage is also the key to understanding much of the rage to be found in modern Western literature. When we discuss *bībhatsa* and *bhayānaka rasas* we will deal with these kinds of literature — Existential literature, Absurd literature etc. There, in fact, we see a hoard of emotions like anger, fear, courage, etc., in the face of what is terrifying and disgusting. The rage to be found both in John Osborne's *Look Back in Anger* and

Allen Ginsberg's *Howl* can be related to these.

Look Back in Anger, a post-Second World War play, presents an outsider in the form of its central character, Jimmy. It is to be noted that in *Metamorphosis* alienation gives rise to sorrow. But to the same alienation, Jimmy reacts with fury. Sadness is latent, but it is the fury that is emphasized. The causes or the *vibhāvas* of his anger are many. For instance,they can be traced back to his traumatic childhood, his suffering and the injustice of fate. At the age of ten he saw his father dying a humiliating death, slowly, everyday:

> You see, I learnt at an early age what it is to be angry — angry and helpless. And I can never forget it. (*Sits.*) I knew more about love . . . betrayal . . . and death, when I was ten years old than you will probably ever know all your life.
>
> — *Look Back in Anger*, p. 58: Act II, Scene 1

Another reason is his sense of alienation, his feeling that he is an outsider, an outcaste, that the world has treated him unjustly. As Alison's (his wife's) recollection of their first meeting suggests:

> I met him at a party. I remember it so clearly. I was almost twenty-one. The men there all looked as if they distrusted him, and as for the women, they were all intent on showing their contempt for this rather odd creature . . .
>
> — *Look Back in Anger*, p. 45: Act II, Scene 1

On top of all that he feels purposeless, without a meaning which he desperately, urgently searches for:

> Nobody thinks, no body cares. No beliefs, no convictions and no enthusiasm. Just another Sunday evening.
>
> — *Look Back in Anger*, p. 17: Act I, Scene 1

What he complains about the others is also true of him. He

has tried out many things and now has a sweet-stall. It is these that lead to his fury, that makes everyone's life (including his own) miserable:

> Why do I spend nine pence on that damned paper every week? Nobody reads it except me . . . . You two will drive me round the bend soon — I know it, as sure as I'm sitting here. I know you're going to drive me mad . . . Let's pretend we're human beings, and that we're actually alive.
>
> — *Look Back in Anger*, p. 15: Act I, Scene 1

and the way he looks at Helena, Alison's friend, whom he considers his enemy, shows the depth of his anger:

> HELENA (*pondering*) : It's almost as if he wants to kill someone with it. And me in particular. I've never seen such hatred in someone's eyes before.
>
> — *Look Back in Anger*, p. 23: Act.I, Scene 2

The effects or the *anubhāvas* are manifold. Alison, his wife, almost goes over the edge. Her friend, Helena, reacts to his fury with fury by slapping him, and his friend Jeff finally decides to leave his house.

But this fury generates more an atmosphere of sadness than that of terror. This is so because the reader or the audience is made to feel that Jimmy really does not mean any harm. Since his fury (like the gambler's dice) hurts him and the people whom he loves (and who love him), it leads to distress.

True, the play ends with a sense of reconciliation, but it does not mean that the fury in their lives does not leave its marks on their lives. Alison loses her baby even before it is born. Friends part. Here the protagonist thus, both causes and reaps the consequences of his own fury.

Raudra, the Frenzy and the Grotesque

But in Ginsberg's *Howl* the fury is intermixed with a kind of spiritual frenzy. What we have noticed in all these instances is a kind of fury that is born of suffering. It is, in fact, the agony of the characters that finds vent in fury rather than in sorrow. Thus, in all these cases, the fury is a desperate effort to come to terms with life. Here also, the same features are to be found. *Howl* is a *howl* of anger and anguish at the loss and waste of so much of good and the speaker seeks to transcend his anger through poetic experience. *Howl*, thus, has the ability to lead towards *śānta rasa*.

Since *Howl* is a long poem which is not a narrative, we do not have any specific story-line. What, nonetheless, is understandable is the injustice which causes of alienation of talented young men by the society. Thus, it is as if a character were letting out his angry and frenzy in words:

> I saw the best minds of my generation destroyed by madness, starving hysterical naked,
> dragging themselves through the negro streets . . .
>
> — *Anthology of American Literature*, Vol. II.
> p. 1749: lines 1-2

Here, the sense of alienation from the society, the sense of injustice, is distinct. This 'howl' is for those:

> who cowered in unshaven rooms in underwear, burning their money in wastebaskets and listening to the Terror through the walls . . . .
>
> — *Anthology of American Literature*, Vol. II.
> p. 1749: line 8

or

> who went out whoring through Colorado in myriad stolen night-cars
>
> — *Anthology of American Literature*, Vol. II.
> p. 1750: line 43

or

> who copulated ecstatic and insatiate with a bottle of beer a sweet heart . . .
>
> — *Anthology of American Literature*, Vol. II.
> p. 1750: line 41

Here is depicted a world of frenzy, fury and violent sexuality — a sexuality, which is at times repulsive and at other times ecstatic. In all these thefts and sex, what is lurking again is their seeking and their discontent. In fact, their fury is the result of their endless seeking which is frustrated at every corner: for they pine for *śānta* (calm) or a religious resolution, and there are (illusory or real) moments, that after they are gone, only heighten their fury. Hence this 'howl' is for those:

> who fell on their knees in hopeless cathedrals praying for each others' salvation and lights and breasts, until the soul illuminated its hair for a second . . . .
>
> — *Anthology of American Literature*, Vol. II.
> p. 1750: line 61

or for those:

> who cut their wrists three times successively, gave up and were forced to open antique stores where they thought they were growing old and cried . . . .
>
> — *Anthology of American Literature*, Vol. II.
> p. 1751: line 56

Here, fury gives way to self-destruction and to *karuṇa*. But in some instances it leads to one-minute illumination of the "hair of the soul" that once gone only leads to greater discontent.

An interesting thing to be noted in this poem is that the fury is two-fold — the fury and the frenzy that is depicted, and the fury and the frenzy felt by the narrator.

Besides, we have here almost all the accompanying states of *raudra rasa*. In the narrator's sense of injustice there is the sense of disgust at those who have made these people outcasts. In these men's lives we see courage in their brave efforts and their seeking. Their suffering gives rise to sorrow. But in the end the poem moves away from fury and suggests the possibility of a transcendence of the alienation. The speaker becomes some kind of institution in himself to whom these suffering souls can come for solace. There is still the possibility of meaning left:

> I'm with you in Rockland
> in my dreams you walk dripping from a sea-journey on the highway across America in tears at the door of my cottage in the Western night.
>
> — *Anthology of American Literature*, Vol. II. p. 1753

The use of the word 'tear' here is ambiguous. It might mean tears of joy or tears of sorrow or both. But in coming to the narrator, it is as if they were reaching a place of comfort, where their restless souls could find peace. Thus, as mentioned earlier, the possibility of *śānta rasa* is hinted at.

Fury and Waste

Before we end this discussion, let a remarkable feature of *raudra rasa* which was mentioned earlier be highlighted. In *vīra* we find dynamic energy while here we find **anger**. As already pointed out, while dynamic energy is properly channellised, anger involves a lot of waste, for it involves an excited emotional state which is not very decided, which does not judge and act. But in the literature that we have scanned, what is to be noted is the fact that fury is usually associated with a sense of impotence. At times, however, it appears that at that moment the manifestation of fury is the only outlet. It is as if a lot of energy were suddenly brought alive, which is directed, but irrationally or unreasonably. It is thus that fury can result in uncalled for devastation which eventually leads to *karuṇa rasa.*

From the above discussion we can conclude that *raudra rasa* can be considered an intermediary stage where one is not sure how exactly to act. He knows his grouse, he might even know at what it is directed, but the action is not controlled as it is in *vīra rasa.* Thus, in Mayakovsky's short poem, 'You', behind the fury there is contempt and disgust, but not much possibility of directed action:

> You, wallowing through orgy after orgy
> owning a bathroom and a warm, snug toilet!
> How dare you read about awards of St. George
> From newspaper columns with your blinkers oily?
>
> Do you realize, multitudinous nonentities
> thinking how better to fill your gob,
> that perhaps just now Petrov the lieutenant
> had both his legs ripped off by a bomb?
>
> Imagine if he, brought along for slaughter,
> suddenly saw, with his blood out-draining,
> you, with your mouths still dribbling soda-water
> and vodka, lasciviously crooning Severyanin!
>
> To give up my life for the likes of you,
> lovers of woman-flesh, dinners and cars?
> I'd rather go and serve pineapple juice
> to the whores in Moscow's bars.
>
> — *Mayakovsky: Selected Verses*, Vol. I, p. 56

Fury and Disgust as Responses

A reason for quoting the above verse is, we find that fury if intermixed with contempt and disgust loses its force. When disgust rules, fury automatically gets diluted — for here at the end, the bourgeois becomes too low for the speaker's fury. This also points to a psychological mechanism. The possibility is that when the fury is impotent, it tries to find an outlet in the form of disgust.

It is similar in W.B. Yeats's poem, "The Spur":

You think it horrible that lust and rage
Should dance attention upon my old age;
They were not such a plague when I was young;
What else have I to spur me into a song?
— *Yeats : Selected Poetry*, p. 190

It is the 'rage' and 'lust' of old age that channellized his life in the productive direction of poetry. But this poetry comes out of the fury at getting old. Hence, a certain sense of impotence against fate is suggested. Here is a sense of 'injustice' (by fate) that can be even more amply illustrated in Black American poetry much of which is born out of rage against discrimination. In "Slave Story", a poem by the Black American poet Hodding Carter, the life of a plantation slave is described in a capsule:

At twenty-one Jupe ran away
To join the Yankee jubilee.
The word had trickled to Mount Pine,
Old Abe had set the niggers free.
The hounds retrieved him in a swamp,
His master gave him ten yards grace
Then shot him just above the calf
To make him realize his place.
— *The Poetry of the Negro*: 1746-1970, p. 540

Times change and Jupe gets a chance to vote. He is happy. But then:

Four reeling years, and the Klan
Rode through the state and dragged him out.
They strung him skyward by his heels
And beat him with a leaded knout,
— *The Poetry of the Negro*, p. 540

And so this is how the poet remembers Jupe:

I can remember old Unc' Jupe
Who could remember nothing much
. . . .
And dragged his leg beneath a crutch,
And foretold weather by the pains
. . . .
And when he dies the head line read
A faithful former slave set free.

— *The Poetry of the Negro*, p. 541

What is remarkable about this poem is that nowhere is the narrator's rage suggested. As in a drama, a situation is given and it makes the reader's blood boil, while compassion for the old man lurks behind. This happens because we have the cause and effects of *raudra* clearly spelled out here. The white men, acting like 'monsters' or 'demons', manifest their rage and cruelty upon this black victim. Out of that madness suffering follows. It is this suffering that moves us to rage. Thus, interestingly, through the manifestation of the various *anubhāvas* and *vyabhicārībhāvas* (consequent and accompanying states) rage or fury is generated by the injustice.

Langston Hughes, another black writer, in "Song For a Dark Girl", writes:

Way Down South in Dixie
    (Break the heart of mine)
They hung my dark young lover
    To a cross roads tree.

Way down South in Dixie
    (Bruised body high in air)
I asked the white Lord Jesus
    What was the use of prayer.

Way Down South in Dixie
    (Break the heart of mine)
Love is a naked shadow
On a gnarled and naked tree.

— *I Am the Darker Brother: An Anthology of Poems by Negro Americans*, p. 67

This poem leads us to ask a vital question — even though it is about sorrow why does it generate anger as a response? It is so because what comes through is the outcome — the destruction. As much as we are moved by sorrow, anger is directed at the source. But then one might ask, what about the works discussed in the chapter of *karuṇa rasa*? We can answer that it is the way the situation is painted and the way things are treated that decide the outcome or the response. In *karuṇa* the manifestation of sorrow is emphasized rather than the cause. Here, in this poem of separation, what caused the anguish has been highlighted — and so the difference in response.

Another thing noticeable in both the poems is the element of irony. Especially in "Slave Story" the handling is satirical (the disjunction between Jupe's dream and the reality is shown). In other words, the **satirical** mode is equally applicable to *raudra rasa* as to *hāsya*. But here, the outcome is serious and hence, what it generates is anger.

Thus, *raudra* is a very vital element in modern Western literature. But it has a tendency to dissolve or get transformed into something else. It cannot sustain itself for a long time, and thus its outlets are sorrow and action (heroic or devastating) and where it is impotent, it usually leads to a sense of incomprehension — the Absurd. In the *rasas* like *vīra*, *bhayānaka* and *bībhatsa* which will follow, *raudra rasa* always holds an important secondary position.

7

Vīra Rasa

HE was an inch, perhaps two under six feet and he advanced straight at you with a slight stoop at the shoulders, head forward, and a fixed from-under stare which made you think of a charging bull. His voice was deep and loud, and his manner displayed a kind of dogged self-assertion which had nothing aggressive about it.

— *Lord Jim*, p. 9

This is how Joseph Conrad describes his hero at the beginning of the novel *Lord Jim*. In the *Nāṭya Śāstra* (VI.67) Bharata says:

Vīrarasa is properly acted out by firmness, patience, heroism, pride, dynamic energy (*utsāha*), bravery, might, and profound emotions.

— *Aesthetic Rapture*, Vol. I, p. 54

The Manifestations of Vīra Rasa

Here, already, some of the qualities of the **heroic emotion** are perceivable in the description by Conrad. The physical appearance, apart from the height and the powerful built, suggests a certain strength of a 'charging bull'. But even though there is a certain self-assertion, it has nothing 'aggressive' about it. This is very important for 'aggression' and 'violence' might lead to the manifestation of *raudra rasa*. Not that *vīra* cannot be associated with fierceness, but it is the degree of violence and the degree of self-control suggested that makes the difference.

Firmness and Patience

The basic qualities that suggest heroism in a person are 'firmness', 'patience' etc. Now, 'firmness' and 'patience' go together and complement each other. 'Firmness' suggests steadiness — a certain rootedness. In other words, in the presence of danger or threat one does not give way. 'Patience' is what helps this steadfastness to sustain itself. Both are sustained by what is the essence of *vīra* (in fact, its **primary state**) — 'dynamic energy'. It is this positive outlook and energy that sustain the qualities of firmness and patience.

Even so, 'dynamic energy' gets its anchorage and outlet in 'patience' or 'steadfastness' where it is correctly channellised.

Strength

'Might' or 'strength' can suggest (as we have seen in the above passage from *Lord Jim*) courage. 'Profound remarks' can come only from the insights that a heroic man gets from his struggles with life. Thus, such remarks will come from the heart, from what is actually felt, and the deep insight in them will make them profound.

When we first meet Jim in *Lord Jim*, he is actually an outcast. All his youth he has been a dreamer dreaming of brave deeds:

> On the lower deck in the babel of two hundred voices he would forget himself, and beforehand live in his mind the sea-life of light literature. He saw himself saving people from sinking ships, cutting masts . . . . always an example of devotion to duty, and as unflinching as a hero in a book.
>
> — *Lord Jim*, p. 11

Here again, some of the basic traits of heroism are to be found in what constitutes Jim's daydreams — 'devotion to duty', an 'unflinching quality' etc,., which show patience as well as courage.

A chance comes his way, but before he can react, another seaman saves the drowning man. But the way the rescuer boasts of his valour fills Jim with disgust:

> "Fancy such a big chap fainting like a girl . . . ." "No silly! It was not his flesh that held him — his breeches did. Lots of blood of course."
>
> Jim thought it a pitiful display of vanity.
>
> — *Lord Jim*, p. 13

Thus, 'pride' (which we see listed in the *Nāṭya Śāstra*) should not be confused with 'vanity' or boast. Pride is not displayed like vanity. It is something which comes out of one's sense of achievement, or even competence. Hence, here it should be understood as a positive quality which manifests itself through poise or elegance.

One day, the long-cherished dream of Jim is upon the threshold of coming true. He is on board of a sinking ship (or what all the mates think to be one) and the quail is about to break. But in that confusion of noises and images, Jim loses his bearing:

> Eight hundred living people, and they yelled after the one dead man to come down and be saved. 'Jump, George! Jump! Oh, jump!' . . . . 'Jump, George! we'll catch you! Jump! . . . .
>
> "I had jumped . . . ." He checked himself, averted his gaze . . . "It seemed," he added . . . .
>
> "I knew nothing about it till I looked up," he explained

> hastily. And that's possible too. He didn't know. It had happened somehow.
>
> — *Lord Jim*, pp. 82-83

Thus, from a ship which contained eight hundred helpless souls, he jumps in a confused daze (without realizing it) at the call from his mates which hypnotize him. Now, since, in the inquiry he has nothing really to say for himself, he lives the life of an outcast, moving from port to port, never going to the sea again.

What is emphasized here is the fact that Jim does not act out of cowardice. It is just that he loses his head and so it is not strange that we see Jim at the beginning of the novel very much composed and with a certain poise and control: for it also needs a lot of 'courage', 'patience' and 'dynamic energy' to face the world when one is considered a coward. It needs a lot of conviction to believe in oneself after all that has happened — to still consider oneself a brave man.

Jim leaves the ports (for invariably his story follows him) and settles down among the natives of Patusan Island. It is here that his potential is recognized (since no one knows his past) and he is in his element. But courage tests him again and at a point in his life when he is already married and is very much in love with his wife. Among the natives, it is trust that matters. Jim introduces a petty thief and trader, Brown, (who is jealous of Jim) to the natives. But in an act of betrayal Brown and his party, just before leaving the island, shoot and kill the chief's son. When Jim comes to know of this, he knows of the consequence. Even though the chief loves him like a son, it will be death for him:

> All at once Jim, who seemed to be lost in quiet thought, turned to him and said, "Time to finish this."
>
> 'Tuan?" said Tamb' Itam, advancing with alacrity. He did not know what his mater meant, ...
>
> — *Lord Jim*, p. 290

and when his wife asks him:

> "Will you fight?" she cried. "There is nothing to fight for," he said; "nothing is lost." Saying this he made a step towards her. "Will you fly?" She cried again. "There is no escape," he said, stopping short, and she stood still also, silent, devouring him with her eyes. "And you shall go" she said slowly. He bent his head. " . . . . Do you remember you said that you would not leave me? Why? I asked you for no promise. You promised unasked — remember." "Enough, poor girl," he said. "I should not be worth having."
>
> — *Lord Jim*, p. 290

In fighting he would show courage, but what kind of courage is it when you fight your own people? If he ran away for the sake of his wife, he would feel so contemptible about himself that he "would not be worth having". A final opportunity comes to test his courage and this time he does not fail and walks to his death.

Correct Perception

A key factor that is discernible from the passage is that Jim lost his bearing or 'correct perception' (*Nāṭya Śāstra*, VI.66) which is the key to directed action. This led to a certain 'confusion' and to his acting wrongly. Thus, in *vīra rasa*, it is the 'correct perception' which is the source of directed activity. But in *raudra* 'confusion' (*Nāṭya Śāstra*, VI.63) leads to distortion of perception (on many occasions) and hence 'confusion' is a very important accompanying state there.

The *Nāṭya Śāstra* (VI.66) also notes the following regarding the *vīra rasa* :

> Now (the *rasa*) called *vīra* has (only) noble people for its characters and consists in dynamic energy (*utsāha*).
>
> — *Aesthetic Rapture*, Vol. I, p. 54

Before we proceed, let one thing be clarified — the "nobility" of the character need not necessarily be determined by birth. What determines nobility is the **action**. Jim, in fact, is a common seaman. But when he starts living among the natives of Patusan his qualities of honesty, poise and courage are recognized and he is called "Lord Jim". Here, thus, it is his conduct and action that elevate his stature.

Dynamic Energy

Earlier, we have briefly mentioned that *utsāha* or dynamic energy is the *sthāyībhāva* or the primary state of *vīra rasa.* In other words, without the enthusiasm or the 'dynamic energy' — however prudent or insightful or calm one is — one cannot act. Thus, this positive state of excitement is at the root of any action, or even 'patience' that causes a courageous act of waiting.

Talking of 'patience', one might ask, how can patience (which involves no action but a stasis) lead to *vīra*? For one thing, as in *The Old Man and the Sea* which we will discuss shortly, patience is what determines the right moment to strike. Valour without prudence will lead only to disaster. Even otherwise, as in Marquez's *No One Writes to the Colonel*, the very act of patience, of waiting against all despairs, is an act of courage.

The Causes of Vīra

The causes or the *vibhāvas* of *vīra* are the following (*Nāṭya Śāstra*, VI.66):

> Correct perception, decisiveness (*adhyāvasāya*), political wisdom (*naya*), courtesy (*vinaya*), an army (*bala*), eminence (*prabhāva*) etc.
>
> — *Aesthetic Rapture*, Vol. I, p. 54

Here, one might, quite justly, point out that *vīra* is usually generated in the face of some 'arrogance', 'injustice' or challenge. It is some provocation or opposition (be it that of man or fate) that leads to the necessity and display of courage. But we do not find any mention of them in the *Nāṭya Śāstra*. This is true. But unless one has the necessary qualities, no amount of provocation will elicit the response of courage. It might lead to sorrow or fear instead. Hence, here, the *vibhāvas* (or those possibilities that lead to *vīra*) must act upon the qualities already innate in one, and must stimulate them, before the courageous act can follow.

'Correct perception' is at the root of any positive act. If it is not there (as happened in the case of Jim when he abandoned the ship) even in the face of challenge, one might act rashly. In other words, it is 'correct perception' only that can lead to any decisive (and positive) action. *Naya* has been translated as "political wisdom". The word also implies goodness and a sense of justice. Thus, when one is good and just, it leads to 'correct perception' and thus to right action.

'Bravery in battle', 'courage' etc., are inner qualities that lead to or cause heroic action. But 'courtesy' or *vinaya* is a little problematic. *Vinaya* also means humility. We can understand it as an accompanying state of *vīra rasa*. But one cannot see how it can cause *vīra rasa* since it neither provokes, nor suggests the possibility of any dynamic action.

Bala can mean both 'an army' and 'power'. *Śakti*, similarly, can mean both 'skill in battle' as well as 'strength'. These give one confidence in oneself and thus can lead to heroic action in the face of necessity. But if power and skill (which again gives one power) are misutilized, they can lead to *raudra* or *bhayānaka rasa*. Thus, these must be accompanied by nobility of character and 'correct perception'.

The Responses of Vīra

The *Nāṭya Śāstra* (VI.66) tells us that *vīra*:

> . . . should be acted out by such *anubhāvas* as firmness, patience, heroism, generosity and shrewdness (*vaiśāradya*).
>
> — *Aesthetic Rapture*, Vol. I, p. 54

The manifestations or effects of *vīra rasa* should depict such qualities as mentioned above. We have already discussed 'firmness' and 'patience'. 'Heroism' is a rather vague categorization which includes valour, courage, correct perception etc.

'Generosity' and 'shrewdness' need to be elaborated. In fact, we will come across both these possibilities in *The Old Man and the Sea*. 'Generosity' is associated with 'courtesy' or humility. Here the element of sympathy figures prominently; and it is kindness and understanding that lead to 'generosity'.

'Shrewdness' is the opposite of 'foolishness' (in the present context) and not of 'goodness'. Any kind of war (in *vīra* warring is a very important element), action should be prudent and 'skilful', for along with the clash of strength, there is also the clash of intelligence. 'Shrewdness' is thus to be related to 'skill' and involves a clear and 'correct perception' of things.

Determination in the Face of Odds

Ernest Hemingway's *The Old Man and the Sea* is a short novel in which the various possibilities of heroism come out clearly. In fact, when we read it, we are reminded again and again of a passage in the *Nāṭya Śāstra* (VI.66):

> *Vīrarasa* is a dynamic energy (*utsāha*) which arises from various causal factors (*arthāvśeṣa*) such as decisiveness, not giving way to depression, not being surprised or confused (emphasis supplied).
>
> — *Aesthetic Rapture*, Vol. I, p. 54

We have already talked of 'decisiveness' and 'confusion'. But here are two other very important elements — 'not being surprised' and 'not giving way to depression'.

In *Lord Jim*, it was the fact that Jim was not ready for the storm when it really arrived that made him lose control. It was his 'surprise' at the unexpected that led to 'confusion' and ultimately to the wrong act of abandoning a ship full of helpless people.

But, in *The Old Man and the Sea*, Santiago (the old fisherman) is a veteran fighter and is prepared for anything. Even when he is surprised at the size of the marline, he does not lose his self-control in the excitement or get confused. But what is remarkably more important, he never gives up hope and so is like the old colonel in *No One Writes to the Colonel*:

> He was an old man who fished alone in a skiff in the Gulf Stream and he had gone eighty-four days now without taking a fish. In the first forty days a boy had been with him. But after forty days without a fish the boy's parents had told him that the old man was definitely and finally *salao*, which is the worst form of unlucky, ... It made the boy sad to see the old man come in each day with his skiff empty . . . .
>
> — *The Old Man and the Sea*, p. 5

Though the element of sadness (*karuṇa*) is innate here, what holds our attention is the old man's stubborn perseverance. Even when the boy is gone and he is alone, he still continues with his efforts. When the narrative begins, he is going out for the eighty-fifth time without a fish. This single-minded and dogged determination becomes more clear as the narrative proceeds.

Humility

The old man is battle-scarred and there are marks of sea-battles (with fishes) upon him:

> . . . his hands had deep-creased scars from handling heavy fish on the cords. But none of these scars were fresh. They were as old as erosions in a fishless desert.
>
> Everything about him was old except his eyes and they were the same colour as the sea and were cheerful and

undefeated.

— *The Old Man and the Sea*, pp. 5-6

Thus, we have the picture of a warrior who has nerves of steel. Even after eighty-four days out of luck, his eyes are still undefeated. It is perhaps his long experience that has made him overcome anger. Thus, in his action there is always control and never anger, not even when he is ridiculed:

> They sat on the Terrace and many of the fishermen made fun of the old man and he was not angry.
>
> — *The Old Man and the Sea*, p. 7

Thus, he has learnt the ultimate essence of heroism: 'humility' and 'forgiveness':

> He was too simple to wonder when he had attained humility. But he knew he had attained it and he knew it was not disgraceful and it carried no loss of true pride.
>
> *The Old Man and the Sea*, pp. 9-10

Here, two of the contrasting elements — pride and humility — have been resolved in one man. But the simplicity of the old man does not mean that he cannot be 'shrewd' when fighting with the marlin.

Wonder

A very important element — the response of *adbhuta* — is to be found in the reaction of the boy (Manolin) who considers Santiago the best fisherman in the world:

> "There are many good fishermen and some great ones. But there is only you."
>
> "Thank you. You make me happy. I hope no fish will come along so great that he will prove us wrong."
>
> — *The Old Man and the Sea*, pp. 19-20

But actually such a big marlin does come along and challenge the old man. On the eighty-fifth day, the old man goes deep into the sea and there a fish takes the bait on one of his lines — a huge marlin, as the old man comes to know in good time.

From now on it is a battle of courage, patience and intelligence. The old man is 'shrewd' and skilful. But he soon realizes that the fish is also a 'shrewd' old fish. For one thing, it stays way deep inside the sea, away from where fishermen usually fish. But the way it dives in and threatens to capsize Santiago's skiff makes us realize that it is experienced in this game.

What the fish tries to do then is to run the old man out of courage and patience. It does not come out until almost the very end, and hence, the old man has no way of knowing how big he really is. Thus, the battle turns slowly into a test of patience and endurance, a war of attrition:

> He held the line against his back and watched its slant in the water and the skiff moved steadily to the north-west.
>
> This will kill him, the old man thought. He can't do this for ever. But four hours later the fish was still swimming steadily out to sea . . .
>
> — *The Old Man and the Sea*, p. 43

In this battle an entire day and a night pass and now it becomes a battle of sheer will and endurance — for neither is ready to give up:

> "Fish," he said softly, aloud, "I'll stay with you until I am dead."
>
> — *The Old Man and the Sea*, p. 50

and in the process the old man is gradually able to appreciate the fighting calibre of the fish:

> "Fish," he said, "I love you and respect you very much. But I will kill you dead before this day ends."
>
> — *The Old Man and the Sea*, p. 52

It makes us wonder at the courage and endurance of these two warriors.

Weakness

An interesting point to be noted is that the old man is very sensitive about weaknesses. When his left hand cramps he says:

> "What kind of a hand is that," . . . . "Cramp then if you want. Make yourself into a claw. It will do you no good."
>
> — *The Old Man and the Sea*, p. 56

Thus any kind of weakness, indecisiveness etc., is inimical to *vīra* or the **heroic emotion**.

Absence of Confusion

Another quality emphasized in the *Nāṭya Śāstra*, which is to be seen here, is the insistence on the absence of 'confusion':

> " . . . .If you do not sleep you might become unclear in the head."
>
> I'm clear enough in the head, he thought. Too clear. I am as clear as the stars that are my brother. Still I must sleep.
>
> — *The Old Man and the Sea*, p. 76

This, the old man keeps on telling himself, for in the battle to come, he needs a clear head.

As the day progresses, finally the fish comes out and the old man kills him, but that is not the end of his ordeal. On his way back the sharks attack his fish which is tied to the side of his skiff. They come in large numbers and he fights them with his harpoon, and when it is gone, with a knife and then with the tiller. But in the night they eat away most of his great fish. Despair attacks him:

> It was too good to last, he thought. I wish it had been a dream now and that I had never hooked the fish and was alone in the bed on the newspapers.
>
> — *The Old Man and the Sea*, p. 103

But immediately he says:

> "But man is not made for defeat," . . . . "A man can be destroyed but not defeated." I am sorry that I killed the fish though . . . .
>
> — *The Old Man and the Sea*, p. 103

In his courage, he is very much like the old colonel in *No One Writes to the Colonel*. What emerges above everything else is that 'energy' that always latches on to a hope. True, there are elements of sadness in it. For instance, even as he kills the marlin, the old man feels sorry for the fish and, later on, he repents having killed him. Thus, he recognizes the courage of the fish, and respects it. But it is his duty to kill fish (his *dharma*). It is also his livelihood and so he justifies his deed.

As readers, we feel sorry for both the fish and the old man. Hence, the element of *karuṇa* is also to be seen here. But the old man's adventurous spirit and heroic exploits lead to the element of wonder and admiration for his courage, strength and endurance; and thus sorrow is not overemphasized.

Associated Emotions of Vīra

In the *Nāṭya Śāstra* (VI.66), the *vyabhicārībhāvas* or the accompanying states of *vīra rasa* have been listed as follows:

> . . . happiness, attentiveness, pride, panic, violence,

resentment, remembrance, and horripilation.

—*Aesthetic Rapture*, Vol. I, p. 54

'Happiness' and 'pride' follow from a sense of achievement. When the old man finally kills the marlin, he achieves his goal and so is happy. Thus, the possibility of reaching a goal and happiness (and thus the possibility of *śānta*) is to be seen here. 'Resentment' can lead to action. It might also result from an encounter, on the part of the victim of the heroic action. 'Panic' and 'horripilation', thus, apply mostly to the object on which the heroic act is being enacted. But even in the reader, there is the possibility of fear (or awe) at the enactment of a great heroic deed. Thus, there is a scope for both *bhayānaka* and *adbhuta*. In fact, in the *Mahābhārata*, after the war, what is left is only death and devastation. Hence, *vīra rasa* can also lead (apart from *karuṇa*) to a sense of fear and pity at the waste. This holds the possibility of a 'world-weary' feeling and so of leading to *śānta rasa*.

Love, Anger and Vīra Rasa

Love can lead to heroic acts. Intense love leads to a certain steadfastness and courage. A person is moved in a certain direction and when something comes in the way of his achieving his end, he acts courageously to overcome it. In love, the sense of attraction overcomes whatever fear there is in the way.

Similarly, anger can lead to courageous acts. Here again, the element of sorrow is choked, and a more directed act of rage is to be seen. If this rage is properly directed, it can lead to heroic action. As Yeats writes in "Easter 1916":

I have met them at close of day
coming with vivid faces
From counter or desk among grey
Eighteenth-century houses.
. . . .
All changed, changed utterly:

A terrible beauty is born.

— *Yeats: Selected Poems*, p. 93

The common men, ordinary men, hypocritical men, all have been transformed in the Irish Easter uprising. For a common cause, directed against the injustice of British occupation, their rage has given way to courage:

Hearts with one purpose alone
Through summer and winter seem
Enchanted to a stone

— *Yeats*, p. 94

Thus, common men can also become 'transformed' in a moment of intense excitement and in a reader or a perceiver, this transformation gives rise to wonder.

Vīra and the Other Rasas

If a heroic act is handled in a different manner the element of wonder might dominate. In such a case, it will lead to *adbhuta rasa.* In *Jonathan Livingston Seagull* by Richard Bach, the bird's experiences generate wonder, but in the determination and the drive behind the bird's wonderful performance lies the element of the heroic. Similarly, as Abhinavagupta has pointed out, even spiritual pursuits need 'steadfastness', 'patience' and 'courage'. Thus, even there (as we shall see later in Herman Hesse's *Siddhartha*) the element of courage is very important. Hence, even in *rasas* like *adbhuta* and *śānta* the element of the heroic is to be noticed as an accompanying state.

We have already discussed some of the possible relations that *vīra rasa* can have with other *rasas*. But certain other relations are also perceivable. We have already mentioned that *vīra* leads to *adbhuta.* True, if the element of the heroic is the focus, then what comes through is the element of wonder at the remarkable quality of courage, for one admires heroism. Admiration suggests the possibility of being impressed by something. In other words, it holds the connotation of a delightful surprise. This involves a certain element of distancing. But one can also get inspired by seeing an act of courage. This kind of emotion is something very close to the *sthāyībhāva* or the primary state of *vīra* — dynamic energy.

But the consequence of *vīra*, as has been mentioned, can also be sorrowful, terrible or horrible. *Vīra* has always the possibility of (if not controlled or directed correctly) getting transformed into *raudra* and thus again leading to *bībhatsa* and *bhayānaka*. This also holds the possibility of *karuṇa*.

But one very interesting fact worth notice is that it is very difficult to relate *vīra* and *hāsya rasa*. The one relation that comes to the mind is that the imitation of *vīra* can lead to *hāsya*. But here, what lies behind is only the element of incongruity.

As for *śānta* and *vīra*, the spiritual seeker or the one who seeks **peace** must have courage and perseverance. *Vīra*, in itself, can lead to a state of 'happiness' when it **achieves** something, as happens when the old man finally kills the fish in *The Old Man and the Sea*. It is, thus, similar to *śṛṅgāra* in its end, which is happiness. In that moment of achievement (be it heroic achievement or the achievement of union) there is a moment of **complete** satisfaction. But this is only a moment. If this can be transcended, perhaps there is the possibility of *śānta rasa*.

8

Bhayānaka Rasa and Bībhatsa Rasa

Neglected Rasas

BHAYĀNAKA *rasa* and *bībhatsa rasa*, that deal with the **terrifying** and the **disgusting** emotions, are two of the most neglected *rasas* in Indian tradition. They almost invariably occupy a secondary position in works where the **heroic emotion** or *vīra rasa* is to be seen. Thus, in the plays of Bhāsa (Sanskrit playwright of the AD 4th century) which deal with episodes from the *Mahābhārata*, the consequence of heroic deeds are terrifying and horrifying. Of course, in the *Mahābhārata* epic itself, we have ample evidence of both these emotions. For instance, the episode in which Draupadī, the wife of the five Pāṇḍavas, is humiliated by their cousins while her husbands watch on silently after losing her in a game of dice, is disgusting. The battle at Kurukṣetra is terrifying. But in the major part of Indian literature, neither *bībhatsa* nor *bhayānaka* is given much importance. In fact, in the literature of the following two thousand years, very few instances of these are to be found. But it is nothing unusual when we remember that Indian tradition has been strongly influenced by the doctrines of *karma* and the transmigration of the soul. As we have mentioned earlier, they make it almost impossible for one to have a tragic view of life. Moreover, it is this framework, this positive outlook, which is always emphasised.

But these two — *bībhatsa* and *bhayānaka* — in the modern

Western context seem to be the most important *rasas*. So, it is truly unfortunate that after *Nāṭya Śāstra* very few works have emphasized their relevance. It is perhaps with Abhinavagupta that they find some importance—in his discussion of *śānta rasa*. But otherwise, their neglect is to be lamented. On the other hand, their relevance in the modern context cannot be overemphasized, for wherever we look in the West, the elements of disgust, grotesque, distrust, uncertainty, alienation, terror and disillusionment dominate.

But before we go to the relevant texts in the light of these two *rasas* a certain clarification needs to be made. Why have these two *rasas* been put together in one chapter? Is it because they do not have much scope or have not been much elaborated? On the contrary, the answer lies at the other end. Without a discussion of these two, a discussion of modern literature of any culture (in the light of the *rasa* theory) will remain incomplete. But these two *rasas* are so intimately connected (both in theory and in literature) that looking at them in isolation would make their discussion a little incomplete. *Nāṭya Śāstra* (VI.41) writes:

> The sight of the disgusting (gives rise to) the terrifying.
>
> —*Aesthetic Rapture*, Vol. I, p. 48

Thus, of the two *rasas*, *bībhatsa* is considered **primary** and *bhayānaka* is supposed to follow from it. Even otherwise, a lot of their *vibhāvas* and *anubhāvas* are similar. We will discuss these possibilities in a short while. Let us first look at each of these *rasas* individually.

Bhayānaka Rasa

> Now (the *rasa*) called *bhayānaka* has fear as its permanent emotion. It arises from such *vibhāvas* as ghastly noises, seeing of supernatural beings (ghosts), fear and panic due to the (cries) of owls (or the howling of) jackals, going to an empty house or to a forest, hearing about, speaking

about, or seeing the imprisonment or murder of one's relatives.

— *Aesthetic Rapture*, Vol. I, p. 54

The above is noted about *bhayānaka rasa* in the *Nāṭya Śāstra* (VI.68) of Bharata. The primary state or the *sthāyībhāva* of *bhayānaka* is 'fear'. What this means is that within the work, the emotion or state which is (shown to be) generated is that of fear. Interestingly, while *karuṇa* (pity or compassion) gives rise to *śoka* (sorrow) and *hāsya* (comic) gives rise to *harṣa* (laughter), here *bhayānaka* (furious) gives rise to *bhaya* (fear). Thus, as in *raudra rasa* or *vīra rasa*, a relation of opposition exists, here (*vīra* leads to wonder or fear and *raudra* leads to sorrow, fear or even anger) it is fear that is communicated to the reader or perceiver. But a subtle difference is to be noticed which will become clear when we discuss a work like *The Emperor Jones* by Eugene O'Neill. Fear can be transmitted to the audience in two different ways. First, if one is sufficiently distanced, what one will perceive will be the manifestation of fear in the work. In this case, he will recognize and perceive fear, and its accessory emotions and states within the work. But if he is not able to sufficiently distance himself or if he is able to share the fear of the victim, he will feel an empathetic response of fear himself. This is generally the case in horror fiction.

Causes

Within a text, fear is said to be caused by *vibhāvas* such as 'ghastly noises', 'seeing supernatural beings' etc. Now let us look at each of these closely. 'Seeing supernatural beings' is also listed under *adbhuta rasa*. But, it is only when the supernatural beings are of a negative nature (ghosts, demons etc.) that the possibility of fear arises. 'Ghastly noise' indicates the possibility of a threat since it suggests something ferocious at the source of the noise. Thus, here is a case of anticipatory fear and also fear at something which is not (necessarily) known.

'Cry of an Owl' is considered an ill-omen and hence suggests some terrible consequence. 'Jackals' are also of the same nature. 'Empty house' or 'forest' hold, again, the threat of the unknown. 'Imprisonment', when described in its cruel details or shown, can give rise to empathetic fear.

Interestingly, nowhere is any direct threat mentioned, namely wild animals, a ferocious enemy, natural calamities etc. Perhaps, 'ghosts' (supernatural) are the only exception. True, forest holds the fear of wild animals, ghosts or robbers. An empty house holds the possibility of treachery or of ghosts. But explicitly no threat is mentioned. Most of the *vibhāvas* are in the nature of anticipatory fears. This might be so because, like the Greeks, the Indians also did not believe in showing violent and terrifying things on the stage, and *Nāṭya Śāstra* has the stage specifically in mind. But even so, this lack is something that cannot simply be explained away.

What Causes Fear?

What is the nature of the objects that cause fear? Fear, in the long run, is the cause of a threat or even the anticipation or the possibility of threat—and what is the nature of a threat? A threat is one that can bring about some alteration (for the worse) in the normal order of things. Thus, a powerful man's anger can bring ruin to a subordinate. A 'ghost' might torture or kill one. In a 'forest', death or disaster can come from any quarter. Now, again, fear can come from a known quarter or it might come from an unknown quarter. In the *vibhāvas* listed, it is the possibility of the unknown that has been highlighted.

A tiger is a wild animal that can kill a man. It can be seen, known to a certain extent, and thus the fear it will generate is more or less definable. But fear can come also as a result of incomprehension. Now, let us take the instances of 'lonely room', 'darkness' or 'forest'. In all these cases, the cause of fear is always unknown. In the dark, even an odd-shaped tree can generate fear, while revealed in light, it might look quite harmless. Hence, if we probe into one's psyche here, we find that darkness dissolves all identities. In it things become indefinable, unknown. Thus, darkness holds the potential of incomprehension. An incomprehensible object is impossible to judge — whether it is harmful or not. This gives rise to anticipatory fear.

Bībhatsa Rasa

About *bībhatsa rasa Nāṭya Śāstra* (VI.72) writes:

> Now (the *rasa*) known as *bībhatsa* has disgust as its permanent emotion. It arises from such *vibhāvas* as discussing, hearing, or seeing what is ugly, unpleasant, unclear (*acosya*) and undesired.
>
> — *Aesthetic Rapture*, p. 55

Metamorphosis to the Unknown

The contemporary French critic, Julia Kristeva, in her paper entitled, "Approaching Abjection", writes:

> Spasms and vomiting which **protect** me, repulsion and nausea which separate and turn me away from the impure, from the cloaca, from filth . . . . Shudder of fascination which both **leads** me there and **separates** me from it (emphasis supplied). . . . (p. 126)

Here, she is talking of the way the Unconscious reacts to the 'abject'. In defining the 'abject' she says:

> There is in abjection, one of those violent and obscure revolts of being against that which threatens it and which seems to it to come from an outside or an exorbitant inside. . . . (p. 125)

But she also makes it clear that the 'abject' is not an object. "The abject is not an object in front of me . . . . (It is what is) drawing me towards the point where meaning collapses" (pp. 125-26).

It is interesting to see how similar this attitude is to the one we find in the passage above from *Nāṭya Śāstra*. Kristeva point out some of the responses of one to the 'abject' — 'spasms' and 'vomiting'. *Nāṭya Śāstra* (VI.72) lists the following:

> . . . contractions of the whole body (*sarvāṅgasaṁhāra*), facial contortions (*mukhavikūṇana*), vomiting (*ullekhana*), spitting, violent trembling of the body (*udvejana*), and similar gestures.
>
> — *Aesthetic Rapture*, Vol. I, p. 55

Responses like 'vomiting' protect us or try to protect us from what repulses us and most importantly, the 'abject' is not an object. Thus, disgust on the physical plane and the grotesque (as well as disgust) on the metaphysical plane are born when familiar things become unknown, the real becomes the unreal, the natural the unnatural, for when a living body decomposes, it is not the object **in itself** that generates repulsion; it is the **transformation** from the known to the unknown, from the recognizable to the unrecognizable. In this context, we can refer back to our discussion of Kafka's *Metamorphosis* in the chapter on *karuṇa rasa*. Another interesting example is O'Neill's play, *The Hairy Ape*, where the protagonist's disjunction and alienation give rise to his disgust with the world. Yank, a stoker in a steam ship (a kind of strong and powerful primitive man) feels that he **belongs** to the steel of the ship. In that he feels powerful. But then he confronts the ghost-like pale daughter of the capitalist to whom the ship belongs. In that confrontation, the other world (which in fact controls him) confronts him and he realizes that he does not belong there. In his search for his sense of belonging, he wanders around and finally feels a sense of affinity to a huge gorilla inside a zoo. But even the gorilla rejects him and he dies in its hands — the sense of disgust and repulsion at humanity not leaving him till the end.

Ugly-Distortion

Now, what is the nature of the object that is 'ugly', 'unpleasant', 'unclear', or 'undesired'? An object is 'ugly' when it does not look like what it ought to look like. Thus, there is a break of order or of harmony. Here also, we find a disruption in the order of things as in *bhayānaka*. Normalcy is distorted. Now if we look closely, why is it that the 'ugly' is disgusting? Ugliness involves a distortion that can lead to pity. Then when will it lead to disgust instead? It will be so when one feels alienated from the 'ugly' object, and underlying this must be the possibility of incomprehension; for if we can understand the ugly, there is the possibility of comprehension and hence of sympathy. We will see this highlighted when we discuss *The Heart of Darkness* of Joseph Conrad or "There are More Things", a short story by Borges.

Incomprehension

A little earlier we were talking of anticipatory fear and incomprehension. In other words, incomprehension holds the potential of being fearsome and thus, inbetween the **stimulus** and **response** of fear, there is the possibility of *bībhatsa rasa*. In *Nāṭya Śāstra* we have already been told that "the sight of the disgusting (gives rise to) the terrifying" (VI.41). *Bībhatsa* thus, in many cases, is an intermediary step to fear, for in *bībhatsa* as well, the first response is one directed at a certain incongruity which leads to a certain incomprehension. In this sense, it is very close to *hāsya*, but here the incongruity is of a negative kind. It is rather the displacement of the normal by the abnormal. And it is this abnormal that holds the possibility of fear.

But since we are told that the sight of the disgusting is terrifying, the disgusting, thus in a sense, is the analysis of fear. A 'dead body' frightens us not because it threatens us; it is so because it is unnatural. It is a distortion of life and hence generates in us a feeling of insecurity — some day we might all come to this:

Remember, my soul, the thing we saw
    that lovely summer day?
On a pile of stones where the path turned off,
    the hideous carrion —

legs in the air, like a whore — displayed,
    indifferent to the last,
a belly slick with lethal sweat
    and swollen with foul gas.

— *The Flowers of Evil*, p. 35

Baudelaire, thus, describes a decaying corpse in his poem 'Carrion' — and beyond this disgust lies the sense of an insecurity, an incomprehension:

Behind the rocks an anxious bitch
    eyed us reproachfully,
waiting for the chance to resume
    her interrupted feast.

— Yet you will come to this offence,
    this horrible decay,
you, the light of my life, the sun
    and moon and stars of my love!

— *The Flowers of Evil*, pp. 35-36

What can acutely be felt here is the awareness that even the most beautiful and loved object can become ugly in a moment. Thus, any moment, a known thing can become a stinking, unknown carrion.

Another verse in *Nāṭya Śāstra* (VI.81) tells us:

> *Bībhatsa* is of two kinds: *kṣobhaja* (that which arises from agitation) and pure *udvegī* (that which is nauseating). *Udvegī* (*bībhatsa rasa*) comes from (seeing) faeces, worms (etc.), and the other comes from (seeing) blood, etc.
>
> — *Aesthetic Rapture*, Vol. I, pp. 56-57

The passage is not very clear and holds a lot of ambiguities. But we have taken it up here for two basic reasons. One, the mention of 'faeces', 'worms' etc., is interesting. They are disgusting since they are ugly. They are a distortion of all that man stands for (for both can come from a man's body, dead or alive) and thus hold the possibility of not only disharmony but of incomprehension as well.

Secondly, and much more important, Abhinavagupta's commentary on this passage is central to understanding the modern literature of the Absurd and disillusionment. It also shows how *bībhatsa* and *bhayānaka* (that can give rise to disgust owing to the manifestation of mutilation and destruction) hold the possibility of leading to *śānta rasa*. Quoting *Yogasūtra* (2.40, 33) he says, "from purity comes disgust with one's own body" and the desires of the five senses might lead to disgust and thus may lead to renunciation (*Aesthetic Rapture*, Vol. II, p. 94). For instance, Bhartṛhari writes in his *Nītiśataka*:

> She, about whom I think always: she likes me not;
> She loves another man, who loves another girl;
> And yet there is another woman, who seeks my love:
> Fie on her, on him, rebuke me and him and the god of love.
>
> — *History of Indian Literature*, Vol. III, p. 158

Metaphysical Disgust

Disgust need not necessarily arise only from a physical displacement. True, a certain kind of disgust arises out of one's preoccupation with one's body, as we shall see in the case of the Buddha. But this disgust which comes from a disillusionment with one's body is actually linked with a metaphysical position, with a certain conception of what things are. In fact, in all cases, the disillusionment is the result of realization of the gap between the ideal and the real; between what ought to be and what things really are. In T.S. Eliot's "The Hollow Men", it is this disillusionment at the modern man's metaphysical position that leads to disgust:

We are the hollow men
We are the stuffed men
Leaning together
Headpiece filled with straw. Alas!
— *Selected Poems*, p. 77

Here is a displacement of the **inner stuff** of man. Instead, what we find is straw 'stuffing'. A little later the displacement is even more clearly projected:

Shape without form, shadow without colour,
Paralysed force, gesture without motion;

Those who have crossed
With direct eyes, to death's other Kingdom
Remember us — if at all — not as lost
Violent souls, but only
As the hollow men
The stuffed men.
— *Selected Poems*, p. 77

Interestingly, the sense of disgust comes not out of any insecurity or any incomprehension, but out of cowardice. It is the lack of courage that gives way to disillusionment — modern man is only this!

Towards Śānta

But in many instances it is, in fact, the strife to overcome the sense of insecurity and the sense of incomprehension at a transformation that may lead to both the absurd and renunciation. In fact, in Bhartṛhari, this is distinctly noticeable. An effort to face it can get manifested in various ways. For instance, Baudelaire ("Carrion") attempts to immortalize some 'essence' that cannot decay:

Yes, you will come to this, my queen,
after the sacraments,
when you rot underground among

the bones already there.

But as their kisses eat you up,
my Beauty, tell the worms,
I've kept the sacred essence, saved
the form of my rotted loves!

— *The Flowers of Evil*, p. 36

Another attempt to face this insecurity can manifest itself in the form of a **transcendence** of an order of reality.

It can take the shape of renunciation as it did in the case of Gautama Buddha. In the *Buddha Carita*, Aśvaghoṣa narrates that after seeing the 'four signs' (the sight of sickness, old age, death and renunciation) the Buddha, who had never known of such things, is shocked. The sight of beautiful women only make him exclaim, 'one must die' (*The Bible of the World*, p. 192). Later that night, when Buddha wakes up from a brief slumber he perceives the sleeping women in an entirely different light:

> . . . some with their bodies wet with trickling phlegm and spittle; some grinding their teeth, and muttering in their sleep; some with their mouths open; and some with their dress fallen apart so plainly to disclose their loathsome nakedness . . . . To him that magnificent apartment, as splendid as the palace of Sakka, began to seem like a cemetery filled with dead bodies impaled and left to rot. . . .
>
> — *The Bible of the World*, p. 194

It is this sight (which both horrifies as well as disgusts) which precipitates renunciation. Similarly, in Śaṅkara's "Hymn of Renunciation" disgust at the distortion of things leads one towards renunciation:

While man's soul remains in his body
Fondly family wishes him well.
But when the life-breath leaves its dwelling
Even his wife flees in fear.

— *Self Knowledge*, p. 242

Pointing at such realities Śaṅkara tells one to give up this world of illusions. These possibilities hold the potentials of *śānta rasa*.

Thus, *bībhatsa* like *bhayānaka* also centres around an insecurity. The transcendence of this insecurity is possible, but only when there is an alternative metaphysical system in which harmony can be achieved. But this need not always be the case. In fact, in the West, especially in modern literature, we do not find a very convincing alternative system in which the crisis can be resolved. This is at the root of what can be roughly classified as the literature of the Absurd.

The Absurd

Briefly, the genesis of the **Absurd** can be traced as far back as to *The Origin of the Species* by Charles Darwin. This work, tracing back the origin of man to the monkeys, shattered the Christian image of man 'made in the image of God'. A scientific world order, in replacing a religious world order, cannot do very much about one's insecurities and faith, itself being based on **reason**. Following in its wake, we had two World Wars, made all the more gruesome with the help of science. It is in this background that we see the crisis of identity in the modern man. What is profoundly noticeable is a disjunction, a displacement, an incongruity. An order is broken, and there is no substitute order to take its place. It is this unnaturalness that holds the possibilities of both *bībhatsa* and *bhayānaka rasas*.

Another thing that is distinct in both these *rasas* and also in Absurd literature is alienation. The response of fear is a response of repulsion. It is so also with disgust. One tends to move away from what is fearsome or disgusting. At the root of both these responses is a certain sense of alienation, of lack of recognition. Since this cannot be rejected or substituted (by renunciation as in Indian tradition), it has to be endured or at least experienced.

Albert Camus, in his 'The Myth of Sisyphus', observes the following:

> The gods had condemned Sisyphus to ceaselessly rolling a rock to the top of a mountain, whence the stone would fall back of its own weight. They had thought with some reason that there is no more dreadful punishment than futile and hopeless labour.
>
> — *The Myth of Sisyphus*, p. 107

This is the penalty that he pays for his impudence against and disobedience of the gods:

> Mercury came and seized the impudent man by the collar and, snatching him from his joys, led him forcibly back to the underworld where his rock was ready for him.
>
> You have already grasped that Sisyphus is the absurd hero. He is, as much through his passions as through his torture. His scorn of the gods, his hatred of death, and his passion for life won him that unspeakable penalty in which the whole being is exerted towards accomplishing nothing.
>
> — *The Myth of Sisyphus*, p. 108

Interestingly, here, courage manifests itself in the face of this absurd situation, for it is a mixture of the elements of disgust and fear-horror; and yet in this labour Camus sees a transcendence:

> It is during that return, that pause, that Sisyphus interests me. . . . I see that man going back down with a heavy yet measured step towards the torment of which he will never know the end. . . . At each of those moments when he leaves the heights and gradually sinks towards the lairs of the gods, he is superior to his fate. He is stronger than his rock.
>
> — *The Myth of Sisyphus*, pp. 108-9

Thus, in Camus, we see the response of *vīra* to a situation which is both horrifying and terrifying. It is thus that *bībhatsa* and *bhayānaka* can lead to a response of courage. Interestingly, even in that absurd situation, there is a transcendence of itself: "he is stronger than his rock". It is in this transcendence that there is the possibility of calm, of resolution, and thus of *śānta rasa*. It is similar in Camus' novels like *The Outsider or The Fall*, where the victim-heroes face their absurd world courageously.

But usually we find a response of horror (a mixture of fear and incomprehension) in the face of the absurd. For instance, in Kafka's parable, "At the Door of Law" the man never really understands anything:

> Outside the law there stands a doorkeeper. A man from the country comes up to the doorkeeper and asks to be admitted to the law. But the doorkeeper says he cannot admit him at the moment. . . .The man from the country had not anticipated such difficulties; access to the law ought to be available to everyone at all times, he thinks, but after a closer look at the fur-coated doorkeeper, at his great pointed nose and his long, straggly, black Tartar beard, he decides that he will in fact wait. . . . There he sits for days, for years on end. . . . The man . . . invests everything, no matter how great its value, in attempts to bribe the doorkeeper. . . .
>
> — *Kafka: Stories 1904-1924*, p. 194

It is thus that the man keeps on waiting until he is old, desperate and almost hopeless. In the end when death is approaching, he calls the doorkeeper:

> "What do you want to know now?" the doorkeeper asks. "You're insatiable." "Everybody seeks the law," says the man, "so how is it that in all these years no one but me has demanded admittance?" The doorkeeper sees that it is all over for the man, and to penetrate his growing deafness he shouts at him, "no one else could gain admittance here because this entrance was meant for

you alone. Now I am going to close it."

— *Kafka: Stories 1904-1924*, p. 195

It is this revelation which gives rise to the element of the absurd and the horrifying. Now, one might ask, since the consequence is so terrible, it should be discussed directly under *bhayānaka* and not under both the headings. But if we give more attention, we shall find that the element of the **grotesque**, the distorted, pervades everywhere. 'Law' is distorted. The function of the 'gate' (which is to give admittance) is distorted. In the distortion lies the element of the repulsive, the absurd and the 'ugly'. In the implications lie the possibility of the terrible. Thus, both together give rise to horror.

Bībhatsa and Hāsya

Talking of this element of distortion, it will be interesting to notice how close *bībhatsa* and *hāsya* are. We have already discussed in the earlier chapter (on *hāsya rasa*) about how both the *rasas* are based upon the possibility of incongruence, of displacement. Thus, 'deformity' which is to be found in *bībhatsa*, which, in fact, is the cause or *vibhāva* of the disgusting is also to be found in *hāsya rasa* (*Nāṭya Śāstra*, VI.48). In that context, we have also discussed the "comedy of the grotesque". In many modern Absurd writers (this tag is being applied rather generally here), a similar element of 'black comedy' is to be noticed, e.g., in the works of Eugene Ionesco or of Samuel Beckett.

In Ionesco's story, "The Rhinoceros", though the depiction is comic, a gradual darkening of the world is to be seen as the story progresses. Here, the element of the grotesque is very subtly poised. What makes us laugh in the beginning is capable of arousing disgust at a later stage. Thus, we are in a position to realize how closely *hāsya* and *bībhatsa* are related and consequently, how a single change (in consequence) can make the comic terrifying.

The narrator and his friend are sitting in a cafe when a

rhinoceros rushes past them. An excited and interesting discussion follows in which a lot of speculations are made about where the rhinoceros came from. In a few days more rhinoceroses are to be found. One day in the office one of the employees, Madame Boeuf comes in excited:

> "I was pursued by a rhinoceros all the way from home," she stammered.
>
> "With one horn or two?" I asked.
>
> — *The Short Story and the Reader*, p. 106

Very soon, that same rhinoceros is found at the door of the office. It has two horns. An excited argument is going on about whether African rhinoceroses or the Indian ones have two horns when:

> . . . Madame Boeuf, who had got up and come to join us, and who had for some minutes been staring attentively at the rhinoceros, which was turning round and round below us, suddenly uttered a terrible cry:
>
> "It's my husband! Boeuf, my poor dear Boeuf, what has happened to you?"
>
> The rhinoceros, or rather Boeuf, responded with a violent and yet tender trumpeting, while Madame Boeuf fainted into my arms and Botard, raising his to heaven, stormed: "It's sheer lunacy! What a society!"
>
> — *The Short Story and the Reader*, p. 107

The narrative is comic. But soon the whole population of the town is metamorphosed into rhinoceroses. In fact, the narrator's friend, Jean, undergoes the transformation right in front of his eyes, and then charges at him trying to kill him. In the nightmare atmosphere that follows, the narrator and the typist girl (from the office) are the only ones who have not undergone any transformation. Yet, one day she cannot take it any more:

> "I'm rather ashamed of what you call love, that morbid thing. . . It cannot compare with the extraordinary energy displayed by all these beings we see around us."
>
> — *The Short Story and the Reader*, p. 112

Soon she is also gone and the narrator is left alone, alienated and agonized.

> . . . looking at myself in the glass, I took a dislike to my long face: I needed a horn, or even two, to give dignity to my flabby features.
>
> . . . . My conscience was increasingly uneasy, unhappy. I felt I was a monster. Alas, I would never become a rhinoceros. I could never change.
>
> I dared no longer look at myself. I was ashamed. And yet I couldn't, no, I couldn't.
>
> — *The Short Story and the Reader*, p. 113

Thus, in the end, the narrator becomes a victim of alienation and identity crisis. The story is farcical and yet the consequence intensifies not the comic dimension (which nonetheless is present) but the horrifying. Thus, this black comedy manifests a certain displacement which leads to an alienation. It is not disgust here in any physical sense, but incomprehension which comes from the alienation. In fact, in the end, this holds the possibility of *śoka* or sorrow.

Bībhatsa and Black Comedy

In Beckett's *Waiting for Godot*, a play, a similar kind of dark comedy is to be found. There, it is of course much darker and the implications much more terrifying. Interestingly, in it, since it has much of the element of pantomime, a lot of the *anubhāvas* or consequences of both *bībhatsa* and *bhayānaka* are to be found. For instance, the physical condition of the two tramps who are waiting for an unknown mysterious entity — Godot — evokes both pity and disgust.

Here, it must be pointed out that even though incomprehension, which is at the root of the sense of the absurd, is a very important element of *bībhatsa rasa*. This aspect, in Indian tradition, has never really been highlighted. But even so, if we look closely, the distortion (which leads to incomprehension) gradually leads to (through insecurity) fear and thus to *bhayānaka rasa*. It is in this way that, in Absurd literature, it is the ominous consequences of incomprehension that are usually emphasised. Nonetheless, the element of the grotesque persists throughout, and this leads to the possibility of *bībhatsa*. For instance in William Faulkner's short story "A Rose for Emily", it is discovered on the death of old Emily that she had been living with and sleeping near the dead body of her lover (whom she had killed so as to keep him for ever) for a number of years (*The Faulkner Reader*). In this instance, a distortion, through an incomprehension (which repels) leads to a sense of **horror**. This horror is a mixture of disgust and fear.

Fear and Disgust

There can be pure disgust, without the accompaniment of fear, as in "The Hollow Men" of T. S. Eliot. But it is very rarely that fear can be separated from one of the most essential features of disgust — incomprehension. Fear of a tiger is comprehensible. But what is it that makes us fear a tiger? The possibility of death, and death is something whose nature is unknown, and hence it is frightening. This is, of course, a rather implicit relation between *bībhatsa* and *bhayānaka* that is being located. But usually, the two are to be seen together in a more explicit relation in the majority of works. Eliot, in his epigraph to "The Hollow Men", quotes a line from *Heart of Darkness*: "Mistah Kurtz — he dead" (*Selected Poems*, p. 75). In the poem, he talks of "lost violent souls" referring to the central character of Conrad's novel — Mr Kurtz. Here, we have an intense mixture of horror and terror; of disgust and repulsion which Marlow, the narrator of the story, feels.

Heart of Darkness is about a journey to the interior of Africa. It is also a symbolic journey to the "heart of darkness". In a land of superstition and ignorance, Marlow joins as a replacement for one of the Company's men who is killed there in a skirmish. In fact, when he reaches the place the body is still there:

> Afterwards nobody seemed to trouble much about Fresleven's remains, till I got out and stepped into his shoes. I couldn't let it rest, though; but when an opportunity offered at last to meet my predecessor, the grass growing through his ribs was tall enough to hide his bones.
>
> — *Heart of Darkness*, p. 23

And when he meets the so-called "savages" what he finds is:

> . . . nothing but black shadows of disease and starvation, lying confusedly in the greenish gloom. Brought from all the recesses of the coast in all the legalities of time contracts, lost in uncongenial surroundings, fed on unfamiliar food, they sickened, became inefficient, and were then allowed to crawl away and rest.
>
> — *Heart of Darkness*, p. 32

Thus, at the heart of Africa, Marlow discovers not the darkness of the native souls, but the darkness within the souls of the white men, and he finds a perfect example of it in Mr Kurtz.

Mr Kurtz is an agent of the Company who has alienated himself from it. When he had come, he had lofty ideals. He had said:

> "Each station should be like a beacon on the road towards better things, a centre for trade of course, but also for humanizing, improving, instructing.
>
> — *Heart of Darkness*, p. 52

In fact, one of his writings had impressed Marlow very much:

> But this must have been before his — let us say — nerves, went wrong and caused him to preside at certain midnight dances ending with unspeakable rites. . . . But it was a beautiful piece of writing.
>
> — *Heart of Darkness*, p. 74

But once, in Africa, he had discovered the darkness within his soul, he had scrawled at the end of the paper, "Exterminate all brutes" (*Heart of Darkness*, p. 75). It is this unusual transformation that strikes terror at one's heart. This terror, interestingly, comes from the fear of death, and thus from a sense of distancing. But more interestingly, the revulsion and the horror that Marlow feels comes directly from the sense of identity. Like Marlow, he also had lofty ideals. Thus, the horror and the revulsion suggest the possibility of an unconscious attraction, from a fear that Marlow might thus become transformed, for Marlow discovers the 'dark interiors' of a white man's civilized heart. He also realizes that Kurtz discovers this at the end:

> I think the knowledge came to him at last — only at the very last. But the wilderness had found him out early, and had taken on him a terrible vengeance for the fantastic invasion.
>
> — *Heart of Darkness*, p. 85

Thus, the idealist Kurtz had become a killer obsessed with hoarding ivory. His hut was surrounded by stakes holding human skulls. When the Company finds him (from which he had cut himself off) he is dying. When they bring him into the boat, Marlow is the last to see him alive:

> Anything approaching the change that came over his features I have never seen before, and hope never to see again. Oh, I wasn't touched. I was fascinated. It was as though a veil had been rent. I saw on that ivory face the expression of sombre pride, of ruthless power, of craven terror — of an intense and hopeless despair. Did he live

> his life again in every detail of desire, temptation, and surrender during that supreme moment of complete knowledge? He cried in a whisper at some image, at some vision — he cried twice, a cry that was no more than a breath —
>
> "The horror! The horror!"
>
> — *Heart of Darkness*, p. 99

Later, Marlow is able to understand that stare better:

> I understand better the meaning of his stare, that could not see the flame of the candle, but was wide enough to embrace the whole universe, piercing enough to penetrate all the hearts that beat in the darkness. He had summed up — he had judged. "The horror!"
>
> — *Heart of Darkness*, pp. 100-101

Marlow's complex response of attraction, repulsion and terror is understandable:

> It is his extremity that I seem to have lived through. True, he had made that last stride, he had stepped over the edge, while I had been permitted to draw back my hesitating foot.
>
> —*Heart of Darkness*, p. 101

And so, it is neither surprising nor strange that he does not rush out with the others when he hears of Kurtz's death:

> I believe I was considered brutally callous. However, I did not eat much. There was a lamp in there — light, don't you know — and outside it was beastly, beastly dark.
>
> — *Heart of Darkness*, p. 100

Here, the fear of 'darkness' is the terror of undefinable evil. It is thus that horror, repulsion and raw terror grip the work, and in the last moment of his life Kurtz also sees the 'horror' clearly and cries out. Interestingly, this is possible only because he is able to alienate himself from what is so horrible in the core of his soul. A similar kind of thing happens in Eugene O'Neill's *The Emperor Jones* where Jones (the dictator of a small island), while making an escape from his enemies, confronts the very core of fear in the 'forest'. Jones, the cruel dictator, at the beginning of the play finds himself in the midst of a plot to assassinate him. As he makes his escape, he loses his way in the forest. This forest, a very symbolic one, makes him slowly regress into the very core of his primitive soul — and as he makes this regression, in the ignorance of darkness, he is gripped with raw terror. It is thus that his running (into the forest and through it) is a running from himself, from the terror which is within him, with the discovery of the darkness inside his heart. Here, though fear is very distinctly to be felt, it does not affect the audience directly. It is so because Jones is a tyrant. Hence, when he confronts fear, one cannot identify or sympathize with him. This leads to a certain distancing where the fear is perceivable, but only in a detached sort of way.

The States That Accompany Fear and Disgust

In *Heart of Darkness* disgust, fear, repulsion etc. are so closely intermixed that it is hard to distinguish among them. This is nothing unusual as various accompanying states or *vyabhicārībhāvas* of the two *rasas* are similar. In *bhayānaka* they are (*Nāṭya Śāstra*, VI.68):

> paralysis, sweating, stuttering, horripilation, trembling, a break in the voice, change of colour, anxiety, confusion, depression, panic, rashness, lifelessness, fright, apoplexy, death and so forth.
>
> — *Aesthetic Rapture*, Vol. I, p. 54

The *vyabicārībhāvas* of *bībhatsa* are the following (*Nāṭya Śāstra*, VI.72):

> apoplexy, agitation (*udvega*), panic, confusion, sickness, death and the like.
>
> — *Aesthetic Rapture*, Vol. I, p. 55

Many of the accompanying states are identical. It is in this light that Borges's story, "There Are More Things", can be seen. Here disgust and fear are intermixed. The narrator returns home to find that his uncle is dead and his house has been auctioned off. But what intrigues him is the mysterious nature of the man who has bought the house. What persists all through the story, till the very end, is the sense of the unknown. This new owner, a Jewish man named Preetorious, wished to completely demolish the house and build a new structure there. But Mr Muir, an old friend of the narrator's uncle refused to make another plan. The man threw out all the furniture, all the books, and with the help of a carpenter had certain alterations made:

> It was also by night that the new owner of the Casa Colorada moved in. The windows no longer opened, but chinks of light could be made out in the dark. One morning, the milkman found the sheepdog dead on the walk, headless and mutilated. That winter they felled the araucarias. Nobody saw Preetorious again.
>
> — *The Book of Sand*, pp. 36-37

Another man also recounted his adventure at night near the house:

> A few nights ago, I was returning from a party. A hundred yards or so from the house I saw something. My horse reared up, ... "What I saw justified the horse's fright."
>
> — *The Book of Sand*, p. 38

When the narrator meets the carpenter, he tells him that the furniture he made were outrageous:

> On saying goodbye, he confided to me that even for all the

> world's gold he would never again set foot in Tudera, let alone that house.
>
> — *The Book of Sand*, p. 39

Curiosity overwhelms the narrator so much so that he finally ventures into the house:

> A sweet, sickening smell filled the house . . . . The dining room and the library of my memory were now, with the wall between them torn down, a single great bare room containing one or two pieces of furniture. . . . Let me explain myself. To see a thing one has to comprehend it. An armchair presupposes the human body, ... None of the meaningless shapes that night granted me correspondence to the human figure, for that matter, of any conceivable use. I felt revulsion and terror.
>
> — *The Book of Sand*, pp. 40-41

The horror does not end there for the narrator saw:

> . . . a sort of long operating table, very high and in the shape of a U, with round hollows at each end. I thought that maybe it was the bed of the house's inhabitant, whose monstrous anatomy revealed itself in this way, implicitly, like an animal's or a god's by its shadow.
>
> — *The Book of Sand*, p. 41

And finally:

> My feet were touching the next to last rung of the ladder when I felt that something, slow and oppressive and twofold, was coming up the ramp. Curiosity overcame my fear, and I did not shut my eyes.
>
> — *The Book of Sand*, p. 40

Thus, fear and disgust are accompanied by associations such as 'panic', (of the horse) 'death', (of the dog) 'confusion' (of the carpenter, of Mr Muir, the inhabitants) etc.

In fact, what is intrinsic in all the stories of Borges, and which is also to be found here — the strangeness — indicates the presence of *adbhuta rasa.* This possibility is something which we have mentioned in the chapter on *adbhuta rasa.* This is very strikingly noticeable in *Chronicle of a Death Foretold* by Marquez as well as in *The Name of the Rose* by Umberto Eco.

Relation with Other Rasas

Wonder and Disgust

In *Chronicle of a Death Foretold* what is remarkable is the fact that almost everyone is aware, prior to his death, that Santiago Nasar is going to be killed. Everyone tries his best to save Nasar (including the killers), and yet he dies. It is this which is baffling, strange, awesome. Santiago's mother has the ability to interpret dreams. Yet she is not able to foresee his death. It is as if his death had been inevitably written down. The two killers (the two brothers of the girl he had seduced) are also not so much inclined to the act:

> Pedro Vicario . . . . was the one who made the decision to kill Santiago Nasar, and at first his brother only followed along. But he was also the one who considered his duty fulfilled when the mayor disarmed them, and then it was Pablo Vicario who assumed command.
>
> — *Chronicle of a Death Foretold*, pp. 60-61

And when the killing actually takes place:

> Through the door she saw the Vicario brothers running towards the house with their knives out. From the place where she was she could see them but she couldn't see her son . . . . Then she ran to the door and slammed it shut. . . . Santiago Nasar only lacked a few seconds to get

in when the door closed.

— *Chronicle of a Death*, p. 119

Thus, strangely, it is the mother who seals the fate of her son. If this same element of the inevitable (that is surprising) had been in a different context, it might have given rise to *adbhuta rasa*. But here, the element of wonder is diluted by the consequence or rather, the inevitability of death, and thus gives rise to horror.

It is similar in the case of Umberto Eco's novel, *The Name of the Rose*. Briefly, it is about the mysterious killings that go on within the compounds of an Italian monastery during the time of Medieval Christianity. Williams, a travelling brother who comes to the monastery, manages to solve the mystery. But in the end we discover that his scientific methods, though they have been able to take care of a part of the problem have not been able to grapple the totality, which strangely is a series of coincidental deaths. Thus, Williams, in the end, realizes in a flash the tremendous insignificance of the scientific method in the face of the cosmos. One is marvelled by the brilliance of William's method. The gruesome killings are both terrifying and revolting. But, the very insignificance of man, in the face of the immensity of living, gives rise to awe and to horror; for as foretold, the beautiful monastery with its immense collection of books goes up in flames.

This also makes us aware that in mystery thrillers, the possibility of all the three — *adbhuta*, *bhayānaka* and *bībhatsa* — are there. What is highlighted depends on the treatment.

Vīra, Bībhatsa and Bhayānaka

As for the relation of these two *rasas* with *vīra*, we have already seen the response of courage to the incomprehensible in the works of Albert Camus. Interestingly, a reverse relation is also possible — *vīra* can lead to revolting and terrifying consequences. For instance, in Isaac Rosenberg's "The Dead Man's Dump", the consequences of war are terrifying:

The wheels lurched over sprawled dead
But pained them not, though their bones crunched;
. . . .
A man's brains splattered on
A stretcher bearer's face;
His shook shoulders slipped their load,
But when they bent to look again
The drowning soul was sunk too deep
For human tenderness.

— *The Golden Treasury*, pp. 447-48

In the *Mahābhārata* also this is what is felt, when at the end, almost all the important characters are dead. *Raudra* can also lead to disgust and fear. For instance, in the episode of the killing of Duryodhana by Bhīma (they are cousins) in the *Mahābhārata*, Bhīma's fury leads to the act of ripping apart Duryodhana's thighs.

Karuṇa

Karuṇa and these two *rasas* are inimical. But they can co-exist as they do in the works of Kafka. We have already discussed the possibilities in the chapter on *karuṇa rasa*. Another interesting possibility (just the reverse of what we saw in *Metamorphosis*) is that when compassion is not felt for the victim, it leads to disgust in case of *bībhatsa rasa*. But in case of *bhayānaka* this kind of distancing results in a detached participation in the drama of fear. For instance, in O'Neill's *The Emperor Jones*, the tyrant Jones, when he makes his escape into the dark forest, is hounded by the fears of the mind. In this case, his terror cannot be shared by us, since he has alienated himself from our sympathies by his abominable cruelties. But in a detached observation of his terror, one can feel his fear, though in a distanced sort of way. Thus, though the atmosphere is that of terror, in the reader, the response need not be that of fear. Another interesting thing is that, it is only because we feel disgust and horror at Jones' crimes (the elements of *bhayānaka*) that we are not able to identify with him and feel his terror.

ŚṚṄGĀRA

The relation of *śṛṅgāra* with *bībhatsa* and *bhayānaka* is also inimical: for a distortion of love or any violation can lead to horror and disgust. Similarly, mere lust can generate disgust as we saw in the verse of Bhartṛhari.

Coming to the relation of *bībhatsa* and *bhayānaka* with *śānta rasa*, some of the possibilities have already been mentioned earlier. A more comprehensive discussion of their relation will follow in the chapter on *śānta rasa.*

Problems

Finally, before we end this discussion, some of the limitations and inadequacies of these two *rasas* as discussed in *Nāṭya Śāstra* must be mentioned. In *Nāṭya Śāstra* (VI.69) it is said:

> Pretended (*kṛtaka*) *bhayānaka* results from an offence against a Guru or a king.
>
> — *Aesthetic Rapture*, Vol. I, p. 55

Abhinavagupta interprets this as fear in the noble men. "In the case of people who possess primarily *sattva* (*guṇa*), (fear) is only artificial." The purpose of displaying fear in front of the teacher or the king is to show that one is modest and has humility (*Aesthetic Rapture*, Vol. II, p. 92). But if this is so, we cannot accept this simulated fear under *bhayānaka rasa.* Earlier we have said that the two kinds of *bībhatsas* mentioned — "that which arises from agitation" and "that which is nauseating" — are not very clear (*Nāṭya Śāstra*, VI.81). However, we might say that the first refers to a metaphysical disgust, while the second refers to disgust that arises from concrete objects. However, if we look closely, all cases of disgust have a tendency to move from a physical to a metaphysical plane — for it always involves the unnatural, the abnormal, which is a mental construct. Earlier in

Nāṭya Śāstra (VI.73) it is said:

> *Bībhatsarasa* arises from seeing something one doesn't like, from unpleasant smells, tastes, physical contacts, words and from many violent tremblings of the body.
>
> — *Aesthetic Rapture*, Vol. I, p. 55

Here, though the basic possibility of repulsion has been suggested, the list is inadequate and does not emphasise the metaphysical aspect which is important in Indian literature — in the *Mahābhārata*, in the works of Bhartṛhari or the poetical works of Śaṅkara.

9

Adbhuta Rasa

ADBHUTA *rasa* or the **emotion of wonder** is an important though a much neglected *rasa*. It is interesting to note that in *Nāṭya Śāstra* it comes just before *śānta rasa*; and if we look closely we will find that it has greater affinity to *śānta* than any of the other *rasas*.

Surprise and Delight

If we refer back to the first chapter where the reader's participation is discussed, we will remember that *camatkāra* or **delight** is a very important element in the reader's response to a work of art. If we look closely, we will find that it is also a very important ingredient in a work which contains *adbhuta rasa*. Of course, it is obvious that inside a work it will generate a response of wonder which is its primary state. But even in the reader, it will generate an emotion which can be roughly translated as a mixture of surprised delight and awe that is the result of something surprising, for in *Nāṭya Śāstra* (VI.74) it is said:

> Now (the *rasa*) called *adbhuta* has for its permanent emotion wonder. It arises from such *vibhāvas* as seeing heavenly beings, gaining one's desired object, going to a temple, a garden (*upavana*) or a meeting place, or (seeing) flying chariot, a magic show (*māya*), or a juggler's show.
>
> — *Aesthetic Rapture*, Vol. I, p. 56

In whichever way we look at the relation between a work of art and a reader or perceiver, there is an inherent relation of attraction. If the basis of this attraction is personal, then it cannot be an experience which all readers can (to some extent) share. But if this is not the case, what is it that attracts a reader to a text? The answers will be numerous and this would involve going into very deep problems. But one of the reasons (which cannot be overlooked) will be the way the work is presented. In other words, whatever it is that the work depicts, it is the manner of organization and presentation that makes it attractive; for a text deals with possibilities (of reality or fantasy). Our everyday world is also a world in which we move through, and in, possibilities. Then what is it that attracts us to a work? Everything else remaining common, the basic difference is that a consciousness reorganises the material. Thus, what is latent here is the possibility of doing things in a remarkable way and this leads to surprise and wonder.

Causes of Adbhuta

The *vibhāvas* or causes listed above are the following: "seeing heavenly beings", "a magic show" or a "juggler's show". Here, what is to be noticed is the element of surprise. But more importantly, what does this surprise lead to? If it leads to fear (pure) or a sense of incongruity, we might have *bībhatsa* or *bhayānaka rasa* instead. It is only because here the most important emotion or state generated in the work and transmitted to the reader is wonder, that the outcome is a surprised delight. As Abhinavagupta says, *camatkāra* is the response of a reader to any work of art. Thus, even *rasas* like *bībhatsa* and *bhayānaka* hold the possibility of leading to *camatkāra*.

Skill and Wonder

Another important resemblance is in the category, "seeing . . . a juggler's show". What this involves is skill and brilliance which is surprising. If we trace back a work of art to its origin or source (which is a man or a group of men), our admiration also involves an admiration of the skill of the artist. Thus, *adbhuta rasa* is very close to the kind of emotion generated in the reader. It is also essentially a part of what is transmitted along with every other *rasa*, which is a **delight**. It is unfortunate that this aspect has not been highlighted by Abhinavagupta or the later aestheticians since *Nāṭya Śāstra* (VI.75) puts it thus:

> One should know that all the following are *vibhāvas* of *adbhuta*: any speech that contains an unusual idea, any unusual work of art (*śilpa*) or any remarkable act (*karma-rūpa*).
>
> — *Aesthetic Rapture*, Vol. I, p. 56

Earlier, we mentioned in passing that *adbhuta* involves a certain distancing. What this means is that if we can share and empathize with the act (that generates wonder) then it will no longer generate the sense of wonder — say, a juggler watching another juggler. Thus, what wonder involves is something strange and not a part of the regular order of things. It is out of the ordinary — extraordinary. Most important, there is a positive response to this stimulus. Thus, what is latent (and sometimes explicit) is an admiration at what is being done. It is in such a frame that we must understand "seeing a heavenly object", "a flying chariot", "a magic show" etc. But what about "going to a temple", "a garden" or "a meeting place?" The first, temple, holds two possibilities. A temple might be an immense creation, a product of skill and devotion with which sometimes miracles and wonderful legends are associated, and it may thus be an object of wonder. It holds the possibility of God revealing Himself, or bringing about some miracle. A garden has associations of beauty and beauty holds the possibility of wonder. A meeting place is related to *sṛṅgāra* or union. It also holds the possibility of beauty and admiration (of the beloved object). Similarly "gaining one's desired object" holds the possibility of surprise. It is like a dream coming true. Hence, the result is a delighted surprise.

Adbhuta Rasa and Love

Adbhuta rasa can also be related to *śṛṅgāra* since in *śṛṅgāra* each (lover or beloved) gets the object of desire — the other. For instance, Pablo Neruda says in "Adonic Angela":

> Her bosom like a two-flamed fire
> burned raised in two regions,
> and in a double river reached
> her large, clear feet.
>
> — *Residence on Earth*, p. 50

Here, the object of desire is also the object of wonder.

Thus, *śṛṅgāra* is closely related to *adbhuta* for in love we find attraction and admiration. Since attraction also involves an alien that is admired and that is desired to be absorbed into one's being, the possibility of *adbhuta* is always there. In this context we can cite a few lines from Lorca's poem "The Faithless Wife":

> And I took her to the river believing her a maid, but she had a husband.
>
> It was on St James's night, and almost as in duty bound. The street-lights went out and the crickets flared up. By the last street corners I touched her sleeping breasts, and they opened to me suddenly like spikes of hyacinth. The starch of her petticoat sounded in my ear like a piece of silk rent by ten knives. The trees, without silver light on their tops, have grown larger, and a horizon of dogs barks very far from the river.
>
> — *Lorca*, pp. 44-45

This is an erotic love poem (the above passage is a prose translation of it) in which we find the element of wonder at seeing or experiencing the desired object.

In fact, in *Nāṭya Śāstra* (VI.82), the following is stated about the *adbhutarasa* :

> *Adbhutarasa* has been said to be two-fold: that which is divine and that which is born from joy. . . . the *adbhutarasa* born from joy comes from delight (i.e. the fulfilment of one's desires.)
>
> — *Aesthetic Rapture*, Vol. I, p. 57

Thus, unusual occurrences give rise to surprise and hence to wonder.

"Fulfilment of one's desire", in the second category, has been emphasized by Abhinavagupta (*Aesthetic Rapture*, Vol. II, p. 79). A key element here is that of 'joy' and this joy is the consequence of 'delight' which holds the possibility of wonder. This is a very important factor in Haiku poems that we shall discuss below. Besides, like *śṛṅgara*, *adbhuta* also involves a positive state of excitement.

Wit and Wonder

Earlier, in the context of *śṛṅgāra*, we have talked of the intervention of intellect. It is necessary here to discuss that possibility again. A major trend in modern Western literature has been that of intellectualization. Perhaps, the influence of T.S. Eliot in this respect has been great. But it can be said to be more of a revival than a new tradition. In all cultures, **wit**, at some time or the other, plays a very important role. This involves unusual figures of speech and thought, new words etc. In Sanskrit poetry, in the *Alaṁkāra* School, this has been given much emphasis. In England, in the writings of John Donne, Andrew Marvell and others, this is also to be seen. As T.S. Eliot put it in his essay "The Metaphysical Poets", what this involves is a unity of sensibility, i.e., of thought and feeling (*Norton Anthology*, Vol. II, p. 2235). If this possibility is extended, as has been done by French writers like Gennet and others, it leads to a pure delight in the very use of language for its own sake. Thus, in much of modern writing, be it Absurdist or Imagist, the element of a delightful surprise intervenes before the final response. Even in works that finally generate emotions like fear or disgust (in writers like T.S. Eliot, Samuel Beckett, George Luis Borges, Gabriel Garcia Marquez etc.) an intervening element of surprise or even wonder is to be seen.

Surprise and Delight

Before we proceed to individual works, unless the genre of **haiku** is mentioned, a discussion of *adbhuta rasa* will remain incomplete. A haiku is a Japanese verse, consisting of seventeen syllables, which creates an **intensity** of mood. It tries to compress in a few words a totality (of an object in time and space) and elicits a response to that intensity. What is generally to be found here is an unusual connection which bursts into realization in a moment of poetic concentration. Since the influence of Buddhism and Taoism upon it is substantial, the possibilities of wonder, delight and calm are inherent here. A few illustrations from Japanese haiku poet Basho (16th century AD) will suffice:

> In my new robe
> this morning —
> someone else.
>
> — *On Love and Barley: Haiku of Basho*, p. 25

> Autumn storm —
> wild boars tossed
> with leaves.
>
> — *On Love and Barley: Haiku of Basho*, p. 43

Sengai's haiku on Basho's "Frog" goes like this:

> Under the cloudy cliff, near the temple door,
> Between dusky spring plants on the pond,
> A frog jumps in the water, plop!
> Startled, the poet drops his brush.
>
> — *On Love and Barley: Haiku of Basho*, p. 21

All these poems are poems that are born of 'delight' at an unusual association which gives rise to 'joy'.

We have another reason for mentioning the Haiku here, for it would not be wrong to say that the Imagist school of Ezra Pound was influenced (at least technically) by it. Thus, Pound writes:

> The apparition of these faces in the crowd:
> Petals on a wet, black bough.
>
> — *The Japanese Haiku*, p. 17

T.E. Hulme writes in his poem "Above the Dock":

> Above the quiet dock in midnight,
> Tangled in the tall mast's corded height,
> Hangs the moon. What seemed so far away
> Is but a child's balloon, forgotten after play.
>
> — *The Golden Treasury*, p. 445

Its influence on the Greek poet George Seferis is also noticeable. In his poem "Haiku" he writes:

> I
>
> Pour into the lake
> Only a wine drop
> And the sun's gone.
>
> II
>
> In the Museum Garden
> Chairs empty
> Statues returned
> To the other museum.
>
> — *Poems:George Seferis*, p. 41

In all these poems, an unusual connection is made, a thing which is surprising (for though it existed it had not been discovered) is recognized and this leads to delight. But this delight can be of two types—delight at an unusual discovery and a delight that inheres even beyond the discovery, in the relation itself. Thus, the next two sections of Seferis's poem:

III

Is this the voice
Of our dead friends
Or of the gramophone?

VI

What's wrong with the rudder?
The boat goes in circles
And not one gull.

— *Poems:George Seferis*, p. 41

In these sections, after the initial surprise at the surface texture or at the unusual connection, there lurks the possibility of sadness, fear and the unknown. Hence, through the element of surprise or even wonder, the movement can be in a different direction altogether.

Which Way Does Wonder Move?

It is also important to discuss works where wonder dominates all through and moves in a positive direction. Lorca's poem, "Dream", is an example:

My heart rests by the cool fountain. (Fill it with your threads, spider of oblivion.)

To it the water of the fountain sang its song. (Fill it with your threads, spider of oblivion.)

My awakened heart sang its loves. (Spider of silence, weave your mystery.)

The water of the fountain listened sombrely. (Spider of silence, weave your mystery.)

My heart tumbles into the cooling fountain. (White

> hands, far away, halt the waters.)
>
> And the water takes it away with joy. (White hands, far away, nothing remains in the water.)
>
> —*Lorca*, pp. 10-11

It need not be emphasized here that a dream always holds the possibility of wonder.

Similarly, in Juan Ramon Jimenez's *Platero and I* (a long prose poem), in the relationship between the poet, his donkey (Platero) and the world, beyond all poverty and sadness, a sense of wonder persists:

> Platero is a small donkey, a soft, hairy donkey: so soft to the touch that he might be said to be made of cotton, with no bones. Only the jet mirrors of his eyes are hard like two black crystal scarabs. . . . When on Sundays I ride him through the lanes in the outskirts of the town, slow-moving countrymen, dressed in their Sunday clean, watch him a while, speculatively:
>
> "He is like steel," they say.
>
> Steel, yes. Steel and moon silver at the same time.
>
> — *Platero and I*, p. 9 : Section 1

Here, the element of wonder comes from love. Unusually, the object of love here is a donkey.

But as we have again and again found, it is the way one looks at things that makes the difference. Even in the midst of darkness, one can discover something delightful, as in Han-Shan's poems that we discussed in the chapter on *hāsya rasa*. Here for instance, in *Platero and I*, in "Lullaby" (Section 45) Jimenez says:

The charcoal-burner's little daughter, as pretty and dirty as a coin, with eyes of burnished black and full lips that seem about to burst with the red blood behind the grime, is at the cabin door, sitting on a tile, rocking her baby brother to sleep.

. . . . Feelingly, sweetly, the charcoal-burner's daughter sings:

"Sleep little one, sleep
To please the good Shepherdess . . . "

Platero, who is walking gently among the pines, approaches, little by little . . . Then he lies down on the hard earth, and, smoothed by the monotonous lullaby of the singer, he falls asleep, like a child.

— *Platero and I*, p. 27

Vīra, Adbhuta and Śānta

Adbhuta rasa comes from *vīra rasa* (*Nāṭya Śāstra*, VI.38). What this involves is an admiration (either inside the text, or on the part of the reader) and the 'joy' born out of this. Richard Bach's *Jonathan Livingston Seagull* holds the possibility of *śānta rasa* through *adbhuta rasa*. Here, let it again be emphasized that *adbhuta* has a very close relation to *śānta* and any inimical *rasa* (like *śṛṅgāra*, *hāsya* etc.) can lead to *śānta* through the intermediation of *adbhuta rasa*.

The book by Bach is basically about flying. But it also involves much more. Since the central character is a bird, the element of fantasy or the unusual (almost supernatural) is present. But beyond the fairy tale element, what is striking is the courage of a seagull to attempt to fly beyond its normal capacity. When the story begins, Jonathan is learning to fly:

But way off alone, out by himself beyond boat and shore,

> Jonathan Livingston Seagull was practising. A hundred feet in the sky he lowered his webbed feet, lifted his beak, and strained to hold a painful hard twisting curve through his wings. . . . Then his feathers ruffled, he stalled and fell.
>
> — *Jonathan Livingston Seagull*, pp. 11-12

All the other gulls are against this kind of flying. They do not appreciate it and it makes him an outcast:

> "Why, Jon, why?" his mother asked. "Why is it so hard to be like the rest of the flock, Jon? Why can't you leave low flying to the pelicans, the albatross? Why don't you eat? Son, you're bone and feathers!"
>
> — *Jonathan Livingston Seagull*, p. 13

But Jonathan replies:

> "I don't mind being bone and feathers, mom. I just want to know what I can do in the air and what I can't, that's all. I just want to know."
>
> — *Jonathan Livingston Seagull*, pp. 13-14

Here is a remarkable bird, a courageous seeker who can do anything, who can go through any amount of difficulty to learn what he wants. He risks his life, but soon he knows all about high flying and low flying and speed. It is this that makes him an outcast:

> A seagull never speaks back to the Council Flock, but it was Jonathan's voice raised. "Irresponsibility? My brothers!" he cried. "Who is more responsible than a gull who finds and follows a meaning, a higher purpose for life? For a thousand years we have scabbed after fish heads, but now we have a reason to live — to learn, to discover, to be free! Give me one chance, let me show you what I've found . . ."
>
> — *Jonathan Livingston Seagull*, pp. 39-40

Here, Jonathan's courage to fight back generates a sense of wonder. His speech also holds the possibility of a transcendence, the possibility of moving towards *śānta rasa.*

Jonathan is thrown out of the Flock and in his seeking and his meditation (on flying) he reaches a higher level of understanding. Since a transcendence of ordinary living involves something unusual, it gives rise to wonder. One day while flying alone a strange thing happens:

> They came in the evening, then, and found Jonathan gliding peaceful and alone through his beloved sky. . . . Without a word, Jonathan put them to his test, a test that no gull had ever passed. He twisted his wings, slowed to a single mile per hour above stall. The two radiant birds slowed with him . . . . At last he turned that speed straight up into a long vertical slow-roll. They rolled with him, smiling.
>
> He recovered to level flight and was quiet for a time before he spoke. "Very well," he said, "who are you?"
>
> "We're from your Flock, Jonathan. We are your brothers." The words were strong and calm. "We've come to take you higher, to take you home."
>
> — *Jonathan Livingston Seagull*, pp. 52-53

It is thus that Jonathan reaches heaven. But he is disappointed since he finds that even there things have a limit:

> In the days that followed, Jonathan saw that there was as much to learn about flight in this place as there had been in the life behind him. But with a difference. Here were gulls who thought as he thought. For each of them, the most important thing in living was to reach out and touch perfection . . . .
>
> — *Jonathan Livingston Seagull*, p. 60

And with the help of the Elder Jonathan learns:

> "Chaing, this world isn't heaven at all, is it?"
>
> The Elder smiled in the moonlight. "You are learning again, Jonathan Seagull," he said.
>
> . . . . Is there no place as heaven?
>
> "No, Jonathan, there is no such place. Heaven is not a place, and it is not a time. Heaven is being perfect." He was silent for a moment. "You are a very fast flier, aren't you?"
>
> "I . . . I enjoy speed," Jonathan said, taken aback but proud that the Elder had noticed.
>
> "You will begin to touch heaven, Jonathan, in the moment that you touch perfect speed. And that isn't flying a thousand miles an hour, or a million, or flying at the speed of light. Because any number is a limit, and perfection doesn't have limits. Perfect speed, my son, is being there."
>
> *Jonathan Livingston Seagull*, pp. 64-65

Thus, Jonathan learns of transcendence, where one is not limited since he does not believe that a limit exists, and reaches perfection. But he does not stop there. He comes back to his old flock and guides the ones who have the inclination towards perfection. This is not unusual. Any kind of seeking can lead to *adbhuta* and then to *śānta rasa*, for all seekings are directed towards a perfection. Once it is achieved, a transcendence is achieved as well. But all seekings involve 'steadfastness', 'patience', and 'courage' and, hence, are heroic. This perseverance as well as the transcendence to an intenser world (which is unusual and hence wonderful) generate *adbhuta rasa*.

In this work, we have 'unusual deeds' and the conversation contains 'unusual ideas' (*Nāṭya Śāstra*, VI.75). This possibility — 'unusual ideas' — suggests that even brilliant ideas or profound thoughts can be included in *adbhuta rasa.*

Adbhuta and Terror

Adbhuta involves the element of surprise, of something extraordinary, a break (transcendence) of normalcy. All these, as we have already seen earlier, point to the possibility of both the terrible and the disgusting. All that is needed is a slight twist — a foreboding or a negative consequence. This is what is to be persistently noted in the short stories of Borges.

In his story, "The Other" the old Borges meets the young Borges accidentally:

> "Sir," I said, turning to the other man, "are you an Uruguayan or an Argentine?"
>
> "Argentine, but I've lived in Geneva since 1914," he replied.
>
> There was a long silence. "At number seventeen Malagnou — across from the Orthodox church?" I asked.
>
> He answered in the affirmative.
>
> "In that case," I said straight out, "your name is Jorge Luis Borges. I, too, am Jorge Luis Borges. This is 1969 and we're in the city of Cambridge."
>
> "No," he said in a voice that was mine but a bit removed.
>
> — *The Book of Sand*, p. 4

An argument follows and the older Borges manages to convince the younger one that they are both really the same person by recounting the past and some secrets. In the end they decide to meet again:

> I told him that the supernatural, if it occurs twice, ceases to be terrifying. I suggested that we plan to see each other the next day, on this same bench, which existed in two times and in two places. He agreed at once and, without looking at his watch, said that he was late. Both of us were lying and we each knew it of the other. . . .
>
> I have brooded a great deal over that meeting, which until now I have related to no one. I believe I have discovered the key. The meeting was real, but the other man was dreaming when he conversed with me, and this explains how he was able to forget me; I conversed with him while awake, and the memory of it still disturbs me.
>
> — *The Book of Sand*, p. 10

Here, for the narrator, the encounter is terrifying. Thus, the element of fear is also there. But, for us, it is the element of awe that dominates. In the end, the explanation (which usually reveals the mystery and diminishes wonder), is in itself so extraordinary that it adds to the element of wonder. But the sense of wonder generated here is not really positive. It does not really hearten one. The encounter with the supernatural usually (along with fear) holds the possibility of certain positive emotions and is thus somewhat different from seeing ghosts etc. But, here it is almost like seeing a ghost, and so it leaves one slightly disturbed. This tendency towards the terrifying is even more persistent in the story, "The Book of Sand."

"The Book of Sand" is a story about an unusual book that the narrator gets from a stranger, a man who collects and sells books:

> He opened the suitcase and laid the book on a table. It was on octavo volume, bound in cloth. There was no doubt that it had passed through many hands. Examining

> it, I was surprised by its unusual weight. . . . "Nineteenth-century, probably," I remarked.
>
> "I don't know," he said. "I never found out."
>
> — *The Book of Sand*, p. 88

And then, the stranger reveals to the narrator that the book has an infinite number of pages and no page or illustration is ever repeated. Such a book is unusual and an object of wonder. Thus, the book elicits *adbhuta*. If the narrative had ended here, it would have been a case of pure *adbhuta rasa*. But as the narrative continues, we see the effect of this book upon the narrator:

> I showed no one my treasure. To the luck of owning it was added the fear of having it stolen, and then the misgiving that it might not truly be infinite. These twin preoccupations intensified my old misanthropy. I had only a few friends left; I now stopped seeing even them. A prisoner of the book, I almost never went out anymore. . . . I set about listing them alphabetically in a notebook, which I was not long in filling up. Never once was an illustration repeated. At night, in the meagre intervals my insomnia granted, I dreamed of the book.
>
> Summer came and went, and I realized that the book was monstrous. . . .
>
> I thought of fire, but I feared that the burning of an infinite book might likewise prove infinite and suffocate the planet with smoke. . . . at the Argentine National Library, which contained nine hundred thousand volumes . . . . I lost the Book of Sand on one of the basement's musty shelves.
>
> — *The Book of Sand*, p. 91

The implications are terrifying. *Adbhuta* slowly gives way to *bhayānaka*. It is true that the narrator escapes it. But the book lurks in the old shelves, waiting for an unknown victim.

Wonder Beyond Terror

This does not mean that even in the environment of terror, one cannot give way to wonder. It is possible, but involves a transcendence. In "Returning We Hear the Larks" by Isaac Rosenberg, when the soldiers are marching back towards the camp, suddenly the music of a lark makes the poet transcend the immediate fear of death into another world where wonder dominates:

> Sombre the night is.
> And though we have our lives, we know
> What sinister threat lurks there.
> Dragging these anguished limbs, we only know
> This poison-blasted track opens on our camp —
> On a little safe sleep.
>
> But hark! Joy — joy — strange joy.
> Lo! heights of night ringing with unseen larks.
> Music showering on our upturned list'ning faces.
>
> Death could drop from the dark
> As easily as song —
> But song only dropped,
> Like a blind man's dreams on the sand
> By dangerous tides,
> Like a girl's dark hair for she dreams no ruin lies there,
> Or her kisses where a serpent hides.
>
> — *Norton Anthology*, Vol. II, pp. 1931-32

But, nonetheless, immediately following the sense of wonder follows the foreboding of something sinister.

Like Borges, Marquez also writes in a way that elicits a sense of wonder. As we have discussed earlier (in a different context), while talking of the intervention of 'wit', here also, the medium through which we get our narrative is full of surprises and unusual occurrences. This lends an element of the unusual and the unreal, the magical, as is amply to be found in *The Chronicle of a Death Foretold.*

Effects of Adbhuta Rasa

In this chapter, we have not really said much about the *anubhāvas* or the effects of *adbhuta*. The reason is that they are basically the effects (listed) that are to be shown upon the stage, for *Nāṭya Śāstra* (VI.74) says:

> It should be acted out by such *anubhāvas* as opening one's eyes wide, staring, horripilation, sweat, tears, ecstatic delight, . . . nodding one's head (in admiration).
> — *Aesthetic Rapture*, Vol. I, p. 56

All the effects listed are such as suggest surprise and in almost all cases, they lead to admiration. 'Tears' can be tears of delight or awe. 'Horripilation' and 'sweating' can be the result of seeing something strange or awesome.

But the *vyabhicārībhāvas* or the accompanying states hold the possibilities of 'paralysis', 'fear', 'panic', 'lifelessness', 'fainting' etc. (*Aesthetic Rapture*, Vol. I, 56). Thus, though *adbhuta rasa* is basically a positive *rasa*, it can lead to certain negative manifestations in one who has a weak constitution. For instance, a man with a weak heart can die of happiness.

Adbhuta and the Other Rasas

As we have mentioned earlier, *adbhuta* is similar to *bībhatsa*, *bhayānaka* and *hāsya* in that they all suggest something which is out of the ordinary. But fear and disgust are negative states while laughter and wonder are positive ones.

The comic emotion (*hāsya rasa*) is also similar to the emotion of wonder (Masson and Patwardhan translate it as 'awesome emotion'), or *adbhuta rasa*, in that in both, delight plays an important role. Both suggest states of happiness. But in *hāsya* the element of incongruity is more persistent while is *adbhuta* it is the element of surprise that is more persistent. As in *śṛṅgāra* it is the state of happiness that is important, so also in *hāsya rasa*, it is the element of the comic or the humorous.

But it is very difficult to relate *adbhuta rasa* with *karuṇa* or *raudra rasa*. Apart from some of the accompanying states like 'crying', 'trembling', 'fainting' etc. not much else can be found common with them.

Children's Literature usually contains the second kind of *adbhuta rasa* — the one that is born of 'delight'. Similarly, in detective fiction, though the gruesome deed elicits horror, the skilful solving of the mystery is what gives rise to delight and even wonder.

10

Śānta Rasa

ŚĀNTA *rasa* implies a state of **calm** or of **equilibrium**; a state of **quiet** or of **repose**. But this does not mean that it can be achieved effortlessly, on its own, as easily as one falls back into sleep. Of course, sleep implies a state of rest with not much to distract the senses. But it is also a state of dreams which indicates emotions and hence unrest.

In basic opposition to *śānta* are the five restless senses that can never for a moment remain unstimulated and the desires that they generate and satisfy. It is only when the desires created by the senses are transcended or satisfied that the possibility of repose or of calm arises.

Thus, from whatever emotional state one moves to *śānta*, two possible ways are to be seen. One, when there is a fulfilment and hence the end of desire. Secondly, when from and due to excess, there is disgust and thus a rejection which leads one away from the state of excitement and away from desire.

Thus, even in the case of *śṛṅgāra rasa* there is the possibility of moving into *śānta*, not only through disgust but also through a positive transcendence in union. This is, in fact, not alien to Indian thought, since in *Bṛhadāraṇyaka Upaniṣad* (IV.3.21) we have an instance where the realisation of *Brahman* is compared to a state of union with one's wife:

> Just as when a man is embraced by his dear wife, he knows nothing outside nor anything inside; similarly when the individual Self is embraced by the universal Self, he knows nothing outside nor anything inside; for he has attained an end which involves the fulfilment of all other ends, being verily the attainment of Ātman which leaves no other end to be fulfilled.
>
> — *A Constructive Survey of Upanishadic Philosophy*, p. 255

The Uniqueness of Śānta

Śānta has been emphasized again and again as being unique among the *rasas* and as being different from the other eight *rasas*. The reasons are many.

For one, as mentioned in *Nāṭya Śāstra*, all the *rasas* arise from it and finally merge into it (*Śānta Rasa*, p. 93). Both in *Nāṭya Śāstra* and the *Abhinavabhāratī* it is considered the original or the 'natural' state of mind from which, due to various causes (desires or the obstruction of desires), the different emotions arise.

Secondly, in the absence of stimuli, desires abate and lead to a calm. Thus, it is different from the other *rasas*, leading one **away** from the emotions.

Is Śānta Really a Rasa?

If *śānta* leads away from emotions, how can it be a rasa, many argue, for if it is the very negation of emotions, how can it have a *sthāyībhāva* or permanent state? On the other hand persists the possibility that all the eight *bhāvas* can lead to *śānta*. If through the various *sthāyībhāvas* or primary states of the various *rasas* one can go to *śānta*, one cannot simply reject its possibility — for the desire to transcend all desires, must, in some way, be considered a desire.

In fact, Abhinavagupta, instead of being deterred by the possibility that all the eight *sthāyībhāvas* can be the *sthāyībhāvas* of *śānta*, points to the fact that some common factor in all these cases must be leading to *śānta*. He identifies it as the 'perception of truth' (*Śānta Rasa*, p. 130).

Besides, *bhāva* though mostly used in *Nāṭya Śāstra* in the sense of emotion is a much more potent word. Its connotations also include contemplation (*bhāvanā*). Thus, an awareness of or an insight into Truth, which arises from and is intermixed with any specific emotion (here it is paradoxically **tranquillity**), can also be known as a *bhāva*.

The Stable State in Śānta

Hence, *śānta* according to Abhinavagupta has 'right knowledge' or *sama* (right knowledge is the pre-requisite of *sama* or the state of calm and thus *sama* implies 'right knowledge') as its *sthāyībhāva* or primary state.

In *Nāṭya Śāstra* (or in the interpolated verse on *śānta*) it is said:

> Now *Śānta*, which has *sama* for its *sthāyībhāva*, and which leads to *mokṣa*, arises from *vibhāvas* such as knowledge of the truth, detachment, purity of mind etc.
>
> — *Śānta Rasa*, p. 92

Sama, equanimity or tranquillity is the primary prerequisite of *mokṣa* or the state of bliss. This indicates a state where one has overcome his desires.

But in order for this state to be achieved, certain factors must **stimulate** one towards *sama*. Earlier, we found that the eight other *sthāyībhāvas* can lead to *sama*. As Abhinavagupta has also pointed out in his *Abhinavabhāratī*, no one is born **into** self-realization. At some critical point in one's life, one is directed away from the emotions due to some reason or the other.

This, if taken with a positive frame of mind, leads one towards *mokṣa* which is considered in Indian tradition as the realization of the Ultimate Truth. In fact, the division of the stages of life into *āśramas* indicate *sanyāsa āśrama* after *bramhacārya*, *gārhasthya* and *vāṇaprastha*; and *sanyāsa* implies the renunciation of desires.

Causes of Śānta

What is it that leads to or causes (*vibhāva*) one to reach the state of *sama*. According to Abhinavagupta, as we have already seen earlier, in each instance (in case of the eight *sthāyībhāvas*) it is the realization of 'the Truth' that gives rise to *sama*. 'Purity of mind' thus is a pre-requisite, as is 'detachment' or *vairāgya*. Purity can be achieved only when one knows what is impure, and hence this involves this prior distinction at some point of time (which might lead to disgust and thus to detachment). *Vairāgya*, translated as 'detachment', is actually a much more potent word. It connotes a certain transition. It indicates a prior state of disillusionment which leads to detachment.

What can be considered a limitation in the above list of *vibhāvas* or causes is the fact that none (excepting *vairāgya*) indicates an emotional cause which leads to *sama*, while in the case of *vairāgya* there is the suggestion of disgust or *jugupsā*.

Seen this way, Abhinavagupta's indication of the way the various *sthāyībhāvas* can lead to *sama* have substantive claim to be the *vibhāvas* or the causes leading to *śānta*.

What is Really the Sthāyībhāva of Śānta

In fact it would be relevant to make a detailed analysis of the passage from Abhinavagupta (quoted earlier in chapter on the relation of *rasas*) in which these above possibilities have been mentioned.

Now, let us look at how each of the various *sthāyībhāvas* can lead to *śānta* separately.

Harṣa or Laughter

Of the *sthāyībhāva hāsya* or **laughter** Abhinavagupta says:

> . . . we find that a person attains to liberation if he realizes the oddity of everything in the world.
>
> — *Śānta Rasa*, p. 129

Here, he is referring to the discrepancy between the ideal and the real; to the realization of how things are different from what we think them to be — 'oddity'.

This is amply evidenced in the writings of Han-Shan that we have quoted earlier. Let us again quote them here:

> In the house east of here lives an old woman.
> Three or four years ago, she got rich.
> In the old days she was poorer than I;
> now she always laughs at me for not having a penny.
> She laughs at me for being behind;
> I laugh at her for getting ahead.
> We laugh as though we'd never stop,
> she from the east and I from the west!
>
> — *Cold Mountain*, p. 51

It is the 'oddity' of life that is here realized and this holds the possibility of a disillusionment that can lead one to *śānta*. Similarly, in the 'comedy of the grotesque' which we have discussed earlier, there is the awareness of a discrepancy between the ideal and the real. It is laughter that lightens the situation. Thus, laughter is a way of rejecting that which gives rise to the emotion of sorrow. It, in this way, can lead to an insight into the nature of sorrow and the way to go beyond it.

Śoka or Sorrow

Abhinavagupta says that *śoka* or **sorrow** can lead to *śānta* in one:

> . . . if he sees the whole world as lamentable.
>
> — *Śānta Rasa*, p. 129

This involves the possibility of disillusionment which arises along with a desire to escape from the world of sorrows. In case of Gautama Buddha, it was a desire to escape sorrows and sufferings that lead towards *śānta* as we see in Aśvaghoṣa's *Buddha Carita*. After seeing the four great signs the Buddha realizes the profound truth, 'One must die' (*The Bible of the World*, p. 192).

Later that night when the Buddha wakes up from a brief slumber he perceives the beautiful courtesans differently:

> . . . some with their bodies wet with trickling phlegm and spittle; some grinding their teeth, and muttering in their sleep . . . . To him that magnificent apartment, as splendid as the palace of Sakka, began to seem like a cemetery filled with dead bodies impaled and left to-rot . . .
>
> — *The Bible of the World*, p. 194

In Owen's poems, "Futility" and "Strange Meeting" what gives rise to sadness is the futility of war. This pain, in order to abate, seeks to escape from itself, and this is possible when one renounces attachments which are in fact the cause of all sufferings.

On the other hand, as in the case of *Metamorphosis* by Kafka, in the end, Gregory transcends his sorrows. At the moment of death:

> He recalled his family with sympathy and love. His own belief that he must go was even firmer that his sister's. He remained in this state of vacant and peaceable

> reflection until the church clock struck three in the morning . . . . Then, independently of his will, his head sank to the floor and his last breath streamed feebly from his nostrils.
>
> — *Franz Kafka*, p. 141

Here is a transcendence of sorrow without any disillusionment.

Krodha or Anger

Abhinavagupta feels that from *krodha* or anger one can move towards *śānta*:

> (if one) . . . perceives the happenings of the world as harmful to his spiritual well-being (and angry with them desires to conquer them). . . .
>
> — *Śānta Rasa*, p. 129

What is indicated here is the possibility of anger leading to disillusionment. Anger also arises from desires (from the refutation of desires or the bereavement of desired objects) and it may lead to disillusionment.

Besides, as in *Howl* by Ginsberg, it can be due to obstructions to one's 'spiritual well-being' and can lead to *śānta*:

> who fell on their knees in hopeless cathedrals praying for each other's salvation and lights and breasts, until the soul illuminated its hair for a second . . . . (line 61)

But, first the anger, the rage, the madness has to be itself overcome and must give way to the 'knowledge of the Truth'.

Utsāha or Dynamic Energy

About the relation of *utsāha* (**dynamic energy**) of *vīra rasa* with *śānta*, Abhinavagupta says that the former can lead to *śānta*:

> . . . if he resorts to extraordinary energy dominated by the absence of delusions (in order to overcome worldly temptations).
>
> — *Śānta Rasa*, p. 129

Now, *vīra* and *śānta* have certain similarities. The *vibhāva* or cause of *vīra* is 'correct perception'. The cause of *śānta* is 'knowledge of Truth'. Both have 'steadfastness', determination, patience etc., among their *vyabhicārībhāvas* or accompanying states. But the basic difference between the two is that while in *vīra* pride plays an important role and thus there is the affirmation of ego, in *śānta* ego gets diluted in the realization of the bigger Self (*Śānta Rasa*, p. 93).

But in order for one to achieve self-realization, a lot of difficulties, temptations etc., have to be overcome and this needs courage — a basic ingredient of *vīra*. On the other hand, in a life of courage, one learns 'humility' as we saw in *The Old Man and the Sea*:

> He was too simple to wonder when he had attained humility. But he knew he had attained it and he knew it was not disgraceful and it carried no loss of true pride.
>
> — *The Old Man and the Sea*, pp. 9-10

Once 'pride' is transmoted there is the effacement of the ego and one is on the road towards Self-realization. Thus, in the end, even if the old man is tired, dead tired, he has nothing to be sad about. In his sleep in the end, we find him dreaming of Africa and of lions.

Similarly, in *Jonathan Livingston Seagull*, Jonathan's strong dedication to his art (of flying) shows courage, and his total immersal in it demonstrates transcendence of both temporality and space, and thus the acknowledgement of *śānta*:

> You will begin to touch heaven, Jonathan, in the moment that you touch perfect speed. And that isn't flying a

> thousand miles an hour, or a million, or flying at the speed of light. Because any number is a limit, and perfection doesn't have limits. Perfect speed, my son, is being there.
>
> — *Jonathan Livingston Seagull*, pp. 64-65

Thus, where steadfastness and perseverance are (at one point of time) detached from egotism, *vīra* gets transformed into *śānta.*

BHAYA OR FEAR

Bhaya or **fear** can lead to *śānta*, Abhinavagupta says:

> . . . if he feels afraid of all the objects of the senses . . .
>
> — *Śānta Rasa*, p. 129

This is possible in various ways. When one is aware that the objects of senses are the cause of pain and suffering and so fears them, it leads to disillusionment and hence to *vairāgya* (or renunciation). We can take the case of Gautama Buddha.

Secondly, when one is terrified, it might lead to a desire to overcome this terror (*vīra*) and thus through heroic effort to *śānta.*

Thirdly, fear intermixed with disgust or leading to disgust can further lead to disillusionment and thus to *śānta.*

For instance, in Baudelaire's poem "Jewels", both fear and disgust persist at the realization that all beautiful human beings must one day become corpses:

> — Yet you will come to this offence,
> this horrible decay,
> you, the light of my life, the sun
> and moon and stars of my love!
>
> — *The Flowers of Evil*, pp. 35-36

Similar is the frightening realization of the facts of life, as in

Śaṅkara's verse:

> While a man supports his family,
> See what loving care they show!
> But when his aging body falters,
> Nearing the time of dissolution,
> None, not even his nearest kin,
> Will think to ask him how he fares.
>
> — *Self Knowledge*, p. 242

This horror (both fear and disgust) can lead to disillusionment and hence to *śānta.*

Jugupsā or Disgust

Jugupsā or **disgust** can lead to *śānta* as has been much emphasised:

> . . . if he feels disgust for young women etc., though they are desirable for all other people. . .
>
> — *Śānta Rasa*, p. 129

This also indicates how *śṛṅgāra* holds the potential of being reversed into *bībhatsa* due to some realization or when the way of seeing things is reversed. In the illustration from Aśvaghoṣa's *Buddha Carita* above we see its possibility as also in the poem of Baudelaire we discussed a little earlier.

In a poem by Bhartṛhari we see the possibility of disgust arising from desire amply evidenced:

> She, about whom I think always: she likes me not;
> She loves another man, who loves another girl;
> And yet there is another woman, who seeks my love:
> Fie on her, on him, rebuke me and him and the god of love.
>
> — *History of Indian Literature*, Vol. III, p. 158

VISMAYA OR WONDER

Vismaya or **wonder** can also lead to *śānta* according to Abhinavagupta:

> . . . if he feels astonished at his unprecedented realization of his own self.
>
> — *Śānta Rasa*, p.129

Wonder always accompanies anything that is extraordinary. Thus it comes in the process of realization of the Truth as a *vyabhicāribhāva* or an accompanying state. But wonder (which is an excited state) is inimical to *śānta*.

This, of course, does not mean that wonder cannot lead to *śānta*. As we saw in *Jonathan Livingston Seagull*, it is the element of the **wonderful** nature of 'flying' that first attracts Jonathan. In the reader's response to the depiction of *śānta* there is always the possibility of wonder at the ability of a man to achieve self-realization. But coming back to the point, wonder at the unique nature of the realization of *mokṣa* can attract one and then lead to (in due course) *śānta*. It is in fact this aspect which is highlighted in many of the Japanese Haiku. For instance, Shiki's "The Mist":

> I turned back to see,
> But the man I passed was veiled
> In mist already.
>
> — *Japanese Haiku*, p. 194

Or Basho's "The Galaxy":

> Wild the rolling sea!
> Over which to Sado Isle
> Lies the Galaxy.
>
> — *Japanese Haiku*, p. 184

In both the haiku, the element of wonder at the vast and incomprehensible nature of the world leads towards a desire to understand the true nature of things.

Rati or Love

About *rati* or **love** Abhinavagupta comments:

> Bharata . . . does admit their ability to lead to liberation, provided they are the result of extraordinary causes.
>
> — *Śānta Rasa*, p. 92

Later he says:

> . . . *rati* alone is the *sthāyin* in *śānta*. For it has been said:
>
> "The man whose love is centred in the Self, who is gratified in his Self, and who takes all delight in the Self — for such a man there is nothing any longer to be accomplished."
>
> — *Śānta Rasa*, p. 129

This is substantiated by the verse from *Bṛhadāraṇyaka Upaniṣad* which we have quoted earlier. Another illustration to the point is Rilke's poem which we quoted in the chapter on *Śṛṅgāra*:

> How shall I hold my soul, that it may not
> be touching yours? . . . .
> You and me — all that lights upon us, though,
> brings us together like a fiddle-bow
> drawing **one** voice from two strings it glides along.
> Across what instrument have we been spanned?
> And what violin holds us in his hand?
> O sweetest song.
>
> — *Collected Poems*, Vol. II, p. 114

Cause and Effect of Śānta

Coming back to *śānta rasa* proper, Abhinavagupta has commented that the verse quoted below (from *Nāṭya Śāstra*) indicates the *vibhāva* (cause), *sthāyībhāva* (primary state) and the *anubhāva* (result) of *śānta rasa*:

> *Śāntarasa* is to be known as that which arises from a desire to secure the liberation of the Self, which leads to a knowledge of the Truth, and is connected with the property of highest happiness.
>
> — *Śānta Rasa*, p. 139

Thus, *śānta rasa* arises from a "desire to secure the liberation of the Self". At the beginning of the chapter, we have already discussed the various causes (also mentioned in *Nāṭya Śāstra*) like 'knowledge of the truth', 'detachment' etc.

Coming to the *anubhāvas* or consequences, we have a certain issue to resolve. Here, the result mentioned is "the property of highest happiness". But earlier (to this stanza) in *Nāṭya Śāstra* we find the following:

> It should be acted out by means of the *anubhāvas*, such as *yama* and *niyama*, meditation on the Self, concentration of the mind on the Self (*dhāraṇā*), devotion (*upāsanā*), compassion towards all creatures and the wearing of religious paraphernelia (*liṅgagrahaṇa*).
>
> — *Śānta Rasa*, p. 92

The 'highest happiness' is a state that cannot really be shown. But the associated things that lead to it can be shown, and it is these that have been listed here. Besides, it is categorically said, "It should be acted out by means of . . . ." In other words, these are the outward manifestations which result from a desire to achieve *śānta*; and the inward realization achieved is that of bliss.

Yama or 'abstentions' refer to the five abstentions mentioned in Patañjali's *Yoga Sūtra* — *ahiṁsā* (non-violence), *satya* (truth), *asteya* (absence of the desire to steal), *bramhacarya* (celebacy) and *aparigraha* (non-posession). It is in fact when these 'abstentions' are achieved that one can be truly detached (from desires) and hence achieve the state of *sama* or tranquillity.

It is also similar in the case of the *niyamas* or 'observations' — *śauca* (cleanliness), *saṅtoṣa* (sense of fulfilment), *tapas* (meditation), *svādhyāya* (study of the *Vedas* or the pursuit of knowledge) and *īśvarapraṇidhāna* (contemplation of the Almighty).

In the same way "meditation on the Self", 'devotion'. 'compassion towards all creatures' etc., are manifest when **bliss** is achieved.

Accompanying Emotions

> Its *vyabhicārībhāvas* are disgust with the world (*nirveda*), remembrance, firmness of mind, purity in all the four stages of life (*āśrama*), rigidity (of the body) (*stamba*), horripilation, etc.
>
> — *Śānta Rasa*, p. 92

Thus are the major accompanying states listed. 'Disgust with the world' is usually what leads to the abatement or the rejection of desire. 'Purity of mind' must persist through 'firmness of mind' so that *śānta* can be reached.

In other words, it is usually in works that move **away** from the ordinary world in the exploration of some other reality that we find *śānta*. Thus, though science fiction or fantasy do not in themselves help in achieving *śānta*, if they go in some deep pursuit (as in *Jonathan Livingston Seagull*) they can lead to *śānta*. In fact, in the *Gītā*, one of the ways to *mokṣa* is through *karma* or one's work, duties or action. Thus, in *Seagull*, it is through action that Jonathan achieves *śānta*.

Śānta in Meditative Literature

Rilke's *The Book of Hours* is a long poem where the element of *śānta* seems distinct. It is a long and complex work, but is basically written as a series of meditation-explorations of the relationship between man and God by a monk in a monastery. It, in fact, begins in "unbelief not as the result of doubt but as the result of not-knowing and beginnership" (*Selected Works*, p. 27). A few illustrations here will suffice:

> Nothing's between us but a slender wall,
> fortuitously; for if there came perhaps
> from your mouth or from mine a sudden call,
> it might collapse
> forthwith, quite noiselessly.
>
> — *Selected Works*, p. 29

Or

> With this onsurging of mine, this over-
> outflowing, wide-armed, to the open sea,
> with this increasing recurrency,
> I want to confess you, proclaim you, as never
> one previously.
>
> — *Selected Works*, p. 32

Here, what we find is a contemplation of the relation of man and eternity, of the relation of time and timelessness. It is a movement towards a 'creative understanding' of this relation in order to achieve **equilibrium** or *śānta.*

In fact, in T.S. Eliot's *Four Quartets* a similar kind of relationship of man with space, time, eternity etc. is explored. As with the monk in Rilke's poem, here also the meditative voice has already achieved a certain detachment from the passions of the world. But it is a voice that is yet to achieve a complete understanding. The poem is an exploration of these various possibilities in order to understand the true nature of things:

Time present and time past
Are both perhaps present in time future
And time future contained in time past.
. . . . My words echo
Thus, in your mind.
            But to what purpose
Disturbing the dust on a bowl of rose-leaves
I do not know.

— *Collected Poems*, p. 189

It is from this uncertainty that the poem progresses through a series of reflections towards some resolution of time and space, for our essential problem arises within space and time:

Yet the enchantment of past and future
Woven in the weakness of the changing body,
Protects mankind from heaven and damnation
Which flesh cannot endure.

— *Collected Poems*, p. 192

And yet it is within time that illumination comes:

But only in time can the moment in the rose-garden,
. . . Be remembered; involved with past and future.
Only through time time is conquered.

— *Collected Poems*, p. 192

This basic theme is echoed all through the other three sections as well.

In the second section, the narrator is acutely aware of time and change:

In my beginning is my end. In succession
Houses rise and fall, crumble, are extended,
Are removed, destroyed, restored, or in their place
Is an open field, or a factory, or a by-pass.
Old stone to new building, old timber to new fires,

Old fires to ashes, and ashes to the earth . . .
— *Collected Poems*, p. 196

It is as if he is outside of time, observing its manifestation through centuries and ages. This is a kind of realization not easily noticeable in everyday living. It is only such a detachment that can lead to this insight and this insight can lead to *śānta.*

In this section another thing that is highlighted is the impossibility of knowledge (in the conventional sense):

The only wisdom we can hope to acquire
Is the wisdom of humility; humility is endless.
— *Collected Poems*, p. 199

Through this realization comes the realization that transcendence can only be achieved beyond emotions:

I said to my soul, be still, and wait without hope
For hope would be hope for the wrong thing;
wait without love
For love would be love of the wrong thing . . .
— *Collected Poems*, p. 200

The third stanza begins with a series of intuitive understandings that lead to further contemplation:

The river is within us, the sea is all about us;
The sea is the land's edge also, the granite
Into which it reaches . . .
— *Collected Poems*, p. 205

Along with it is also the awareness that on many occasions we miss the opportunities given to us:

We have the experience but missed the meaning,
And approach to the meaning restores the experience
— *Collected Poems*, p. 208

Hence, the approach he suggests is that of 'contemplation' — a detached attempt at re-understanding the meaning of life through humility and beyond passions. It is thus that the poem progresses towards something that corresponds to the Indian doctrine of *karma yoga*:

> And do not think of the fruit of action.
> Fare forward.
>
> — *Collected Poems*, p. 211

In the final section of the poem he says:

> We shall not cease from exploration
> And the end of all our exploring
> Will be to arrive where we started
> And know the place for the first time.
>
> — *Collected Poems*, p. 223

The exploration comes a full circle, and like the realization of the oneness of the beginning and end comes the realization of 'oldness' and 'newness'; of familiarity and unfamiliarity together.

But what is more relevant for our purpose, apart from the metaphysical explorations, is the way language has been used by both Rilke and Eliot. It is a language that is soothing, slow and unhurried. The images generated are such as quieten desire and encourage meditation. Thus, it is very much justifiable to see them as illustrations of *śānta rasa*. In both the poems, the *anubhāva* or cause for the explorations is the desire for the 'knowledge of Truth'. The dominant mood is that of calm. Though there are uncertainties, there are questions, doubts etc. these are not impetuous or violent. Rather, they are of the nature of doubts which come at the end of worldly desire, from seeking something beyond them. In the moments of resolution and understanding, the experiences are those of the nature of stilling one beyond space and time. For instance, this passage from *Four Quartets*:

> At the still point of the turning world. Neither flesh nor fleshless;
>
> Neither from nor towards; at the still point,there the dance is,
> I can only say, there we have been; but I cannot say where.
> The inner freedom from the practical desire,
> The release from action and suffering, release from the inner
> And the outer compulsion, yet surrounded
> By a grace of sense, a white light still and moving, . . .
>
> — *Collected Works*, p. 192

It is such a state, a more or less indescribable state, that is *sama* or tranquillity, the *sthāyībhāva* or permanent state of *śānta.*

The Seeker of Peace

In Herman Hesse's *Siddhartha*, we find that the hero, Siddhārtha, is a seeker. In him we find courage, but it is not a courage which is attached to an ego, but one that is interested only in finding an Ultimate. On the other hand, he has very little attachment to anything else. He explores all the possibilities of life, but in a more or less 'detached' way:

> In the shade of the house, in the sunshine on the river bank by the boats, in the shade of a sallow wood and the fig tree, Siddhartha, the handsome Brahmin's son, grew up with his friend Govinda. . . . Already he knew how to pronounce Om silently — this word of words, to say it inwardly with the intake of breath, when breathing out with all his soul . . . . Already he knew how to recognize Atman within the depth of his being, indestructible, at one with the universe.
>
> — *Siddhartha*, p. 3

This is how we are introduced to Siddhārtha. But he is not happy. Perhaps, since he 'recognizes *ātman*' within him, he is not satisfied with the ordinary way of life:

> Siddhartha had begun to feel the seeds of discontent within him. He had begun to feel that the love of his father and mother, and also the love of his friend Govinda, would not always make him happy, give him peace, satisfy and suffice him.
>
> — *Siddhartha*, p. 5

Thus, the anxiety or fear of loss of happiness makes Siddhartha desire something which can transcend the human insecurities. One day, seeing some *sāmanas* (wandering ascetics) Siddhārtha's mind is made up:

> "Oh, Siddhartha," he cried, "will your father permit?"
>
> Siddhartha looked at him like one who had just awakened. As quickly as lightning he read Govinda's soul, read the anxiety, the resignation.
>
> "We will not waste words, Govinda," he said softly. "Tomorrow at daybreak I will begin the life of the *Sāmanas*. . . ."
>
> — *Siddhartha*, p. 8

When he asks his father his father is very displeased. But Siddhārtha is 'steadfast' in his decision. He waits outside his father's room all night.

> "Siddhartha," he (his father) said, "why are you waiting?"
>
> "You know why."
>
> — *Siddhartha*, p. 9

He finally lets Siddhārtha go. Siddhārtha spends his time with the *sāmanas*, but even there, with their torture of the body, he is dissatisfied. In his restless seeking, one day he has to part with his dear friend, Govinda, when they come in contact with Gautama Buddha. In fact he is angry with the Buddha for having robbed him of his friend. But he is unable to follow the Buddha's path. He, in fact, says it on the Buddha's face:

> The teaching of the enlightened Buddha embrace much, they teach much — how to live righteously, how to avoid evil. But there is one thing that this clear, worthy instruction does not contain; it does not contain the secret of what the Illustrious One himself experienced. . . . That is why I am going on my way — not to seek another and better doctrine, for I know there is none, but to leave all doctrines and all teachers and to reach my goal alone — or die."
>
> — *Siddhartha*, p. 28

But the Buddha warns him:

> "You are clever, O Samana," said the Illustrious One; "you know how to speak cleverly, my friend. Be on your guard against too much cleverness."
>
> — *Siddhartha*, p. 29

In fact, what the Buddha is warning him against is the ego which is still there; and Siddhārtha is also able to discern that:

> The Buddha has robbed me, thought Siddhartha. He has robbed me, yet he has given me something of greater value. He has robbed me of my friend, who believed in me and who now believes in him; he was my shadow and now is Gotama's shadow. But he has given to me Siddhartha, myself.
>
> — *Siddhartha*, p. 29

In this awareness, there is the awareness of his earlier illusions which he has now been able to break and find himself. But along with it is the awareness of the ego which is sad that its 'shadow' is now gone.

It is as the Buddha had predicted. Siddhārtha loses his way. As he proceeds, he slowly finds that the world is beautiful, that his goal is not on the other side. He becomes aware of sexual desire for the opposite sex in himself. Then on his way to the city, he sees Kamalā (the beautiful courtesan) for the first time and is drawn to her. During his interaction with Kamalā, he is for the first time initiated into the ways of the world. Kamalā tells him that if he is to get her he must have money. So he works for a businessman called Kāmaswāmī. But through all this he still retains his detachment. As Kamalā herself recognizes, Siddhārtha is like a caged bird. He always wants to fly away, for towards everything — even love — Siddhārtha's attitude is detached:

> Why should I not attain what I decided to undertake yesterday? — to be your friend and to learn the pleasures of love from you. You will find me an apt pupil. Kamala. I have learned more difficult things than what you have to teach me.
>
> — *Siddhartha*, p. 44

Talking about himself to Kamalā, he says:

> Listen, Kamala, when you throw a stone into the water, it finds the quickest way to the bottom of the water. It is the same when Siddhartha has an aim, a goal. Siddhartha does nothing; he waits, he thinks, he fasts, but he goes through the affairs of the world like the stone through water, without doing anything, without bestirring himself . . .
>
> — *Siddhartha*, p. 49

This is the most important quality about Siddhārtha — his 'steadfastness' towards a goal once he has a goal. But he does not get what he is seeking in it. Many years pass, and Siddhārtha's hair turns grey. He is successful in the world, but then that was not what he had wanted:

> This game was called Sansara, a game for children, a game which was perhaps enjoyable played once, twice, ten times — but was it worth playing continually?
>
> Then Siddhartha knew that the game was finished, that he could play it no longer.
>
> — *Siddhartha*, p. 67

So, he renounces everything and starts out again. It is then that he comes to the river again (across which he had come when he had come to the city for the first time) and discovers it anew. He decides to remain by the river. In the river he discovers new truths:

> But today he only saw one of the river's secrets, one that gripped his soul. He saw that the water continually flowed and flowed and yet it was always there . . .
>
> — *Siddhartha*, p. 81

But still he is not rid of the world. Kamalā, also fed up with the world, wants to seek shelter at the feet of the Buddha. But on the way, near the river, dies of snake-bite and leaves her son (by the seeds of Siddhārtha) with him. This boy suddenly becomes the object of attachment for Siddhārtha. But the delicate young man, used to the ways of the city, is unable to feel happy near the river. When Siddhārtha reluctantly parts with him, he is very much hurt:

> The wound smarted for a long time. Siddhartha took many travellers across the river who had a son or a daughter with them, and he could not see any of them without envying them . . .
>
> — *Siddhartha*, p. 102

But as he listens to the river's voice, his soul is gradually awakened again:

> When Siddhartha listened attentively to this river, to this song of a thousand voices; when he did not listen to the sorrow or laughter, when he did not bind his soul to any one particular voice and absorb in his Self, but heard them all, the whole unity; the great song of a thousand voices consisted of one word: Om — perfection.
>
> — *Siddhartha*, p. 107

There he remains by the ferry, by the river where Govinda (his old friend) still seeking unsuccessfully for the Ultimate, crosses the river. Siddhārtha recognizes Govinda and it is then that Govinda discovers that Siddhārtha has **found**:

> . . . Govinda stood yet a while bending over Siddhartha's peaceful face which he had just kissed, which had just been the stage of all present and future forms. His countenance was unchanged after the mirror of the thousand-fold forms had disappeared from the surface. He smiled peacefully and gently, perhaps very mockingly, exactly as the Illustrious One had smiled.
>
> — *Siddhartha*, p. 119

Thus, the 'perception of Truth' in Siddhārtha finally leads to *sama* or a state of calm. Siddhārtha's restless seeking comes to an end.

Śānta and Mokṣa

Before we conclude this chapter, let it be mentioned that according to Abhinavagupta, any sustained work of literature must (as we have seen in the discussion of *śānta rasa* in the chapter on the relation of *rasas*) inevitably lead to *śānta*. He, in this context, cites the example of the *Mahābhārata* where the epic war (where almost everyone is destroyed) leads to a disillusionment with the world — power, lust, desires etc. — and thus to *śānta rasa* (*Śānta Rasa*, p. 106). In the Indian context all arts lead to *mokṣa*. In the *Gītā* it is said that one can attain to *mokṣa* or **self-realization** through *karma* (one's work or profession), *bhakti* (devotion) as well as through *jñāna* (knowledge through contemplation and meditation). Thus, any art — dance, music, literature (one's *karma*) — can lead one to *mokṣa*. Even otherwise, any path followed earnestly can lead to *mokṣa*. *Tantra*, for instance, suggests the possibility of *mokṣa* through sex. Thus, a reader, a *sahṛdaya*, if he pursues the path of seeking through literature, can also attain *mokṣa* with the help of appropriate works filled with *rasa*.

This is not unique to the Indian tradition only. In Chinese **Taoist** literature, this is amply evidenced. In Taoist tradition a painter pursues **self-realization** through the principles of Tao. Similarly, a Japanese (as well as a Chinese) poet or painter also strives towards a transcendence through the principles of **Zen**. If these traditions are looked at closely what one discovers is the fact that what they indicate is a concept very close to *śānta rasa*.

11

Conclusion

In the preceding chapters on the nine *rasas*, we came across works dealing with a varying range of emotions. Here, the question that needs to be asked is, do the nine *rasas* manage to hold within themselves the totality of human emotions?

Now, if Aristotle, within the broad division of tragedy and comedy, could fit in all the various emotions then why not the nine *rasas*? True, the *rasa* theory raises some important problems which we have discussed in this work. P.V. Kane points out that modern psychologists have categorized the basic human instincts and emotions many of which can be equated with the various *rasas*. But at the same time, he also shows that the various psychologists do differ both in regard to the number of basic emotions and the specific emotions/instincts themselves (*History of Sanskrit Poetics*, pp. 357-58). If we look at the history of the *rasa* school, we find a similar interesting feature. After Abhinavagupta, the number of *rasas* have slowly multiplied (even during his time he was aware of this tendency and argued against it) and if we make a list of them, we have about thirty or forty *rasas*.

Here, we need not debate about the validity of the various *rasas* that have sprung up later. If the nine *rasas* suffice, then why bring in more? One of the advantages of the nine-fold *rasa* system is that it helps one realize that many of our most complex emotions are actually the manifestations of (an organization of) some very basic instincts and emotions — as in the case of the complex feeling of the **Absurd**, which contains within itself a primary insecurity, and certain repulsions and fears. Hence, the nine *rasas*, in various degrees of co-existence, in a work — like the mixture of food stuff in cooking — create unique and complex emotional possibilities.

Another interesting thing is that the eight-fold (later nine-fold) division suggests that in ancient times, prior to *Nāṭya Śāstra*, these eight basic emotions must have been recognized in Indian culture. Perhaps the eight *rasas* go back to those times when the emotions were being detected, defined and differentiated from one another. What reinforces this supposition is the fact that in Vedic poetry — our most ancient poetry — all these emotions figure.

An important point that may be highlighted here is the unique nature of *śānta rasa*. True, in all probabilities, it is a later addition to *Nāṭya Śāstra*. But, as Abhinavagupta points out (we have already discussed this in the chapter on the relation of *rasas*), *Nāṭya Śāstra* indicates the possibility implicitly.

Śānta rasa, apart from the *rasa* theory, is perhaps the most unique contribution of India to aesthetics, for it seems to have a lot of psychological potentials. It has been pointed out earlier that *śānta* comes at the beginning of all *rasas* and is there at the end of all *rasas*. This indicates a state of stasis, which is broken and restored in our lives again and again; towards which we strive ceaselessly. It also shows that emotions are caused by stimuli and when the stimuli are controlled or modified and channellized, they can lead to a state of equilibrium. More important, it is also suggested that in combination with *śānta* (in a work) and *rasa*-realization, one can transcend one's ordinary life and experience a unique experience of bliss — *ānanda*.

Nonetheless, modern literature poses certain problems for the *rasa* theory that cannot be simply overlooked. While discussing

Neruda and Eliot, we saw how important a role intellectualism plays in the works of many modern poets. In Eliot, we have innumerable allusions — historical, religious, mythical and cultural — which have to be first grasped and understood if one is to understand the poem. And with most modern poets, the idiom is rather a private one — the use of language remarkably personal. Thus, the possibility of ambiguity comes in.

Such problems definitely hamper *rasa*-realization. This is so because *rasa* emphasizes the role of emotions both in the text and in the reader. What is intended is that the language should become so transparent, so invisible, that the emotions are conveyed and transmitted effortlessly. But this cannot be so when one reads a modern thinking poet. In other words, there must be at least two levels or two phases of reading. In the first phase, the ambiguities, the intellectual barrier etc., are to be tackled, digested and accepted (as the writer's conventions) into the general convention that guides a reading. In the second phase of reading, owing to this insight, the barriers and ambiguities are no longer felt, and hence, one can again move towards the relishment of emotions. This seems to us plausible because there is no literature which can be without an emotional effect in the long-run; for the central place of logic is in philosophy and not in literature.

Another related issue is that of **open reading**. What this broadly implies is that the reader has the freedom to find whatever meaning he wishes from a text. There are certain texts that are so closed that this kind of interpretability is not practicable. Yet, in a work where there is ambiguity, this can very well happen. In Sanskrit literature, Sītā's end in the *Rāmāyaṇa* is ambiguous. We can never be sure whether she went back to her mother earth or she died. The commentaries of Lollaṭa, Tauta and Abhinavagupta on *Nāṭya Śāstra*, which give various interpretations of the same passages, are other cases in point. But this kind of an approach is taking things to an extreme. A more sane approach would be to realize that the reader also creatively participates in a work of art. This has already been indicated by Abhinavagupta when he emphasized the importance of *saṁskāras* and *vāsanās* (conventions absorbed, latent impressions and instincts). In fact, Abhinavagupta indicates this when he says:

> . . . *rasa* (which is only the result of poetry) is not something 'certain' (*niyata*), for convention which lies at the root of denotation is limited. The suggested meaning is however unfixed (*aniyata*) since it depends on intangibles like the culture of the reader, the situation depicted, the persons speaking etc.
>
> — *Aesthetic Rapture*, Vol. I, p. 17

Thus, the primacy of the reader cannot be said to have been overlooked by the Indian aestheticians. The concept of *sahṛdaya* itself speaks volumes on the importance of the reader/audience in Indian aesthetics.

There is the possibility of another misunderstanding which must be removed — that *rasas* are water-tight compartments. We have already seen in the various chapters how different *rasas* co-exist. In fact, I have again and again tried to highlight this possibility. But one might still ask, what happens in case of inimical *rasas*? True, inimical *rasas* like *śṛṅgāra* and *bībhatsa* or *śṛṅgāra* and *śānta* can co-exist. But in such cases, an intermediary *rasa* — say *adbhuta* — can separate the two and hence, there will be no problem. But, still, another question persists. What about the relation of *hāsya* with *karuṇa, bībhatsa* or *bhayānaka*? In Absurd literature, they do co-exist. It is interesting to note that an ancient theory of more that 1500 years ago is capable of application to modern literature while the Western critics had to formulate new theories to cope with it.

There are certain other intriguing doubts. As in *karuṇa* one can dissolve into tears, so also in *hāsya* one might burst out laughing. When are these *rasas* (for that matter any *rasa*) relished — is it in those moments of intensity (outbursts) or is it at the end? This is a living, dynamic debate, and we will not try to assume that we have found a solution. On the one hand, an outburst of fury, anger, courage or tears would suggest that we have been **moved** by the text. It would indicate such a state where our emotions are sufficiently roused to be outwardly manifest. But on the other hand, Abhinavagupta suggests that *rasa* is a state of egolessness, of transcendence of ordinary emotions. Are these two positions compatible? But it is possible that when one gets excited or angry in reading a text, this state, though the manifestation of an **identity**, need not be that of personal identity. In other words, we forget ourselves for that moment, or we empathize (and become that person in the text) and hence the personal identity is forgotten.

Now, what about a text in which the possibility of sorrow lurks behind laughter — is *hāsya rasa* fulfilled in this case? Here, unlike what we discussed earlier, two inimical *rasas* are juxtaposed. There is no intermediate step between them. Such a state is almost non-existent in our tradition and hence the difficulty of answering the question.

Now, before we conclude, one final, troubling issue must be tackled. In modern literature, we find many incomplete works — open-ended — where the artist aims at no resolution. There are also works where the emotions are generated and then blocked; a movement terminated in mid-air; a game played without any end — a situation where language is assumed to be without any fixed intention or meaning. But even here, there is scope for *adbhuta* or wonder and *camatkāra* or delight at the skilful play of words and their possibilities.

In such works, the very essence of the *rasa* theory — *rasa* **realization** or *ānanda* — is not possible although the various *vibhāvas*, *anubhāvas* and even *sthāyībhāvas* (antecedents, consequent and primary moods) can be seen.

But this does not mean that this ancient theory breaks down simply because of this. Language was created for communication

— however imperfect or incomplete. The *rasa* theory is based upon this fundamental assumption. But a literature which negates its very essence of communicability of anything (however vaguely specific), which refutes any kind of **meaningability**, can lead only to an ultimate diffusion where nothing can be said. And thus, it hampers the *rasa* theory in no remarkable way.

Besides, all theories, however good they may be, face certain limitations. If a theory would satisfy every possibility, it would become the only theory. But since all theories are imperfect, there are certain situations where they do not apply too well. A theory is also a living thing. It grows, changes, modifies itself to the needs of the time. What the *rasa* theory needs is to grow. To become dynamic again. And this is very important when we keep in mind the fact that the *rasa* theory has unfortunately seen very little development in the last 400 years. Yet the fact that it can be applied to modern literature only points to its universality, timeless quality and its rich potential. It is hoped that this invaluable theory is taken up again by modern critics and that this ancient tradition continues for a long time to come.

Bibliography

Adoff, Arnold, (ed.), *I Am a Darker Brother: An Anthology of Modern Poems by Negro Americans*, New York: Macmillan, 1968.

Adrados, Franciscor, *Festival, Comedy and Tragedy : The Greek Origin of Theatre*, Leiden: E.J. Brill, 1975.

Amaladass, Anand S.J., *Philosophical Implications of Dhvani: Experience of Symbol Language in Indian Aesthetics*, Vienna: De Nobili Research Library, 1984.

Ānandavardhana, *Dhvanyāloka*, tr. by K. Krishnamoorthy, Delhi: Motilal Banarsidass, 1982.

Ānandavardhana, *Dhvanyāloka*, ed. & tr. by K. Krishnamoorthy, Dharwar : Karnatak University, 1975.

Ānandavardhana, *Dhvanyāloka of Ānandavardhana*, Udyotas I & II. ed. & tr. by B.P. Bhattacharya, Calcutta : Farma K.L. Mukhopadhyay, 1956-72.

Apte, V.S., *The Practical Sanskrit-English Dictionary*, Delhi: Motilal Banarsidass, 1965.

Aristophanes, *Birds and Lysistrata, Themophoriazusai, Frogs, Ecclesiazusai, Plautos*, tr. by Patric Dickinson, London: Oxford University Press, 1970.

Aristotle, *Aristotle on Poetry and Style*, tr. by J.M.A. Grube, Indianapolis: Bobbs-Merrill, 1958.

Aristotle, "On the Art of Poetry", in *Classical Poetics*, tr. by T.S. Dorsch, London: Penguin, 1965, pp.31-95.

Aristotle, *Works of Aristotle*, tr. by Ingram Bywater. Britanica Great Books Series 3, London: Britanica.

Aśvaghoṣa, "The Buddha Carita", *The Bible of the World*, ed. by Robert O Ballow, *et al*, New York: The Viking Press, 1939.

Bach, Richard, *Jonathan Livingston Seagull*, New York: Avon Books, 1970.

Bādarāyaṇa, *The Vedānta Sūtras of Bādarāyaṇa with the Commentary of Śaṅkara*, tr. by George Tibaut, 2 Vols., New York: Dover Publications, 1962.

Barthes, Ronald, *Critical Essays*, tr. by R. Howard, Evanston, Ill: Northwestern University Press, 1972.

Barthes, Ronald, *Elements of Semiology*, tr. by A. Lavers and C. Smith, London: Jonathan Cape, 1967.

Basho, Matsuo, *On Love and Barley: Haiku of Basho*, tr. by Lucien Stryk, London: Penguin, 1985.

Basho, Matsuo, *The Narrow Road to the Deep North and Other Travel Sketches*, tr. by Nobuyuki Yuasa, London: Penguin, 1966.

Baudelaire, Charles, *The Flower of Evil*, tr. by Richard Howard, London: Picador, 1982.

Beardsley, M.C., *Aesthetics from Classical Greece to the Present*, New York: Macmillan, 1966.

Beckett, Samuel, *Waiting for Godot*, New York: Grove Press, 1954.

Bhāmaha, *Kāvyālaṁkāra of Bhāmaha*, ed. & tr. by P.V. Naganatha Sastri, Delhi: Motilal Banarsidass, 1970.

Bharata, *Nāṭya Śāstra*, with "Abhinavabhāratī" by Abhinavagupta, ed. with Sanskrit commentary "Madhusūdanī" and Hindi Translation, by Madhusudana Shastri, 3 Vols., Varanasi: Banaras Hindu University, 1971-81.

Bhartṛhari, *The Vākyapadīya*, tr. by K. Raghavan Pillai, New Delhi: Motilal Banarsidass, 1971.

Bhaṭṭanāyaka, *Śṛṅgāraprakāśa*, ed. by Josyer, 4 Vols., Mysore: Coronation Press, 1955-75.

Bhaṭṭanayaka, *Fragments of Bhaṭṭanāyaka*, ed. by T.R. Chintamani, *Journal of Oriental Research* (Madras) I, (1927), pp. 267-77.

Borges, George Luis, *The Book of Sand*, tr. by Norman Thomas di Giovanni, London: Penguin, 1971.

Byrsky, Cristopher, *Concept of Ancient Indian Theatre*, Delhi: Munshiram Manoharlal, 1974.

Calvino, Italo, *Difficult Loves*: Minerva, 1983.

Camus, Albert, "The Myth of Sysiphus", in *The Myth of Sysiphus*, tr. by Justin O'Brien, London: Penguin, 1975.

Carroll, Lewis, "The Walrus and the Carpenter", in *Norton Anthology of English Literature*. 2 Vols., ed. by M.H. Abrams, *et al.*, New York: Norton, 1974 (Vol. II).

Chari, V.K., "The *Rasa* Theory: Theology or Aesthetics?" in *The Sacred and the Secular in India's Performing Arts: Ananda K. Coomaraswamy Centenary Essays*, ed. by V. Subramaniam, pp. 47-61, New Delhi: Ashish Publishing House, 1980.

Chari, V.K., "Poetic Emotions and Poetic Semantics", in *Journal of Aesthetics and Art Criticism*, 24, (1976), pp. 287-99.

Chari, V.K., *Sanskrit Criticism*, New Delhi: Motilal Banarsidass, 1993.

Chari, V.K., "Rasa as an Aesthetic Concept: Some Comments from the Point of View of Western Criticism", Unpublished Papers, International Sanskrit Conference, March 1972, New Delhi.

Charlton, W., *Aesthetics*, London: Hutchinson University Library, 1970.

Chinese Love Lyrics: From Most Ancient to Modern Times, tr. by various hands, New York: Peter Pauper Press.

Chomsky, N., *Language and Mind*, New York: Harcourt, Brace and World Inc., 1968.

Cohen, Ralph (ed.), *New Directions in Literary Histroy*, Baltimore:

Johns Hopkins University Press, 1974.

Coleridge, Samuel Taylor, "Recollections of Love", in *Norton Anthology of English Literature*. 2 Vols., ed. by M.H. Abrams, *et al.*, New York: Norton, 1974 (Vol. II).

Confucious, Menecious, *et al.*, *The Wisdom of China*, New York: Peter Pauper Press, 1965.

Conrad, Joseph, *Heart of Darkness*, New Delhi: UBS Publishers, 1994.

Conrad, Joseph, *Lord Jim*, Delhi: Surjeet Publishers, 1970.

Coomaraswamy, Ananda K., *The Transformation of Nature in Art*, New York: Dover Publications, 1986.

Coward, Harold G., *Bhartṛhari*, Boston : G.K. Hall, 1976.

Coward, Harold G. (ed.), *Language in Indian Philosophy and Religion*, Waterloo: Wilfrid Laurier University Press, 1978.

Coward, H., *Sphoṭa Theory of Language*, Delhi: Motilal Banarsidass, 1980.

Culler, Jonathan, *Structuralist Poetics: Structuralism, Linguistics and the Study of Literature*, London: Routledge & Kegan Paul, 1980.

Culler, Jonathan, *On Deconstruction: Theory and Criticism after Structuralism*, Ethaca, N.W: Cornell University Press, 1982.

Daṇḍin, *Kāvyādarśa*, ed. with commentary by Pundit Rangacharya Raddi Shastri, Poona: Bhandarkar Oriental Research Institute, 1970.

Dasgupta, S., *A History of Indian Philosophy*, Cambridge: University Press, 1963 (Vol. I).

Dasgupta, S.N., & De S.K., *A History of Sanskrit Literature*, Calcutta: University of Calcutta, 1962.

De, S.K., *Sanskrit Poetics as a Study of Aesthetics*, Berkeley: University of California Press, 1963.

De, S.K., *Some Problems of Sanskrit Poetics*, Calcutta: Firma K.L. Mukhopadhyay, 1959.

De, S.K., *History of Sanskrit Poetics*, 2 Vols., Calcutta: Firma K. L. Mukhopadhyay,1960.

Derrida, Jacques, "Structure, Sight and Play in the Discourse of Human Sciences", in *Modern Criticism and Theory: A Reader*, ed. by David Lodge, London: Longman,1988, pp. 108-23.

Derrida, Jacques, *Of Grammatology*, tr. by G.C. Spivak, Baltimore: Johns Hopkins University Press, 1976.

Deussen, P., *The Philosophy of the Upaniṣads*, New York: Dover Pub. Inc., 1966.

Deutsch, Eliot, *Studies in Comparative Aesthetics*, Honolulu: University of Hawaii Press, 1975.

Dhananjaya, *Daśarūpaka*, with *Dhanika's* Commentary, Bombay: Nirnaya Sagar Press, 1928.

Dimock, Edward C., *et al.*, *The Literatures of India: An Introduction*, Chicago: University of Chicago Press, 1974.

Eco, Umberto, *The Name of the Rose*, tr. by Harcourt Brace Hovanovich, New York: Warner Books, 1984.

Eliot, T. S., "Tradition and the Individual Talent" in *Norton Anthology of English Literature*, 2 Vols., ed. by M.H. Abrams, *et al.*, New York: Norton, 1974 (Vol. II).

Eliot, T.S., *Selected Prose*, Harmondsworth: Penguin, 1963.

Eliot, T.S., *Collected Poems*. London: Faber and Faber, 1963.

Eliot, T.S., *Selected Poems*. London: Faber and Faber, 1955.

Esslin, Martin, *The Theatre of the Absurd*, Garden City, N.Y: Doubleday, 1961.

Faulkner, William, "A Rose for Emily", in *The Faulkner Reader*, New York: Modern Library, 1956.

Finn, F.E.S. (ed.), *Humour*, The Short Stories Series, London: John Murray, 1978.

Foucault, Michel, *The Foucault Reader*, ed. by Paul Rabinov, Harmondsworth: Penguin, 1986.

Gerow, Edwin, "*Rasa* as a Category of Literary Criticism: What are the Limits of its Application?", in *Sanskrit Drama in Performance*, ed. by Rachel Van M. Baumer & James R. Brandon, Honolulu: University of Hawaii, 1981, pp. 226-57.

Ghose, Aurobindo, *On the Veda*, Pondicherry: Sri Aurobindo Ashram Press, 1956.

Ghosh, Manmohan, (tr.), *The Nāṭya Śāstra*, Calcutta: The Royal Asiatic Society, 1950.

Gilbert, W.S., "When I, Good Friends, Was Called to Bar", in *Norton Anthology of English Literature*, 2 Vols., ed. by M.H. Abrams, *et al.*, New York: Norton, 1974 (Vol. II).

Ginesberg, Allen, *Howl*, *Anthology of American Literature*, 2 Vols.

Gnoli, Ranieso, *The Aesthetic Experience According to Abhinavagupta*, Varanasi: Chowkhamba Sanskrit Series, 1985.

Gogol, Nikolai, *The Government Inspector and Selected Stories*, tr. by Christopher English and Gordon McDougall, Moscow: Raduga, 1989.

Gonda, J., *The Vision of the Vedic Poets*, The Hague: Mouton & Co., 1963.

Gupt, Bharat, *Dramatic Concepts, Greek and Indian: A Study of the Poetics and the Nāṭyaśāstra*, Delhi: D. K. Printworld, 1993.

Han-Shan, *Cold Mountain*, tr. by Burton Watson, Boston: Shambhala, 1992.

Hemingway, Ernest, *The Old Man and the Sea*, Delhi: Surjeet Publishers, 1970.

Hesse, Hermann, *Siddhartha*, tr. by Hilda Rosner, New Delhi: Rupa (by arrangement with Pan Books), 1983.

Hill, W.D.P. (tr.), *Bhagavadgītā*, Oxford: Oxford University Press, 1966.

Hughes, Langston, *The Poetry of the Negro*, London: Doubleday and Company, 1970.

Hume, R.W. (tr.), *Thirteen Principal Upaniṣads*, Oxford: Oxford University Press, 1965.

Ionesco, Eugene, "Rhinoceros", in *The Short Story and the Reader*, ed. by Thomas S. Kane and Leonard J. Peters, New York: Oxford University Press, 1975, pp. 101-115.

Jagannātha, *Rasagangādhara* with "Marmaprakāśa" by Nagesa, ed. with Sanskrit Commentary and Hindi translation by Madhusudana Shastri, 3 Vols., Varanasi: Banaras Hindu University, 1964-70.

Jimenez, Juan Ramon, *Platero and I*, tr. by Eloise Roach. *Nobel Prize Books*, pp. 9-99.

Jung, Carl. G., "Archetypes of the Collective Unconscious", in *20th Century Criticism: The Major Statements*, ed. by William J. Hardy, New York: Macmillan, 1974, pp. 205-32.

Kafka, Franz, *Franz Kafka: Stories 1904-1924*, tr. by J.A. Underwood, New Delhi: Rupa, 1992.

Kane, P.V., *History of Sanskrit Poetics*, New Delhi: Motilal Banarsidass, 1971.

Keats, John, *Eve of Saint Agnes*, in *Norton Anthology of English Literature*, 2 Vols., ed. by M.H. Abrams, *et al.*, New York: Norton, 1974 (Vol. II).

Keith, A.B., *A History of Sanskrit Literature*, London: Oxford University Press, 1966.

Knight, G. Wilson, *The Wheel of Fire*, London: Methuen, 1949.

Krishnamachariar, M., *History of Classical Sanskrit Literature*, Delhi: Motilal Banarsidass, 1970.

Krishnamoorthy, K., *Essays in Sanskrit Criticism*, Dharwar: Karnataka University, 1964.

Krishnamoorthy, K., *The Dhvanyāloka and Its Critics*, Delhi: Bharatiya Vidya Prakashan, 1982.

Kristeva, Julia, "Approaching the Abject", in *Oxford Literary Review*, Vol. V, 1 & 2 (1982), pp. 125-49.

Ksemendra, *Aucityavicāracarcā*, Hindi edn., Ramnagar, Varanasi: Harihar Parakashan, n.d.

Kuntaka, *Vakrokti-jīvita*, ed. by S.K. De, Calcutta: Firma K.L. Mukhopadhyay, 1961.

Lahiri, P.C., *Concept of Rīti and Guṇa in Sanskrit Poetics*, New Delhi: Oriental Books Reprint Corp., 1974.

Langer, Susanne K. (ed.), *Reflections on Art*, New York: Oxford University Press, 1958.

Langer, Susanne K., *Feeling and Form*, New York: Scribner's, 1953.

Langer, Susanne K., *Mind: An Essay on Human Feeling*, Vol. I, Baltimore: Johns Hopkins University Press, 1967.

Lawrence, D.H, "Love in the Farm", in *Norton Anthology of English Literature*, 2 Vols., ed. by M.H. Abrams, *et al.*, New York: Norton, 1974 (Vol. II).

Lorca, Garcia, *Lorca*, selected and tr. by J.L.Gili, London: Penguin, 1960.

Lorca, Garcia, *Three Tragedies*, London: Penguin, 1963.

Mammaṭa, *Kāvyaprakāśa of Mammaṭa*, ed. & tr. by Ganganath Jha, Varanasi: Bharatiya Vidya Prakashan, 1967.

Marquez, Gabriel Garcia, *Chronicle of a Death Foretold*, tr. by Gregory Rabassa, London: Picador, 1982.

Marquez, Gabriel Garcia, *Love in the Time of Cholera*, tr. by Edith Grossman, London: Penguin, 1985.

Marquez, Gabriel Garcia, *No One Writes to the Colonel*, tr. by J.S. Pernstein, London: Picador, 1979.

Masson, J. L. and M.V. Patwardhan, *Aesthetic Rapture*, 2 Vols., Poona: Deccan College, 1970.

Masson, J.L. and M.V. Patwardhan, *Śāntarasa and Abhinava Gupta's Philosophy of Aesthetics*, Poona: Bhandarkar Oriental Series, 1969.

Matilal, B.K., *The Word and the World*, Delhi: Oxford University Press, 1990.

Max Muller, F. (tr.), *The Upaniṣads*, 2 Vols., The Sacred Books of the East Series 1 & 15, Delhi: Motilal Banarsidass, 1965.

Mayakovsky, Vladimir, *Selected Works in Three Volumes. Vol. I: Selected Verse*, tr. by different hands, 3 Vols., Moscow: Raduga Publishers, 1986.

Mayakovsky, Vladimir, *Selected Works in Three Volumes. Vol. II: Longer Poems*, tr. by Dorian Rottenberg, 3 Vols., Moscow: Raduga Publishers, 1986.

Mayakovsky, Vladimir, *Selected Works in Three Volumes, Vol. III: Papers/Articles/Plays*, tr. by different hands, 3 Vols., Moscow: Raduga Publishers, 1987.

McMichael, George (ed.), *Anthology of American Literature*, 2 Vols., fourth edn., New York: Macmillan, 1989.

Melville, Herman, *Moby Dick*, London: Chancellor Press, 1985.

Mishra, Hari Ram, *Theory of Rasa in Sanskrit Drama: With a Comparative Study of General Dramatic Literature*, Chhatarpur: Vindhyachal Prakashan, 1966.

Miura, Yuzuru (selected and tr.), *Classic Haiku: A Masters' Selection*, Japan: Charles E. Tuttle Company, 1991.

Monier-Williams, Sir Monier, *Sanskrit-English Dictionary*, Delhi: Motilal Banarsidass, 1899 (reprint 1993).

Munro, Thomas, *Oriental Aesthetics*, Cleveland: Press of Case Western Reserve University, 1965.

Nerudo, Pablo, *Residence on Earth*, tr. by Donald D. Walsh, New Delhi: Rupa, 1993.

O'Neill, Eugene, *The Hairy Ape*, ed. by M.T. David, Delhi: BI Publications by Arrangement with M/s Jonathan Cape, London, 1987.

O'Neill, Eugene, *The Emperor Jones*, ed. by M.T. David, Delhi: BI Publications by Arrangement with M/s Jonathan Cape,

London, 1983.

Orlov, Sergi, *Selected Poems*, tr. by Vladislav Saitser, Moscow: Raduga, 1987.

Osborne, John, *Look Back in Anger*, London: Faber and Faber, 1957.

Palgrave, Francis Turner (ed.), *The Golden Treasury*, Delhi: Oxford University Press, 1964.

Pande, Anupa, *A Historical and Cultural Study of Nāṭya Śāstra of Bharata*, Jodhpur: Kusumananjali Prakashan, 1991.

Pandey, K.C., *Abinavagupta : A Historical and Philosophic Study*, Varanasi: Chowkhamba, 1963.

Pandey, K.C., *Comparative Aesthetics*, 2 Vols., Varanasi: Chowkhamba, 1959.

Radhakrishnan, S. (tr.), *The Principal Upanisads*, Delhi: Oxford University Press, 1953.

Radhakrishnan, S., *Indian Philosophy*, London: Allen & Unwin Ltd., 1962, Vol. I and II.

Raghavan, V., *The Number of Rasas*, Madras: Adyar Library and Research Centre, 1967.

Raghavan, V., *Bhoja's Śṛṅgāra Prakāśa*, Madras: The Theosophical Society, 1963.

Raghavan, V., *Some Concepts of Alaṁkāra Śāstra*, Adyar: Theosophical Publishing House, 1942.

Raja, K., Kunjunni, *Indian Theories of Meaning*, Adyar: Adyar Library and Research Centre, 1942.

Ranade, R.D., *Constructive Survey of Upaniṣadic Philosophy*, Bombay: Bharatiya Vidya Bhavan, 1968.

Rayan, Krishna, *Suggestion and Statement in Poetry*, London: Athlone Press, 1972.

Richard, I.A., *Principles of Literary Criticism*, New Delhi: UBS Publishers (Indian Reprint), 1990.

Rilke, Rainer Maria, *Selected Works*, tr. by J.B.Leishman.

2 Vols., London: The Hogarth Press, 1967 (Vol. II).

Rosenberg, Isaac, "Returning We Hear the Larks", in *Norton Anthology of English Literature,* 2 Vols., ed. by M.H. Abrams, *et al.*, New York: Norton, 1974. Vol.II.

Rudraṭa, *Kāvyālaṁkāra,* Hindi edn. with Nami Sadhu's commentary, Varanasi: Chowkhamba Vidyabhawan, 1966.

Saint-Exupery, Antione de, *The Little Prince,* tr. by Katherine Wood, Mammoth, 1991.

Śaṅkarācārya, *Self Knowledge,* tr. by Swami Nikhilananda, Ramarkrishna Mission.

Sankaran, A., *Some Concepts of Literary Criticism in Sanskrit,* New Delhi: Oriental Books Reprint Corp., 1973.

Sastri, P.S., *Ṛgvedic Aesthetics,* Delhi: Bharatiya Vidya Prakashan, 1988.

Sastri, Kuppuswami, *Highways and Byways of Literary Criticism in Sanskrit,* Madras: Kuppuswami Sastri Research Institute, 1961.

Saxena, S.K., *Art and Philosophy,* Delhi: Indian Council of Philosophical Research, 1944.

Seferis, George, *Poems: George Seferis,* London: Bodley Head, 1960.

Seldan, Raman, *The Theory of Criticism,* London: Longman, 1988.

Shakespeare, William, *King Lear,* ed. by Russel Fraser, New York: Signet, 1963.

Shakespeare, William, *The Works of William Shakespeare,* London: Frederick Warne and Co., 1893.

Sophocles, "Oedipus the King", in *The Complete Greek Tragedies,* Vol. III, New York: Modern Library, 1942, pp. 15-92.

Sophocles, *King Oedipus, Oedipus Colonus, Antigone,* tr. by E.F. Watling, Harmondsworth: Penguin, 1947.

Subramania Iyer, K.S. (tr.), *Vākyapadīya of Bhartṛhari,* Poona: Deccan College, 1966.

Sukla, A.C., *The Concept of Imitation in Greek and Indian Aesthetics*, Calcutta: Rupa & Co., 1977.

Swift, Jonathan, *Gulliver's Travels*, Delhi: Rupa (by arrangement with Collins), 1989.

Tambimuttu (ed.), *Indian Love Poems*, tr. by Tambimuttu and G.V. Vaidya, New York: Peter Pauper Press, 1967.

Udbhaṭa, *Kāvyālaṁkara-Sāra-Saṁgraha*, with Induraja's commentary, ed. by N.D. Banhatti, Poona: Bhandarkar Oriental Research Institute, 1925.

Vālmakī, *Rāmāyaṇa*, Gorakhpur: Gita Press, 1960.

Vāmana, *Kāvyālaṁkārasūtrāṇi*, with "Kāmadhenu" with commentary of Tippa Bhūpāla. Hindi edn., Varanasi: Chowkhamba, 1971.

Vijayavardhana, G., *Outline of Sanskrit Poetics*, Varanasi: Chowkhamba, 1970.

Viśākhadatta, *Mudrārākṣasa*, ed. by M.R. Kale, Bombay: 1916.

Viśvanatha, *Sāhityadarpaṇa*, Chapters 1, 2 and 10. ed. by P.V. Kane, Delhi: Motilal Banarsidass, 1965.

Vyāsa, *Mahābhārata*, 14 Vols., Gorakhpur: Gita Press, 1956.

Walimbe, Y.S., *Abinavagupta on Indian Aesthetics*, Delhi: Ajanta Publications, 1980.

Warder, A.K., *The Science of Criticism in India*, Madras: Adyar Library and Research Centre, 1978.

Warder, A.K., *Indian Kavya Literature*, 2 Vols., Delhi: Motilal Banarsidass, 1972.

Winternitz, Maurice, *A History of Indian Literature*, tr. by V.S. Sarma. 3 Vols., New Delhi: Motilal Banarsidass, 1981.

Yasuda, Kenneth, *The Japanese Haiku*, Japan: Charles E. Turtle Company, 1957.

Yeats, William Butler, *Selected Poetry*, London: Pan Books, 1974.

Glossary

Adbhutapuṣpa :	wondrous flower. Abhinavagupta compares the *rasa* experience to a magical flower which is self-created and has neither beginning nor end.
Ālambana :	support.
Alaṁkāra :	literary figure.
Ānanda :	bliss.
Anubhāva :	the consequent, the effect, the response to situations, states of mind and body etc., generated and depicted in a work.
Āsvāda :	savour.
Ātman :	self or soul.
Aucitya :	propriety.
Bhāva :	emotion or feeling. I translate it as psycho-physiological state.
Bhāṣya :	commentary.
Bhaya :	fear.
Brahmacārya :	state of celibacy. In Vedic times a man's life was divided into four phases : *brahmacārya* (bachelorhood — from birth until initiation into marriage), *gr̥hasthya* (household life), *vāṇaprastha* (withdrawal into the forest with the purpose of renunciation of worldly life) and *sanyāsa*

	(life of asceticism with which one is expected to end his life).
Brahman :	the Absolute; the Divine; the Ultimate Reality.
Camatkāra :	state of bliss in which one is oblivious of time and space.
Dharma :	moral duty.
Dhvani :	suggested meaning as distinct from denoted and implied meaning.
Doṣa :	faults or flaws in writing.
Gṛhasthya :	**see** *Brahmacārya.*
Guṇa :	a necessary condition of good writing.
Guṇa-rīti :	a school of poetic theory which emphasizes that the proper combination of style (*rīti*) and canons of good writing (*guṇa*) constitutes the soul of poetry.
Harṣa :	laughter or amusement.
Jñāna :	knowledge.
Jugupsā :	disgust.
Kāvya :	poetry.
Krama :	sequentiality.
Krodha :	anger.
Lakṣaṇa :	literary trait.
Mokṣa :	state of bliss and liberation.
Nāṭya :	drama.
Pratibhā :	poetic genius.
Rasa :	aesthetic rapture. A dominant and sustained emotional and mental state which is the result of an aesthetic experience.

adbhuta : the wondrous or awesome emotion.

bhayānaka : the terrifying emotion.

bībhatsa : the disgusting emotion.

hāsya : the comic emotion.

karuṇa : the compassionate or pathetic emotion.

raudra : the terrifying emotion.

śānta : state of calm, tranquillity and peace.

śṛṅgāra : the erotic emotion.

vīra : the heroic emotion.

Rasadhvani : suggestion of an emotive meaning.

Rati : love.

Rīti : poetic style.

Sādhāraṇī-karaṇa : universalization. It involves the total identification of a perceiver with the work.

Sahṛdaya : the like-minded or emphathetic perceiver who can catch the spirit of a work.

Sama : state of calm.

Saṁbhoga śṛṅgāra: love in union.

Saṁskāra : latent emotions.

Sañcārībhāva : **see** *vyabhicārībhāva.*

Sanyāsa : **see** *brahmacārya.*

Śoka : sorrow.

Sthāyībhāva : stable or permanent state or mood that dominates a work.

Sumana : pure-minded. He is the ideal perceiver whose mind is pure and unbiased and hence like a clear mirror.

Sūtra : aphorism.

Uddīpana : arousing; that which causes or brings forth.

Upagata : arise.

Upaniṣad : The part of *Veda* that deals with Supreme Knowledge.

Utsāha : dynamic energy or enthusiasm.

Vairāgya : detachment and renunciation which arise from disgust with the world.

Vakrokti : indirection.

Vāṇaprastha : **see** *brahmacārya.*

Vāsanā : tendencies of past life; unconscious memory.

Veda : the primary Hindu scriptures including the early hymns, the *Brāhmaṇas* and *Upaniṣads*. The *Vedas* are organised into four collections called *Ṛg, Sāma, Yajur* and *Atharva.*

Vibhāva : the antecedent, the cause, the stimulus which generates a situation, emotion or state in a work.

Vipralambha : love-in-separation.

Vismaya : wonder.

Vyabhicārī-bhāva : fleeting or transitory states that are associated with and accompany *sthāyībhāva.* Also known as *sañcarībhāva.*

Yoga : a practical psychological discipline for achieving release and a state of calm.

Index

"A Rose for Emily", 192

Abhijñānaśākuntalam, 74, 92

Abhinavabhāratī, 6, 16, 45, 82, 98, 104, 226, 227

Abhinavagupta, 6, 8, 24, 35, 39-43, 45, 46, 47-48, 49, 50, 51, 52, 63, 64, 66, 67-68, 72, 73, 81, 82, 86, 88, 104, 107, 117, 141, 143, 145, 176, 183, 202-3, 207, 208, 227, 228-37, 249, 252, 253, 254

Abnormal, 84-86

Absurd, vi, 104, 137, 144, 146, 186-89, 192, 252, 254

Adbhuta rasa, 53, 59, 62-63, 99, 172, 177, 199-200, 205-23, 254, 255

- accompanying emotions of-, 196-97
- causes of-, 205, 206-07
- effects of-, 209-10, 222
- *sthāyī* of-, 205

Adbhutapuṣpa, 42, 52

"Adonic Anglea", 83-84, 208

"Adventure of a Soldier", 117-19

"Adventure of a Crook", 114-16

After Bakhtin, 3

Alaṁkāra, 4, 5, 209

Alaukika, 42, 43

Alienation, 62, 131, 132-36, 150, 152, 186-88, 191

Amaru, 88

Ānanda, 51, 52, 252, 255

Ānandavardhana, 6, 15, 45, 49, 64, 66

Anger, 46, 97, 146, 172 ***see*** *bhayānaka*

Anubhāva, 7, 8, 25, 26, 29-32, 33, 34, 35, 46, 48, 74-75

Appeal, 25

"Approaching the Abject", 179-80

Aristotle, 54, 61, 129, 141, 251

Artha, 56

arthaśṛṅgāra, 56

Artist, 2, ***see*** *pratibhā*

Asvāda, ix

Aśvaghoṣa, 185, 230, 234

"At the Door of Law", 188-89

Atharvaveda, 17

Ātman, 68

Awesome, ***see*** *adbhuta*

Bach, Richard, 214

Basho, Matsuo, 101, 102, 210, 235
Bates, H.E., 104, 107-08
Baudelaire, Charles, 85, 103, 129, 182, 184, 233, 234
Beauty, 24
Beckett, Samuel, 189, 191, 210
Bed Bug, 104, 106-07, 110-13
"Bhaja Govindam", 61
Bhakti, 55, 249
bhaktiśṛṅgāra, 55
Bhāmaha, 4-5, 14, 225-26
Bharata, ***see*** *Nāṭya Śāstra*
Bhartṛhari, 10, 129, 183, 184, 202, 203, 234
Bhāsa, 59, 60, 175
Bhaṭṭa Tauta, 48, 253
Bhaṭṭa Lollaṭa, 6, 16, 33, 35, 38, 253
Bhaṭṭa Nāyaka, 6, 16, 38, 50, 51
Bhāva, 7, 8, 25, 26, 27, 28, 29, 33-35, 46, 47, 227
Bhaya, 27, 36, 67, 177, 233-34, ***see*** fear
Bhayānaka rasa, 28, 30, 32, 53, 54, 57, 58, 60-61, 63, 79, 96, 104, 129, 136, 140, 144, 146, 149, 158, 165, 172, 175, 176-79, 186, 192-99, 200, 201, 202, 203, 204, 206, 218-21, 222, 254
  accompanying emotions of-, 196
  causes of-, 176, 177-79
  sthāyī of-, 176
Bībhatsa rasa, 53, 54, 57-58, 59, 60-61, 63, 104, 106, 112, 116, 129, 130, 135, 136, 137, 140, 146, 149, 158, 172, 179-99, 200, 201, 202, 203, 204, 206, 222, 254
  accompanying emotions of-, 196-97
  causes of-, 179
  effects of-, 181
  sthāyī of-, 179
Black humour, 112
black comedy, 189, 191-92
Bliss, 64, 238
Blood Wedding, 71, 74, 75, 95-98, 124-27
Book of Hours, 239
Book of Sand, 219-21
Book of Songs, 70
Borges, George Luis, 104, 181, 197, 210, 216-19, 221
Brahmacarya, 72, 228
Brahman, 19, 43, 52
Buddhacarita, 185, 230-31, 234
Buddhism, 61

Calm, ***see*** *sama*
Calvino, Italo, 114, 117
Camatkāra, 40, 41, 43, 52, 205-6, 225
Camus, Albert, 186-88, 200
"Carrion", 182, 184-85
Carroll, Lewis, 105
Cause, 7, 31, ***see*** *vibhāva*
Chronicle of a Death Foretold, 199-200, 222
Chuang Tzu, 100

Cloud in Pants, 71, 93-95, 128, 129, 148-49
Cold Mountain, 100-101
Coleridge, Samuel, Taylor, 69
Comedy, 54, 55, 109, 113-15, 251, **see** *hāsya* and *prahasana*
high, 109, 113-15
low, 109, 113-15
black, 189, 191-92
Comedy of Grotesque, 58, 105, 115-19, 137, 189, 229
Comic, **see** *hāsya*
Communication, 30
Compassionate, **see** *karuṇa*
Conrad, Joseph, 159, 181, 192
Consequences, 7, 31, **see** *anubhāva*
Cruelty, 101-05, 109
Culinary, 25, 26, 40

Daṇḍin, 5, 38, 45
Darwin, Charles, 186
De, S.K., 31
"Dead Men's Dump", 200-01
Desire, 66
Dharma, 56, 171
dharmaśṛṅgāra, 56
Dhvani, 2, 6, 14
Dhvanikara, 6
Dhvanyāloka, 6, 66, 141
Disgust(ing), 156, 183-84, **see** *bībhatsa* and *jugupsā*
Disorder, 101-05
Distancing, 113, 141, 196, 201, 207
Donne, John, 209
Doṣa, 4
Drama, 30, 56
"Dream", 212-13
Duḥkhātmaka, 54, 143
Dynamic energy, **see** *utsāha*

"Easter 1916", 172-73
Eco, Umberto, 199, 200
Eliot, T.S., 106, 183, 192, 209, 210, 239, 243, 253
Emotion, 30-31, 32, 34, 55, 65, 254-55, **see** *rasa*
Emperor Jones, The, 136, 177, 196, 201
Erotic, **see** *śṛṅgāra*
Essence as *rasa*, 18, 20, 21, 70, 71
Eve of Saint Agnes, 69
"Express, The", 79-81
"Faithless Wife, The", 208
Fall, The, 188
Fantasy, 131, **see** *adbhuta*
Farce, 114, **see** *prahasana*
Faulkner, William, 192
Fear, 30, 35-36, 39, 60, 77, 78, 129, 176-77, 178, 179, 181, 187, 192-96, 199, 201-02, **see** *bhaya*
Feeling, 38, **see** emotion
Flavour, 25, 26
Flower of Evil, The, 103
"Flying Goat, The", 107-08
Four Quartets, 239-45
Freud, Sigmund, 66

Furious, ***see*** *raudra*
Fury, 62, 154-58 ***see*** *raudra*
"Futility", 136, 230

"Galaxy, The", 235
Gennet, 209
Gilbert, W.S., 103
Ginsberg, Allen, 150, 152, 231
Gītā, The, 238, 249
Gītagovinda, 73
Gnoli, Ranieso, 31
Gogol, Nikolai, 109
Government Inspector, The, 109
Gṛhasthya, 72, 228
Grotesque, 101, 115-16, 118, 132, 145, 152, 154, 155, 189, 192
Gulliver's Travels, 106
Guṇa, 4
  artha, 5
  rīti, 5
  śabda, 5

Haiku, 210-12, 235, 249
"Haiku", 211
Hairy Ape, The, 180
Han-Shan, 55, 100, 102, 213, 229
Harṣa, 27, 100, 177, 229
Hāsya rasa, 27, 53, 58, 67, 99-119, 137, 177, 189-92, 213, 222-23, 254, 255
  causes of-, 99, 109-10
  sthāyī of-, 99-100
Heart of Darkness, 181, 192-96
Hemingway, Earnst, 140, 232
Heroic, ***see*** *vīra* and *utsāha*
Hesse, Herman, 243
"Hollow Men, The", 183-84, 192
Howl, 152-55, 231
Hulme, T.E., 211
"Hymn of Renunciation", 185

Ideal perceriver, 45, 50, ***see*** *sahṛdaya* and *sumana*
Identification, 62
"Improbable Tale, The", 104
Incongruency, 100, 102, 112, 118-19
Ionesco, Eugene, 189

"Jewels", 85-86, 233
Jimenez, Juan Ramon, 110, 213
Jonathan Livingston Seagull, 214-18, 231-33, 235, 238
Jugupsā, 27, 67, 136, 228, 234-35
Jung, Carl, 66

Kafka, Franz, 129, 130, 180, 188, 230
Kālidāsa, 75, 78, 89
Kane, P.V., 8, 28, 31, 251
Karma, 121, 175, 238, 249
Karmayoga, 242
Karuṇa rasa, 53, 56-57, 58, 87, 89, 95, 116, 121-41, 143, 144, 147, 148, 153, 155, 158, 171, 180, 201-02, 223
  accompanying emotions of-, 196-97
  causes of-, 121-23
  sthāyī of-, 121

Kāma, 56
Kāmaśṛṅgāra, 56
Kāvyabhārati, 45
Kāvyālaṁkāra, 4, 8
Kāvyaprakāśa, 7
Keats, John, 69
King Lear, 115
Knight, J. Wilson, 105
Krama, 48
Kristeva, Julia, 179-80
Kāvyādarśa, 5
Krodha, 27, 67, 144, 145, 231, ***see*** anger
Kuntaka, 6

Lakṣaṇa, 4
Lawrence, D.H., 75, 76, 81
Little Prince, 71, 88-92
Locana, 6, 16, 98, 141
Lodge, David, 3
Look Back in Anger, 150-51
Lorca, Gracia, 71, 75, 124, 208, 212
Lord Jim, 159-64, 167
Love, 172, ***see*** *śṛṅgāra* and *rati*
Love in the Time of Cholera, 76, 128
"Love on the Firm", 76-78
"Love Song", 82-83
Love-in-separation, 56-57, 71, 86-91, 92, 96-97, 124, 125
Love-in-union, 56-57, 71-76, 81-83

Mahābhārata, v, 24, 55, 57, 59, 61, 92, 98, 121, 141, 172, 175, 201, 203, 248
Mammaṭa, 7
Marques, Gabriel Garcia, 76, 128, 138, 199, 210, 221
Marula, 70
Marvell, Andrew, 209
Mayakovsky, Vladimir, 71, 93-94, 95, 105, 107, 128
"Meeting after Separation", 70
Meghadūtam, 89
Metamorphosis, 129, 130-36, 150, 180, 230-31
"Metaphysical Poets, The", 209
"Mist", 245
Moby Dick, 145
Mohamudgara, 61
Mokṣa, 56, 68, 227, 238, 248-49
Morality, 49
Mṛcchakaṭikam, 92
Myth of Sysiphus, The, 186-88

Name of the Rose, 199-200
Narrow Road to the North, The, 101
Nāṭya Śāstra, 1, 4, 5-6, 7, 8, 14, 16, 23, 24-34, 37, 38, 39, 42, 43, 47, 49, 53, 54, 56, 58, 63, 64, 65, 66, 71, 72, 73, 74, 86, 99, 100, 101, 102, 109-10, 114, 117, 121, 122, 124, 130, 139-40, 143, 144, 145, 147, 159, 165, 170-71, 176-77, 179, 180, 181, 182, 183, 196-97, 204, 205, 207, 208-9, 222, 226, 227, 237, 238, 253
Neruda, Pablo, 83-84, 208, 253
Nītiśataka, 183

No One Writes to the Colonel, 138-39, 148, 164, 171

O'Neill, Eugene, 177, 201
Oedipus Rex, 61, 123
Old Man and the Sea, The, 164, 166, 167-71, 174, 232
Open Reading, 253
Origin of Species, The, 186
Osborne, John, 150
"Other, The", 218-19
Outsider, The, 188
Owen, Wilfred, 136

Paṇḍitarāja, Jagannātha, 7,9
Patañjali, 237
Perceiver, 23, 26
Pity, 129-30
Platero and I, 110, 213-14
Poetics, 54, 129
Post-Structuralism, 3
Pound, Ezra, 210
Prahasana, 101
Pratibhā, ix, 2, 9, 47, 48
Private Language, 84
Process, 26, 37, 41
Process as *rasa*, 19, 20, 21, 26
Purgation, 141

Rājā Bhoja, 55
Rāmāyaṇa, v-vi, 48, 55, 92, 98, 121, 141, 253
Rasa, 4, 7-9, 15-35, 37, 40-43, 46, 48-55, 65, 86, 226, 251-56
  constituents of-, 25-32
  meaning of-, 13-15
  primary, 58
  secondary, 58
  theory, vi, 1-2,
  theory, history of-, 4-7
Rasagaṅgādhara, 9
Rasāyanaśāstra, 18
Rati, 27, 67, 72, 236, ***see*** *śṛṅgāra*
Raudra rasa, 53, 58-59, 62, 121, 122, 124, 127, 129-30, 93-158, 160, 165, 174, 177
  accompanying emotions of-, 143-44, 145-46
  causes of-, 143, 144-45
  effects of-, 147-51
  sthāyī of-, 143-44
Reader's response, 44-52, 106, 205, 253
"Recollections of Love", 69
Response, 25, 35-37, 48, 61, ***see*** *anubhāva*
"Returning We Hear the Larks", 221
Ṛgveda, 16-17, 18, 80, 123
"Rhinoceros, The", 189-91
Rilke, Rainer Maria, 82-83, 236, 239, 242
Rosenberg, Isaac, 221
Rudraṭa, 4

Sādhāraṇīkaraṇa, v, 41, 45, 50
Sāhityadarpaṇa, 7
Sahṛdaya, 42-43, 49, 50, 129-30, 141, ***see*** reader's response

Saint-Exupury, Antoine de, 71, 72
sama, 64, 67, 227-29, 243
Sambhoga śṛṅgāra, 56-57, 71-76, 81-83
Saṁskāra, 45, 50
Sañcārībhāva, **see** *vyabhicārībhāva*
Śaṅkara, v
Śaṅkarācārya, 61, 185, 203, 234
Sanskrit, 9-10
Śānta rasa, v, vi, 49, 53, 63-68, 76, 81, 82, 88, 135, 137, 138, 152, 153, 172, 174, 176, 183, 184-86, 188, 205, 214-18, 225-46, 252
  accompanying emotions of-, 238
  causes of-, 228, 236
  effects of-, 236-38
  sthāyī of-, 227-36
Saṁnyāsa, 72, 228
Satire, 106-09
Sāttvikabhāva, 7, 26, 33
Seferis, George, 211-12
Self-realisation, 249, **see** *śānta rasa*
Sengai, 210
Sense Perception, 19, **see** space and time
Shakespeare, William, 115
Shiki, 235
Siddhārtha, 174, 243-48
"Slave Story", 156-67
Śoka, 27, 67, 122, 130, 135, 177, 191, 230-31
"Song for a Dark Girl", 157-58
Sorrow, **see** *śoka*
Space, 19, 20, 21, 42, 52
Spender, Stephen, 79
"Spur", 156
Śrī Śaṅkuka, 6, 16, 33, 35, 39
Śṛṅgāra rasa, v, 32, 53, 55, 56-57, 58, 69-98, 99, 117-19, 125, 174, 202, 208-9, 225
  accompanying emotions of-, 78
  causes of-, 172-74
  effects of-, 74-76
  sthāyī of-, 72-74
State, 29, **see** *bhāva*
  transitory, 29, **see** *vyabhicārībhāva*
  stable, 29, see *sthāyībhāva*
Sthāyībhāva, 7, 26-28, 29, 32-33, 36, 37, 39, 41, 47, 64-65, 66-67, 143-44
Stimulus, 25, 30, 35-37, 48
"Strange Meeting", 136-37, 230
Subjectivity, 128
Suggestion, 31, 66
Sukhātmaka, 54, 143
Sumana, 43, 45, 49, 50, **see** reader's response
Surprise, **see** *vismaya*
Swift, Jonathan, 106

Tao, 249
Terrifying, 218-21, **see** *bhayānaka* and *bhaya*
"There are More Things", 181, 197-99
Time, 19, 20, 42, 43, 52
Tragedy, 54, 55, 57, 61, 121, 122,

124, 129, 175
Treatment, 105-06, 111-12, 116, 200

Udbhaṭa, 5
Unknown, 178-79, 180, 182, 197
Upaniṣad, 17-22
Bṛhadāraṇyaka, 225-26, 236
Chāndogya, 24
Īśa, 19
Kauśītakī, 17,20
Taittirīya, 17-21
Utsāha, 27, 59, 67, 159, 160, 174, 231-33

Vakrokti, 5
Vairāgya, 228, 233
Vākyapadīya, 10-11
Vālmiki, 48, 51
Vāṇaprastha, 72, 228
Vāsanā, 46, 50
Veda, 40, 114, 252
Verlaine, Paul, 145
Vibhāva, 7, 8, 25, 26, 27, 31, 33, 34, 35, 46, 48
"Victim", 140
Viewpoint, 95
Violence, 75, 78, 79, 94, 127, 144, 153
Vipralambha śṛṅgāra, 56-57, 71, 86-91, 92, 96-97, 124, 125
Vīra rasa, 53, 59, 62, 99, 137, 139, 143, 145, 147, 155, 158, 159-74, 177, 178, 200-201, 214-18, 231, 232, 233
accompanying emotions of-, 159-64, 171-72
causes of-, 164-65
effects of-, 165-69
sthāyī of-, 160
Vismaya, 27, 59, 67, 206, 207, 235
Viśvanātha Kabirāja, 7
Vyabhicārībhāva, 7, 8, 26, 27, 28-29, 33, 35, 46

"Walrus and the Carpenter, The", 105-06
Wheel of Fire, The, 105
"When I, Good Friends, was Called to Bar", 103-4
Wit, 209-10
Wonder, 209-10, 212-14 ***see*** *adbhuta*

Yeats, W.B., 156, 173
Yoga, 52
Yoga Sūtra, 237
"You", 155

Zen, 249